THE SOCIAL SELF

Volume 144, Sage Library of Social Research

RECENT VOLUMES IN
SAGE LIBRARY OF SOCIAL RESEARCH

THE SOCIAL SELF

Group Influences On Personal Identity

Elisha Y. Babad

Max Birnbaum

Kenneth D. Benne

Volume 144
SAGE LIBRARY OF
SOCIAL RESEARCH

 SAGE PUBLICATIONS
Beverly Hills / London / New Delhi

For information address:

SAGE Publications, Inc.
275 South Beverly Drive
Beverly Hills, California 90212

SAGE Publications India Pvt. Ltd.
C-236 Defence Colony
New Delhi 110 024, India

SAGE Publications Ltd
28 Banner Street
London EC1Y 8QE, England

Printed in the United States of America

Library of Congress Cataloging in Publication Data

Babad, Elisha.
  The social self.

  (Sage library of social research ; v. 144)
  Bibliography: p.
  Includes index.
  1. Social psychology. 2. Self. I. Birnbaum, Max.
II. Benne, Kenneth Dean, 1908-   III. Title.
IV. Series.
HM251.B218 1982   302   82-21553
ISBN 0-8039-1938-7
ISBN 0-8039-1939-5 (pbk.)

FIRST PRINTING

CONTENTS

ACKNOWLEDGMENTS

Many friends, colleagues, and students have helped to make this book possible. James Small made significant contributions to C-Group theory. Irene Allard made a major contribution through her imaginative reconstruction of the processes of the first Clarification Group. Murray Horwitz and Yakov Epstein have been particularly helpful, but other colleagues were important to us in particular stages of thinking and writing. They include Martin Lakin, Warren Bennis, Robert Chin, Peter Kuriloff, Zick Rubin, Robert Rosenthal, and Norman Newberg in the United States; Gavriel Salomon, Yechezkel Darr, and Yaakov Kareev in Israel. Above all, we were "helped" by the late Kurt Lewin, whose ideas provided some large part of the foundation for this book.

Many students and group participants in laboratories at Bethel, Maine, at Osgood Hill, the Boston University Campus Center, and in Israel contributed directly and indirectly to the development of the educational approach exemplified in this book. We are particularly thankful to Bruce Oppenheimer, Irene Melnick, Israel Katz, Michelle Fine, Ilana Rosenzweig, and the anonymous "Susan Goldberg," whose life story is included in Chapter 4. At the University of Pennsylvania, we are grateful to Randy Robinson, Lisa Summers, Maggie Mulqueen, Frank Goodman, and particularly Marsha Tachovsky.

We acknowledge the special assistance and advice we received from Seymour Winegarten, Shifra Babad, Ruth Elraz, Yechezkel Darr, Dorit Rosenblatt, and Gayle Lloyd-Wright. At the University of Pennsylvania, Theresa Singleton and Susan Bosak were a constant source of support and technical assistance, while in Israel, Mrs. Esther Porat was extremely helpful.

We are very appreciative of the Graduate School of Education at the University of Pennsylvania for the varied sources of support and assistance provided to the first author during 1979-1981. Special thanks are extended to Dean Dell Hymes and Peter Kuriloff. We acknowledge the contributions for travel to authors' meetings provided by Staff and Organizational Consultation, Inc.

Yael Babad was a reader, "reflector," adviser, and partner throughout the entire period. Her help was unmeasurable.

B., B., & B.
Jerusalem, Israel
West Orange, N.J.
Washington, D.C.

INTRODUCTION

This book tries to be and do what Kurt Lewin, the eminent social psychologist, was and did: to be theoretical yet practical, basic yet applied, value-oriented yet scientifically detached, eclectic yet committed to one major point of view, a formal teaching instrument yet at the same time a vehicle for *self*-learning. (To facilitate the latter we have studded exercises in self-inquiry throughout the volume, concerned with and adjacent to the particular topics under discussion.) Furthermore, the book deals with issues and processes that were the focus of Kurt Lewin's attention, especially in his later years: identity and value orientation, the social self, the cleavage and struggle between groups in society, the resolution of social conflicts, and personal change through experiential self-learning and self-inquiry.

We have been involved in human relations training and experienced-based laboratory education for many years, following closely the historical developments in the study and application of group dynamics through the last four decades. We have witnessed how various areas of group practice have become independent "professions"—group psychotherapy, personal growth groups, and self-help groups. But we have experienced a growing concern that group and intergroup issues are neglected in these groups, which focus almost exclusively on intrapersonal and interpersonal issues and problems. We have observed, with growing concern, how the study of small groups is disappearing from theory and research in social psychology. Social psychology—a "mother" discipline for group practice—has become a cognitively oriented, individual, and interpersonal psychology. Most of its practitioners seem, in general, to investigate momentary and temporarily induced interactions rather than lasting group memberships and relations.

Issues of personal and interpersonal change are of great contemporary importance, but so are issues of group and intergroup relations. In our work in education and training, we have been concerned with socio-identities and their roots in people's racial, ethnic, religious, cultural, and familial backgrounds; about people's interactions with others who are "different" from them along a variety of dimensions; and about intergroup processes (stereotyping, prejudice, intergroup conflict) that all of us experience inescapably in our lives in a heterogeneous society. These concerns led us to develop the "Clarification Group" (Birnbaum, 1975; Babad, Birnbaum, & Benne, 1978) in efforts further to refine and disseminate this educational approach. It is with this intent that we embarked upon writing this book. The book is an attempt to translate an experiential approach to learning into a guided process of self-inquiry, in which we provide both relevant knowledge and guidelines for applying that knowledge to one's own life and to one's social interactions with others who are different in one or more dimensions of social membership.

This is not primarily a theoretical book, nor a report stressing empirical or field research. Nor is it a "political" book which advocates one solution to problems of social heterogeneity. Nor is it exclusively a book of training exercises. Yet to some extent it is all of the foregoing. It is our attempt to teach readers enough so that they can conduct their own self-inquiries and make meaning of their own life histories, socio-identities, and interactions with different others. We believe that learning is effective when it integrates "universal knowledge" (scientific principles, historical facts, theory, and research) with "personal knowledge" as accumulated in persons' own life experiences. This book provides universal knowledge about heterogeneity, pluralism, intergroup processes, and social change, both on a global level and as characterizing specific dimensions of heterogeneity: race, ethnicity, sex, age, social roles, professional roles, religion, and ideology. But together with this universal knowledge, the book is interspersed with suggested activities intended to guide readers in personalizing the universal knowledge and applying it to their own past development and present quandaries.

The volume is divided into three parts. The first part presents some considerations that precede the process of self-inquiry and examines difficulties inherent in pursuit of self-inquiry. Chapter 1 explores the major problems and challenges facing persons and groups in a heterogeneous society. It also defines central concepts used in this book, such as socio-identity, social perception, minority status, heterogeneity, and pluralism. Chapter 2 reviews the genesis and the major principles and techniques of the method of inquiry used in the book. Chapter 3 discusses several clusters of obstacles to self-inquiry—dynamic, cognitive, and social factors that *prevent* people from attaining relevant "social" knowledge or from applying such knowledge effectively for improving their social functioning. Chapter 4 then expands on a major technique used in clarification groups: the structured group interview. Through a model interview and subsequent guidelines the chapter makes it possible for readers to embark upon inquiries into their own social selves.

The second part of the book provides relevant knowledge about the psychological and sociological processes involved in group and intergroup phenomena. This knowledge is "universal" in the sense that the theory and research presented in this part of the book are not limited to specific dimensions of societal heterogeneity. Chapter 5 discusses the psychology of stereotyping, Chapter 6 discusses phenomena of prejudice and intergroup conflict, and the psychological and sociological theories of prejudice. Chapter 7 analyzes processes of intergroup relations, from the "minimal intergroup situation" to full-blown intergroup conflict in society. Chapter 8 presents relevant major issues, strategies, and principles of personal and social change.

The third part of the book investigates, and attempts to facilitate the readers' own self-inquiry into, the major domains of difference and conflict in our society and, therefore, major dimensions of the social self. Chapter 9 focuses on race, ethnicity, and religion; Chapter 10 deals with gender, sex roles, and the explosive issues of sexism and feminism; Chapter 11 investigates age as a dimension of difference; and Chapter 12 deals with roles and role conflicts, focusing mainly on social and professional roles as determinants of similarity and difference. The closing chapter discusses ideology and its impact on intergroup processes in a heterogeneous society. The chapter explores the special role of ideologies in the development and maintenance of the social self and their immense impact (constructive *and* destructive) in human society.

In writing this book we have tried to integrate our "roles" as scientists, theoreticians, researchers, teachers, and group trainers, as well as our various disciplines: psychology, philosophy, history, sociology, and human relations education. The success of this book will be determined by its capacity to educate, that is, to enhance and deepen readers' understanding of their own lives within their various cultural contexts and to develop their potential for dealing more effectively with intergroup issues in personal, community, and political contexts.

B., B., & B.
Jerusalem, Israel
West Orange, N.J.
and Washington, D.C.

PART I

INITIAL CONSIDERATIONS

1

THE CHALLENGE OF DIFFERENCES

Dimensions of Difference

The United States of America is often described as a pluralistic society. This is, in part, an inaccurate description. That American society is heterogeneous is beyond dispute, and heterogeneity is one component of pluralism in a society. But pluralism also requires an acceptance of the legitimacy of group differences and methods of managing intergroup tensions and conflicts in just and equitable ways. These conditions have not been fully attained in American society.

One dimension of difference in America is *racial*. The concept "race" does not have a clear definition, but most Americans identify themselves as Whites. Other sizable minorities identify themselves as Blacks, as American Indians or Native Americans, as Eskimos, as Polynesians, or as Orientals.

These racial groupings are by no means internally homogeneous. The white majority is marked by internal diversity along *ethnic* lines. Many groups of immigrants have never lost the sense of their cultural differences from other groups. They identify themselves, and are seen by others, as "hyphenated" Americans: Irish-Americans, Italian-Americans, Polish-Americans, Greek-Americans, and the like. Native Americans, even those not segregated in reservations, have not lost their traditional tribal identifications. Within Black America, members often make distinctions between descendants of American slaves and immigrants from the Caribbean Islands. Orientals see themselves as Chinese-Americans, Japanese-Americans, Korean-Americans, and so on.

In the last few decades, there has been a growing consciousness of racial and ethnic *identities*. This consciousness has been stimulated and maintained by social movements of various minority groups, aimed at attaining equality in civil and human rights. If "pluralism" connotes equality in civil and human rights for members of all groups in a society, America is not yet a pluralistic society.

The heterogeneity of American society is not limited to racial and ethnic differences. Another dimension of difference is that of *religious* belief and

17

practice. The Constitution laid a basis for religious pluralism in America through the separation of church and state and the constitutional guarantees of people's right to worship freely. Continuing immigration and missionary efforts have added religious minorities (for example, Eastern Orthodox, Islamic, Hindu, and Buddhist groups) to the three major religious groups in America—Protestant, Roman Catholic, and Jewish.

Another dimension of difference—traditionally denied by many Americans—is *social class*. Sociological studies have shown evidence of a persistent, though changing, structure of social classes in America. The dividing lines between social class groups are often blurred by economic and social mobility and by ethnic and racial diversity. Social class interests often find political expression under other names, in issues such as legal aid, public housing, and conflicts between labor and management.

Two other dimensions of difference have become dramatically evident in recent decades: differences based on *gender* and those based on *age*.

In recent decades, women have organized to challenge male domination in occupations traditionally regarded as "men's work," in access to positions of leadership, and in familial relationships. Of course, the successful struggle for women's right to vote reaches back into the nineteenth century. The current campaign for an Equal Rights Amendment to the U.S. Constitution seeks to lay the foundation for gender-pluralism in the law of the land, comparable to religious pluralism as it was established in the Constitution.

Marked differences in outlook and in lifestyle are associated with membership in particular age groups. Differences between young and old, between adolescents and parents, are known today as the "generation gap." Age has become a significant dimension of heterogeneity in society, and particular age groups (senior citizens, for example) view themselves as minority groups, organizing to protect their rights and interests.

The individual person has no choice about his or her race, ethnic group, sex, or (changing) age group. One has some choice in the *meanings* one attaches to one's race, sex, or age, but these memberships in themselves are not under one's control. However, there are other dimensions of difference in society that do involve personal choice. These dimensions include ideological groups (political ideology, religion of choice as distinct from religion of origin) and professional groups (lawyers, teachers).

Group differences are treated in this book in two general ways: One relates to personal experiences of self and others, of similarity and difference, and to the person's racial, ethnic, religious, or national socio-identity; the other focuses on universal and lawful intergroup processes. These include stereotyping, prejudice, scapegoating, polarization, and intergroup conflict. The general intent of this book is to help readers integrate this objective and subjective information, to increase their awareness of intergroup processes in a heterogeneous society, and to improve their skills for dealing with those who are "different."

Pluralism and Heterogeneity

As already noted, the United States is a heterogeneous society, marked by deep differences among the groups of which it is composed. "Heterogeneity" refers to the existence of differences—in beliefs and ways of life and in cultural history and perspective, as well as in power and privilege. The relations between some groups in American society are characterized by tension and at times by overt struggle and conflict. "Pluralism" is an ideal state of society in which members of diverse ethnic, racial, religious, or social groups maintain their autonomous ways yet share equitable participation in power and in access to society's resources. A heterogeneous society is not necessarily pluralistic. In a way, pluralism is an ideal form of *resolving* the problem of societal heterogeneity.

Pluralism may be more fully developed in some aspects of a heterogeneous society than in others. "Complete" pluralism would encompass the political, economic, and social relationships between groups in a society.

Political pluralism would require that all political offices and positions of power, elective or appointive, be available to any citizen without regard to membership in any subgroup of society. Barriers to public office based on the race, religion, ethnicity, or gender of candidates would be totally eliminated. In a society in which racial, ethnic, religious, and other groups differ in wealth and power, it would be necessary legally to restrain and curb the political advantage of some over others to reach political pluralism.

But political pluralism involves more than equal access of individual candidates to positions of leadership. Political pluralism refers to a structure of society as a union of distinct groups that maintain their cultural uniqueness yet constitute integral parts of the larger society (or nation), with no differences in relative power or status. Political theorists present the ideal image of pluralism in a government that preserves the balance among groups who are in "amiable competition" with each other (see Kariel, 1968).

Economic pluralism would involve equal opportunity for members of all groups in access to jobs in private and public employment. Legislation would be designed to minimize or eliminate the advantage provided to an individual because of his or her socioeconomic status, race, religion, or sex in finding and filling jobs for which he or she is qualified.

Social pluralism involves nonpolitical and noneconomic contacts as they occur in interracial, interethnic, and intergender relationships. Pluralism would mean that persons would suffer no disadvantage in their access to public accommodations and facilities or to educational and cultural resources because of their group memberships. Exceptions would be made for instances that are established by groups to maintain and continue their unique cultural or religious tradition (such as Saint Patrick's day) without intending to propagate ethnocentrism. This is a hard line to draw, but, in a pluralistic society, groups must be free to maintain their distinctive cultural ways as well as participate freely in the public life of their society.

No society has achieved complete pluralism. The United States has probably moved farthest toward pluralism in the political domain. Legal limits to participation in voting due to gender, race, or social class have been eliminated. There are still taboos against members of certain religious, racial, and ethnic groups and against women in achieving the highest office in the land, the presidency. But there are few other elective or appointive posts that have not been filled, at least occasionally in recent years, by minority persons. Furthermore, limits have been put on campaign expenditures and the public financing of campaigns in order to reduce the advantage of wealthier persons in attaining elective offices.

Achieving pluralistic arrangements in the economic domain probably started with the original antitrust legislation and other government attempts to enhance opportunities for smaller business enterprises. Such actions have helped to provide open opportunities for late-arriving immigrants to the United States to establish themselves in the business community. The most massive government interventions into the economic sphere, to equalize employment opportunities for racial, ethnic, and gender groups, took place in the last two decades. (The issue of whether giving preferential treatment to a minority group member violates the rights of individuals not in these "protected groups" is still unresolved, although several high court rulings supported the constitutionality of such preferment.)

Current relationships between the races persist as a major barrier to pluralism in the social domain. Equal access to desirable educational programs—from kindergarten to graduate and professional schools—has long been denied (or partially denied) to many groups in American society. Massive government interventions to remove barriers to equal educational opportunity have met widespread and powerful resistance. The success of pluralistic solutions in the educational sphere has been thwarted by disproportionate access to housing, by white flight from the cities, by increased use of nonpublic (i.e., private) educational facilities, and the like. These responses demonstrate the greater resistance to pluralism in the social as contrasted with the political and economic domains.

Actual pluralism has not been achieved in various domains of society, but "pluralism" operates as an *ideology* concerning the ways of dealing with heterogeneity and its unavoidable tensions and conflicts. Other views with respect to the management of social heterogeneity exist, both in idea and practice. One such view is *totalitarianism*, in which a dominant group, whether party, class, or race, defines public policies and coerces other groups into compliance with those policies. Another view is that of *apartheid*, in which different groups are planfully segregated and operate more or less autonomously within a framework policed by a dominant group. Still another view and practice is that of a *caste system,* in which the place and function of each caste within society is defined by tradition and strong social sanctions operate to prevent fraternization and mobility by persons across caste boundaries. Finally, *socialism* is a vision of equalitarian society based on comprehensive planning and public control of wealth and means of production. Although many varieties of socialism have emerged over the years (see Bell, 1968), all socialists proclaim the need for more equal political rights for all citizens and for a leveling of status differences. Socialism and pluralism share an equalitarian view, but while socialism presents a vision of uniformity in ideal society, wherein group differences are erased, pluralism advocates the maintenance of unique group characteristics and the preservation of cultural differences in an equalitarian society.

Pluralism appears to be the ideology and practice most in keeping with American traditions. As already noted, Americans have adopted pluralism in some areas of life, and even where their practices have historically been inconsistent with pluralism, a majority of Americans have traditionally adhered to pluralistic ideals. With respect to the management of group differences, pluralism seems most fully reconcilable with democratic values.

This book is written with a sharp awareness of the problems and difficulties involved in the translation of pluralistic ideals into social, economic and political practices. But this book is not about "societal" social change; rather, it focuses on *individual* social change; its emphasis is on the challenges faced by individuals living in a heterogeneous society. When individuals comprehend, accept, and cope more effectively with these problems, a heterogeneous society has a better chance of becoming more fully a pluralistic society.

Self-Definition and Group Memberships

Most writers, particularly political scientists and sociologists, view pluralism from a societal perspective, as an ideology and a set of political goals and strategies. We present a more psychological approach, which focuses on the individual person and how he or she experiences heterogeneity and pluralism in private life, as a worker, as a "citizen," and as a member of particular groups.

On the individual level, the initial questions with regard to heterogeneity are: (a) What are my group memberships? (b) Who is "similar" to me and who is "different"? (c) How do I interact with those who are different? (d)

Exercise 1.1 Who Am I?

Please take a sheet of paper, and write "Who Am I?" on the top. Then, take 10-15 minutes to write as many short answers to this question as you can. Please do *not* read further until you have completed the task.

(1) If more than one individual participated in the exercise, discuss with others your reaction to the task and the difficulties you experienced in responding to the question "Who am I?"
(2) Examine your list and distinguish between responses that appear to be primarily descriptive of your unique personal attributes and responses that reflect your group memberships.
(3) Try to divide your list into categories of responses that seem "to go together."

What are my beliefs and attitudes about others who are different from me along various dimensions of difference? Thus, the initial process to investigate is that of *self-definition*. Exercise 1.1 is suggested to launch this investigation.

Sociologists (such as Merton, 1957) distinguish between "reference groups" and "membership groups." Membership groups are groups (racial, sex, and so on) to which people belong, whether they want to or not. A reference group is "any group to which we belong or aspire to belong and which we use as a basis for judging the adequacy of our behavior" (Jones, Hendrick, & Epstein, 1979, p. 486). Writing responses to "Who am I?" clarifies the boundaries between "me" and "not me," defining some of your groups of membership and reference.

To help readers analyze their own responses, the spontaneous responses of two women to the "Who Am I?" exercise are presented.

Jill

I am a mother, a wife, and a full-time businesswoman.

I am proud and outspoken.

I am a friend to the majority of people I know.

I am creative at home.

I am the type of person who can deal with any situation and not be freaked over the load of work or the lack of work.

I am loved by few and disliked by many because of my attitude toward life.

I love music and animals (I have a Great Dane and an alligator).

Sue

I am a woman: I am a feminist.

I am white, 24, and an American.

I live by myself in a large city and worry about walking alone at night.

I have strong feelings and beliefs. I value my questioning outlook and view of the world.

I believe in the power of the individual and I am trying to grow more comfortable with my own power.

My chosen occupation is to help people realize their power and their ability to grow.

I am perceptive, creative, and energetic.

The two women's responses provide information with regard to group memberships they consider significant. Sue states first that she is a woman and a feminist, adding her race, age, and nationality. Jill views herself foremost in terms of her family and work groups. Further down the list Sue focuses on her ideological reference group (the feminists) as well as the implied reference groups of those who are "ideological" and those who "have strong feelings," while Jill emphasizes her *social* style. Jill states that she is disliked by many because of her attitude toward life, and the implied group that shares Jill's "attitude toward life" is probably a significant group for her.

These two lists exemplify several additional distinctions. "Groups" in self-definition can be real or imaginary (that is, with or without an actual, shared membership), and they can range from "demographic" (for example, Catholic, female, black) to "psychological" (jocks, workaholics, responsible persons, and so on). Their significance to the person lies in the person's subjective experiences and meanings. Furthermore, responses to "Who Am I?" clarify the difference between self-perception and perception by others. The two often overlap and confirm each other, but sometimes they can be disparate or even contradict each other. The interesting point is that the perception by others often becomes incorporated into one's own self-definition, even when one's self-perception is dissonant from the way(s) one is perceived by others.

In light of this discussion, responses to the "Who Am I?" task may be reexamined, bearing in mind:

(1) that self-definition is a process of defining who is "similar" and who is "different";

(2) that self-definition delineates one's membership groups and reference groups; and

(3) that groups can be defined not only by demographic and sociological criteria but also by individual psychological criteria.

The Person in Heterogeneous Society

The clusters of problems presented in the remainder of this chapter deal with the effects of heterogeneity on both the societal and the individual level. The challenges facing the individual in a heterogeneous society are the challenges facing society itself. We believe that the first step in a process of self-inquiry is to identify underlying issues and problems, explicating them and examining their relevance to the person's own history and life experiences.

DESTRUCTIVE MANIFESTATIONS OF INTERGROUP CONFLICT

The struggle toward pluralism in a heterogeneous society is often characterized by destructive and violent conflict: thus, many persons experience heterogeneity quite negatively. The tendency to define people in terms of group membership always exists in a heterogeneous society, and conflict makes group boundaries more rigid. Therefore, individuals (of majority as well as minority group membership) find themselves forcibly "grouped" (as WASPs, Jews, blacks, southerners, and so forth)—not only against their will, but often to their direct disadvantage.

The psychological realities of intergroup conflict are very different from the benign images of the early political ideologists about pluralism. Groups are *not* in "amiable competition" with each other, nor does a "spontaneous equilibrium" among groups readily emerge as these theorists had imagined (see Kariel, 1968). Conflicts between groups are intense, bitter, and destructive, and gains attained by one group are almost invariably at the expense of other groups.

Thus, individuals may find themselves as innocent bystanders in a battlefield. Many individuals of goodwill are repelled, and often victimized, by the extreme manifestations of "pluralistic struggle." The mass media further contribute to the destructiveness of intergroup conflict, tending to find higher "newsworthiness" in its more violent manifestations.

In summary, the undesirable manifestations of intergroup struggle are the groupings into which they force persons, often against their wishes; the heightened consciousness of minority and majority groups; the increasing militancy and unreasonableness of embattled minorities and threatened majorities; the influences of the mass media; and in general the resulting atmosphere of warfare and enmity.

Exercise 1.2

Before proceeding, we suggest that you stop to examine if and how you have experienced some of the hostile and destructive manifestations of intergroup conflict. From your own experiences or the experiences of people you know well, try to identify specific instances illustrating the destructive phenomena identified above.

UNDERSTANDING THOSE WHO ARE "DIFFERENT"

People experience great difficulty in understanding others who are significantly "different" from themselves. The basis for understanding others is our understanding of ourselves. According to attribution theorists (such as Harvey, Ickes, & Kidd, 1976; Jones, 1977; Ross, 1977), every person is actually an "intuitive psychologist," holding implicit psychological theories that explain feelings and behaviors. Using these implicit theories, people make sense of their experiences and explain events that take place in their social environments. In order to understand others, people project their theories onto the others' behaviors. As long as the experiences of these others are psychologically similar to the experiences of the interpreter, the latter's "understanding" of others can be quite accurate. When the others are psychologically different, people lose the basis for understanding them. This is most evident when travelers encounter a culture very different from their own. They experience an inability to decode behaviors, to make causal inferences, and generally to "understand" the underlying psychology of those who are so different. They often make embarrassing mistakes by applying their own familiar, but inappropriate, behavioral customs in interaction with those who are different.

In a similar fashion one person may be unable to understand the other sex, another person may be unable to understand the poor and the uneducated, another will not understand religious fanatics, yet another may not understand those who are older—and all of us experience difficulties in understanding those who are "stupid" or who simply disagree with us. Group boundaries (on the basis of nationality, education, social class, age, sex, and so on) define empirically who is "similar" and who is "different." But even within the similarity of a group, the unique experiences of individuals may be so varied as to create personal meanings that make it difficult to understand those who are "similar." On the other hand, most human experiences have common and universal elements, even if they are not experienced in the same context. One does not have to be a member of a particular group to have had experienced rejection and scapegoating—every person experiences being

---

Exercise 1.3

The following list of human roles represents groups of "others" varying in degree of similarity or difference from you.

—grandfather—woman—adolescent—priest—athlete—murderer—student—teacher—salesperson—Frenchman

(1) Rearrange the ten stimuli according to your ease in "understanding" them. Assign the rank of 1 to the person you could most easily understand and with whom you could most easily empathize, and the rank of 10 to the person you would have most difficulty in understanding.
(2) Examine your rankings and try to identify *how* you assigned the rankings and what considerations affected your decisions.
(3) Imagine yourself interacting with No. 3 and No. 8 on your list. How would these experiences differ from each other?

---

an outsider at one time or another and therefore can understand even those who are very different in terms of their life histories and group memberships.

In a parenthetical note, we wish to distinguish *understanding* those who are different from *accepting* those who are different, *empathizing* with those who are different, and *identifying* with those who are different. "Understanding" is the cognitive capacity to know and comprehend the other person's thoughts and terms of reference. "Empathy" is the emotional capacity to take the other person's point of view and experience what the other is experiencing as if in the other's "shoes." "Acceptance" and "identification" add a value judgment to the cognitive or emotional understanding—a judgment that legitimizes the other and his or her actions, or even expresses a wish "to be" like that other.

One can understand others or empathize with them without necessarily accepting their actions. "I can empathize with the frustration of the inner-city youths which led them to loot the neighborhood store, but I nevertheless feel they should be punished!" The first goal of pluralism is to develop people's capacity for understanding and empathizing with those who are different. A further goal of pluralism is to develop people's capacity to accept different ways of life and different value orientations as legitimate, even if they cannot really identify with them.

THE INFLUENCES OF SCHOOLING

School is society's major instrument of socialization. Schools are supposed to provide knowledge, to educate, and to be the arena of experiencing and learning to interact with "different others." It is probably true that the

---

Exercise 1.4

Think back to your years in elementary and high school and examine the extent
to which you received "education for pluralism." Try to note particularly salient events—positive or negative—that influenced your learning to relate to
"different others."

---

majority of schools fail to provide education that could advance pluralism in
society.

It seems that public schools in America have historically served as a major
instrument of a particular, *non*pluralistic kind of socialization: Americanization. They have served to encourage and convert "outside" groups to a central
way of life—that of the white, Protestant, majority culture. Educating toward
pluralism would mean giving equal status to different cultures and teaching
the value of differences. American schoolchildren are often taught to be
"tolerant" but not truly pluralistic.

It is often alleged that, even in educating toward one dominant, "American" way of life, schools are not doing a very good job: Educators are often
preachy; value education tends to be dogmatic and remote from the students'
experiences; and students can witness marked gaps between ideology and
practice when teachers act contrary to the values they preach. Children in
schools indeed experience heterogeneity, but their experience of heterogeneity often includes separatism, fear, hostility, and prejudice.

These issues are reflected in the ways many teachers deal with differences
among children. Schools are publicly committed to an ideology of "treating
every person as an equal human being," but the following studies give ample
evidence that many teachers' behaviors toward students are biased by cultural
stereotypes and preexisting expectations. As *Pygmalion in the Classroom*
(Rosenthal & Jacobson, 1968) and its numerous replications (see Rosenthal,
1971; Rosenthal & Rubin, 1978) have shown, students believed by their
teachers to be "late bloomers" (but actually selected at random from class
lists by the researchers) may indeed show subsequent progress as a result of
the teachers' expectancies. Brophy and Good (1970) showed that teachers
behave differently toward children they believe to differ in ability. Rubovitz
and Maehr (1973), Anderson and Rosenthal (1968), and Babad (1977) have
shown how black and retarded children labeled "brighter" than others may
be discriminated against by their teachers. Recently, Babad, Inbar, and Rosenthal (1982b) have shown that biased teachers' nominations of "high ability" and "low ability" students are influenced by the students' ethnic and
social class background as well as by their level of physical attractiveness. In

another work, Babad, Inbar and Rosenthal (1982a) have shown how the expectations of biased teachers result in negative treatment of children for whom they hold low expectations.

THE "MELTING POT" AND ITS ALTERNATIVES

Perhaps the most widely used catchphrase for Americanization is the *melting pot.* Indeed, in a country as heterogeneous as the United States, the belief that the common hardships and challenges of building a new society would lead to the emergence of a common "American" model of citizenship was quite attractive and very influential. What is confusing to the individual is the indiscriminate praise of both pluralism *and* the melting pot, while actually these two conceptions are very different from, if not contradictory to, each other (see Laumann, 1973; Novack, 1973).

The term "melting pot" implies subjecting different substances to such an intense heat that the result is one, new, uniform entity. This image is the expression of the hope that, in the "new world," differences between groups will disappear and society will be characterized by uniformity, equality, and the acceptance of one salient ideology. Thus, the melting pot ideology seeks to erase differences. In contrast, pluralistic ideology maintains that groups should remain different and distinct from each other, while equal opportunity and equality before the law are preserved.

Rather than talking about the "melting pot," one should perhaps talk about "vegetable soup." Vegetable soup consists of many different vegetables, each making a unique and different contribution to the soup's taste. As Bill Russell, the famous basketball player and advocate of the black cause, is quoted to have said, "You do not expect an onion to taste like a tomato."

Exercise 1.5

From your own personal experiences, try to identify specific events that reflect a melting pot orientation and a vegetable soup orientation. Evaluate the outcomes of these events for you and other participants. What are *your* ideas about this issue?

THE USE OF POWER AND THE POWER OF RIGHTEOUSNESS

Sociologists have characterized our heterogeneous society in terms of power differentials between groups—where the advantages of the majority over the minorities include wealth, education, sophistication, and better access to leadership and decision-making positions. Unlike the South African example, direct use of power against the disadvantaged is totally inacceptable in the United States today, and society is committed to equalitarian ideas and practices.

Under these conditions, a subtle form of paternalistic interaction develops, a pattern that leads to rather destructive outcomes. Those in control of resources decide what is "good" for others and force upon the disadvantaged minorities what is "good for them." Decisions about good or bad are reached from their own point of view, believed to be of universal validity. They may very sincerely wish to help the disadvantaged, but they construe "help" ethnocentrically from their own point of view and are unable to view the situation from the other group's point of view, nor are they aware of the paternalistic overtones of their good intentions. And when the disadvantaged beneficiaries remain resistant, angry, and militant, the helpers become hurt, frustrated, and self-righteous: "We really tried to help them, and they don't even know what is good for them!"

Phenomena of this type take place in a variety of interactions between racial, ethnic, religious, and gender groups in heterogeneous society. They also take place in other situations characterized by power differentials, such as interactions between teachers and students, parents and children, superiors and subordinates, and social workers and poor families.

"Knowing what is good for others," is basically "egocentric" or "ethnocentric"—being able to perceive the world only from one's own perspective. When the majority tries to help the minority from an ethnocentric perspective, a level of superiority is implied, but this superiority is subtle, implicit, and often sugar-coated with professed good intentions. Minority groups are extremely sensitive to this attitude, and it makes them angry and aggressive. Today men often experience the angry responses of women to traditionally "masculine" gestures (such as the address "honey," door-opening, or bag-carrying), wondering why women would consider such behaviors sexist.

Examples of "knowing what is better for them" and its inherent self-righteousness can be found in the international arena as well. During the Vietnam period many American citizens believed that the Asians need freedom, and that "freedom" is defined in the American way (two parties, two houses of congress, free elections, and a president). Similarly, many well-meaning Northern activists of the civil rights movement in the 1960s had miserable experiences in the South. They were unable to understand why they had been rejected as vigorously by some of the blacks they had come to

---

Exercise 1.6

Think of yourself in two of your social roles, one of higher status and one of lower status vis-à-vis "others." For each of these roles, try to recall one example of a self-righteous helping event—as a recipient in one role and as a giver in the other. Compare the outcomes of these two events, your feelings, and those of the other party.

help as by the "bigoted" whites. American Peace Corps volunteers in numerous countries have had similar experiences of rejection and resentment by the local beneficiaries of their help.

We do believe that at times "some may know what is better for others," but the distinction between being "right" and being "righteous" is often hard to make, and one must be aware of the sensitivities of others.

UNINTENDED OUTCOMES OF THE CHANGE PROCESS

Any process of change has intended and unintended outcomes. Intended outcomes are usually positive, at least for their direct target, or beneficiary. Unintended outcomes can be positive *and* negative, affecting the target of change as well as other parties in a larger social context. We focus here on negative unintended outcomes and their social consequences.

Examples of unintended outcomes resulting from "positive" changes are numerous and varied. The growing assertiveness of some women sometimes destroys beyond repair the long-established balance in their families; the "meteoric" success of individuals and companies often carries the seeds of subsequent personal and financial fall; and the implementation of a new teaching method in a school may disrupt the delicate balance of human relations among the staff. The direct experience of negative unintended outcomes can spoil the positive outcomes of the change process, leading to bitterness and frustration even when a positive change has taken place.

Unintended outcomes are outcomes that were not anticipated or predicted before change took place. They are unanticipated either because they were beyond human capacity to foresee or because they *could* have been anticipated but the relevant parties did not anticipate them. Reasons for not anticipating particular outcomes may vary from uncritical thinking to misinterpretation of available information. Individuals and groups often have an explicit interest in *not* anticipating all outcomes, for fear that the change they advocate might be jeopardized if all consequences are anticipated.

In the area of social change, and particularly in change toward pluralism, the probability of the emergence of unintended outcomes is high, and the consequences of such unintended outcomes are very destructive. Changes toward pluralism are usually "tradeoff" situations, in which some positive benefits (say, allocation of funds for a particular purpose) entail potential losses in other areas, and in which one group's gain is almost invariably at the expense of another group. Additional reasons for the high frequency of unintended outcomes in change toward pluralism include the facts that solutions are worked out in an atmosphere of acute tension and conflict, so that they must provide short-range relief of tension; that many pluralistic solutions are compromises between irreconcilable demands rather than products of careful planning (following the famous definition of a camel as "a horse created by a committee"); and the point we mentioned above, that the planners of change—ideologues and/or politicians—often have a conscious or unconscious interest in being blind to potential outcomes of the changes they advocate.

Examples of such unintended consequences of social change are numerous. For example, it has been recognized by now that the construction of high rise public housing for the poor has resulted in disastrous consequences. The concentration of poor people in mass situations with no community norms for controlling delinquent and criminal behavior, and the lack of parental control over children contributed to sharp rises in crime.

Another example is the issue of busing of children to achieve racial integration of the schools. While the desirability of desegregation is largely recognized, the negative unintended outcomes of this policy have been apparent in recent years: Some communities have split into hostile camps; private schools flourish, undermining desegregation plans for the public schools; and the mobility from the cities to the suburbs ("white flight") has received a new impetus.

HETEROGENEITY WITHIN THE PERSON

Persons belong to many groups, and the demands of these memberships are often conflicting and sometimes contradictory. Much as society-at-large cannot readily turn heterogeneity into pluralism, it is difficult for the individual person to turn internal heterogeneity into internal pluralism.

Heterogeneity within the person is perhaps most readily understood through the concepts, role and role conflict. "Role" is a particular group affiliation (daughter, athlete, teacher, salesperson, Democrat, consumer) together with its prescriptive patterns of behavior. Each role embodies expectations by self and others concerning the appropriate behaviors that the role occupant should enact. "Role conflict" means that two or more roles are salient and active at the same time, and their prescriptions are dissonant with each other.

As we show in a later chapter on roles, an important part of socialization is learning how to manage role conflicts with relatively little friction. We view the term "heterogeneity within the person" to refer to conflicts between socio-identities—entities that are not as narrowly defined as social roles. Sometimes one socio-identity (say, racial or ethnic) revolves around a perspective and life experiences of minority, while another socio-identity entails a "majority perspective."

Consider, for example, the conflict of minority group members who devote themselves to attaining "success" in the majority culture. Having reached leadership positions in government or industry, they suddenly find themselves divorced from their groups of origin, wishing to maintain their old membership yet finding it difficult to do so. Another example is the case of the devout Mormon woman who was excommunicated in 1980 due to her public support and advocacy of the Equal Rights Amendment.

Exercise 1.7

Can you recall instances in your own life history when you experienced your internal heterogeneity? Were you able to apply "pluralistic solutions" in these instances? What are your major strategies of resolving internal conflicts?

DISTORTED INFORMATION AND "CRITERIA FOR VALID KNOWLEDGE"

In order to take positions with regard to social issues, people must obtain information, evaluate it, and reach conclusions. We argue that although people receive a lot of information, they neither receive enough *valid* information nor are provided with appropriate criteria for evaluating the information they receive. Much of what is transmitted as "objective truth" over the various media is in fact a mix of facts and opinions, colored by the particular biases and intentions of the sources of information.

When controversial social issues are involved (as, for example, in the Bakke case of 1978, busing and desegregation, and allocation of public funds), the public is exposed to different versions of "the facts"—each distorted by the views held by the particular source of information. Often enough people "do not want to be confused with facts, since they have made up their minds." At other times people mislead themselves into believing that they possess all the relevant facts and that they reach independently their own conclusions, while in effect they receive biasing, conclusive information. Even when one wishes to obtain full, reliable, and valid information, it is not always readily available. The following is a summary of the major sources of social information available to the individual in our society.

(1) "Personal knowledge" and own experiences
(2) Interactions with
    (a) similar others
    (b) different others
    (c) expert others
(3) Mass media
    (a) representatives of groups
    (b) politicians
    (c) random samples
    (d) reporters
    (e) experts

"Personal knowledge" can be the most biased source of information, but people tend to rely on it the most. Persons "know" things because they have experienced them personally or because they have learned them in the past. But personal experience is limited and nonrepresentative, leading to over-generalization and faulty reasoning.

Through interactions with others (friends, acquaintances, relatives, teachers, and so on), persons gain information that contributes to the shaping of their values and attitudes. Because of its directness and intimacy, personal contact often has greater impact than do impersonal media and book information. However, knowledge derived from interactions with others not only suffers the same limitations as personal knowledge but also entails additional distortions, inherent in the exchange of information (for example, selective hearing, miscommunication).

Students of the mass media maintain that it would be naive to think that the media provide the individual with full, objective, and unbiased information, although some media are less distorting than others. Because of the competition among networks and newspapers and journalists' tendency to *create* as well as report news, their credibility as dependable sources of valid information is reduced. They often advocate points of view under the guise of objectivity, and they give unproportional salience to extremely dramatic information. The media can build and destroy political candidates; they can create public issues (consider the role played by Walter Cronkite in engineering the meeting between Sadat and Begin in 1977) and maintain public interest in particular issues; and they can shape public opinion in a variety of ways.

A popular way of providing information on the media is to have "the person on the street," the common citizen, respond to a public issue and voice opinions. The underlying assumption is that this citizen "could be any-body—could be you" and therefore constitutes a representative sample of the "public-at-large." Despite its media appeal, however, this strategy is usually biased and misleading, and the information it provides must be scrutinized carefully.

The final group of informants consists of the "experts." Experts are supposed to be objective and unbiased, providing scientific "knowledge" that is not influenced by group interest. But even experts are not above suspicion: They often cannot separate their ideology from their science; hence the likelihood that two experts would disagree with each other is quite high.

Stephen J. Morse, law professor and psychologist at the University of Southern California, wrote the following comment about experts:

> One of the major news magazines called me the week before last. Since I am a lawyer as well as a psychologist, the reporter wanted to know why I, as a

supposed expert, believed looting had occurred during the blackout in New York City.

I told the interviewer that the only responsible statement a social scientist ought to make is that he or she had no idea why the looting has taken place. After all, little reliable hard data exist concerning infrequent events such as looting after a blackout in a city like New York. The causes are probably so complex, in fact, that determining them is beyond our present competence in social science.

Indeed, upon reading expert statements as ultimately published by the news magazines, I was struck by how thin they were. Most of the assessments were really no more than commonsense reactions.

Consider some examples from *Time's* report. A noted Harvard psychologist said: "When economic conditions get better, those who are left behind get angrier." Another psychologist characterized the looting as "a Robin Hood type of thing—steal from the rich and give to the poor." A third expert said: "It was just like *Lord of the Flies*. People resort to savage behavior when the brakes of civilization fail." These statements may be right or wrong but they certainly don't offer great insight into the events in Brooklyn and the Bronx.

What I did was to ask my interviewer why she thought the looting took place. Her answer was that the looters were people who had less than the majority of Americans, were angry about it and seized the moment to take action. Is there any substantive difference in analytic power between her assessment and that of the "experts"?

Now, experts are also ordinary citizens and, as such, they are entitled to their opinions about current events. But by giving opinions on subjects outside their discipline or by basing statements on insufficient data, they undermine public respect for all experts. Most social scientists are aware of the complexity of events they study and usually their professional publications are full of cautionary words, for they recognize that most social science data are tentative and few questions have been answered authoritatively.

Unfortunately, present social and psychological technology is primitive. Beyond that, all human beings believe—or at least behave as if they believe—that they are the experts on human behavior. There is, of course, much truth in this, which is why, in many cases, I trust my common sense over and above my professional acumen. And I trust common sense in general.

Naturally, my commonsense conclusions will not always agree with someone else's. But then, at least, the two of us can decide what to do on the grounds of whose common sense seems wiser—not on the grounds that I have special knowledge because I am an expert.

I am not suggesting that experts should abandon efforts to analyze rigorously difficult social problems and to share their findings with the public. Rather, I am urging that they, like the larger society, should be more sensitive to the limits of their own expert knowledge. (Reprinted, with permission, from the *Los Angeles Times,* July 29, 1977.)

Exercise 1.8

Focus your attention on one current issue of intergroup conflict (such as women's liberation, race relations, the right of women to abortions, or conflict in the community). Try to trace your sources of information about this issue and your criteria for evaluating the validity of the information you have. On what sources do you rely the most? How do you screen information? How do you test your information in dialogue with others? Do you discuss this issue with people with whom you agree or with people from whom you differ?

THE PRICE OF PLURALISM FOR THE MAJORITY GROUP

The essence of pluralistic ideology is that the "accident" of one's birth into particular groups should not be the source of either advantage or disadvantage in society. Membership in any particular racial, ethnic, religious, or gender group should neither provide higher status nor hinder the individual's social standing. Pluralistic society will not be a uniform society—there will be rich and poor, uneducated and highly educated—but attaining higher status or higher education will *not* be related to a person's race, religion, or sex.

For this to come about, the group(s) enjoying most power in contemporary society must give up their advantageous positions and allow equal access by other groups to political and economic "goods." To ensure equal access and equal opportunity, governmental action must create barriers against the continuous accumulation of wealth and power by any one group.

The price to be paid for the creation of true pluralism by those in advantageous positions is rather high. Human nature and society being what they are, the advantaged groups cannot be expected to pay this entire bill of their own free will. People who are liberal and ideologically inclined toward pluralism would probably be willing to give up *some* advantages they enjoy, but not necessarily *all* advantages. They might like to help the disadvantaged and decrease the gap between groups in society, but it would only be natural that they would wish to maintain at least some edge of advantage. This is true for most issues of pluralistic struggle in our society—race relations, allotment of public funds, equal opportunity and equal rights, education, and so forth. And this is why changes toward pluralism in a society always involve conflict and struggle, enmity and hostility. Minority groups put pressure on those in power to yield more than they might wish. Minority leaders justifiably feel that if they were dependent on what the majority would hand down to them without struggling for better attainments, they would remain at a disadvantage forever. If pluralism is to come to America, it will be an achievement, not a gift. And this achievement will involve intergroup conflict and bitter fighting. But the hope is that conflicts can eventually be resolved productively.

Exercise 1.9

Choose one dimension of your social self where you belong to an "advantaged" group in society (for example, white, male, upper-middle-class).

(1) What will "pluralism" mean for this dimension?
(2) What is the price *you* will be called upon to pay?
(3) What are you willing to give up and what are you not willing to give up to facilitate pluralistic solutions in this domain?

A METHOD OF INQUIRY
INTO THE SOCIAL SELF

Requirements for the Method

Before outlining the method we recommend for readers to use in exploring themselves as social beings, we review briefly the ideas already presented. People in America and in many other nations live and work in societies that are heterogeneous along several dimensions of difference. Persons and groups must deal with other persons and groups who are different from themselves in their cultures, values, aspirations, cognitive styles, and ways of life. In America, there is much tension among different groups, yet most Americans have not been taught how to deal effectively with such tension.

The dominant ideology of America is individualistic. This view of the world emphasizes, rightly as we see it, the importance and worth of the individual person. But it also has led to an unfortunate neglect, sometimes to a willful ignoring, of the powerful influences of group memberships in shaping the values, beliefs, and behavioral patterns of individual persons. A person's "identity" is a complex integration of personality attributes, unique experiences, personal choices, and the individual sense of "self," on the one hand, and "socio-identities," which are the products of various group memberships, on the other hand. This duality is noted by writers such as Stryker (1977), who distinguished between the "two social psychologies" in his treatment of identity and self theory. Birnbaum (1975) wrote that because of social pressures and constraints, the traditional definition of self in "individual-idiosyncratic" terms only is giving way to the need to define and be defined in group terms—black, white, WASP, Catholic, Jew, woman, youth, Spanish-speaking, and so on.

Some socio-identities, such as race, gender, and ethnicity, are outside the range of individual choice—persons are "born" into them. Others, such as vocation, religion, and political identity, are more within the range of individual choice, while the socio-identity of age changes with the passing years.

It has become virtually impossible to ignore the social heterogeneity of American society during the past few decades. Racial, ethnic, gender, and age groups have asserted (sometimes overasserted) their rights to their distinctive ways of life and have demanded a more equitable share in the power and privileges in society. We argued in the previous chapter that pluralistic solutions to these tensions and conflicts are desirable. Moving toward pluralism sets a difficult learning task for individual persons. They must find ways of learning acceptance and understanding of differences that set them apart from other groups. Such empathy is possible only as persons learn to understand their own socio-identities, in terms of both how these were shaped and the ways in which they influence their lives and social interactions.

Learning requires cognitive content: ideas, concepts, and theories. Social-psychological knowledge is particularly appropriate for the required learning, for social psychology links the societal and the individual-personal aspects of human living. However, psychological knowledge will influence people's actual choices, decisions, actions, and interactions only as they learn to apply this knowledge to their own life situations. The application of knowledge is by no means easy, for persons bring to learning situations their own knowledge, beliefs, and implicit theories concerning social-psychological matters. Their personal knowledge, beliefs, and theories have been acquired in the process of growing up, and they influence perceptions and behavior even when they are implicit and their holders are not aware of them. Effective inquiry therefore requires persons to become aware of their own assumptions about themselves and others—assumptions that are often inconsistent with, even contradictory to, the knowledge acquired through scientific studies and theories. Successful inquiry integrates the various bits of knowledge into a richer and more informed social perspective.

There are strong obstacles to the attainment of self-awareness and the pursuit of self-inquiry. These obstacles are discussed extensively in Chapter 3, with the hope that awareness of the obstacles will be a first step toward avoiding, circumventing, or otherwise managing them.

This brief review permits a formulation of the requirements for a productive method of inquiry into the social self.

(1) The method must increase persons' awareness and acceptance of the heterogeneity of society and its resulting personal and social difficulties.

(2) It must draw upon scientific social-psychological knowledge and show its relevance and applicability to learners' life situations.

(3) It must challenge and support persons to become aware of their own unarticulated personal knowledge and underlying psychological theories.

(4) It must help help learners to become aware of the obstacles to self-inquiry and to circumvent them where possible.

(5) It must help persons to understand the social-cultural genesis of group differences and to empathize with others of distinctive perspectives and ways of life.

(6) It must help persons recognize the major psychological manifestations of intergroup process (such as group unity and cohesion, stereotyping, prejudice,

and discrimination) and to examine how these phenomena are reflected in their own life events.

(7) It must help persons to practice pluralistic ways of dealing and working with other persons different from themselves.

Genesis of the Method

A method of inquiry that fits these requirements was first developed in "laboratories" designed for the education of community workers, social services professionals, and volunteers, whose work involved them in multi-group situations. "Laboratories" are residential educational experiences in which participants explore their own behavior patterns, beliefs, and orientations as these affect other people. Participants experiment with alternative patterns, learn new methods and strategies, and share their experiences with other participants. A central feature of laboratories of this type is the face-to-face small group. See Benne (1964) for a historical review of the laboratory method, and Benne's (1976) review of Kurt Lewin's principles of re-education as reflected in 25 years of laboratory education.

In the 1960s, Max Birnbaum and Kenneth Benne developed a special type of community laboratory—the Clarification (or C) Group—to focus almost exclusively on issues of group differences, socio-identities, and intergroup phenomena (see Birnbaum, 1975; Babad, Birnbaum, & Benne, 1978). The Clarification Group consists of 10 to 12 members, heterogeneous with respect to race, ethnicity, religion, gender, social class, occupation, and age as the laboratory population allows. One task of each member is to explore his or her own life history, identify significant group memberships, and examine how these have shaped his or her value orientations, attitudes toward own and other groups, and relations with others who are similar or different. As members compare and contrast the development of their socio-identities and significant life events with those of other members, they become more aware of the social bases of their experiences. Differences and tensions do not disappear, but as they are better understood and accepted, rational collaboration across intergroup boundaries becomes more feasible.

The Clarification Group is ordinarily accompanied by structured laboratory experiences designed to serve several purposes. One purpose is to teach relevant social-psychological theory and concepts in order to assist participants in analyzing the personal material elicited in the clarification groups. Another purpose is to raise into consciousness dimensions of difference that are operating, more or less nonconsciously, within the laboratory population as it lives and learns together. These take the form of designed confrontations between parts of the laboratory population along various dimensions of differences: gender, age, religion, ethnicity, and the like. Still another purpose is to analyze societal issues of public policy that create intergroup tension and conflict in the back-home situations of most participants (such as busing, abortion, and the Equal Rights Amendment). Participants are also grouped, on the basis of similar back-home situations, into consultation groups. They analyze particular intergroup problems confronting them in their back-home situations and receive assistance from other members and from the staff in planning pluralistic strategies for dealing with these problems.

This book is our attempt to convert the Clarification Group methodology into a learning and self-inquiry instrument that can be used in settings other than the experiential human relations laboratory. We provide in this book both the relevant scientific knowledge and guidelines for self-inquiry and for application of that knowledge to readers' own lives and social situations. The method of inquiry is based on the principles that are outlined next.

Principles of the Method

Readers who have done the exercises in Chapter 1, beginning with the "Who Am I?" exercise, have already begun to use the method of inquiry discussed here. In these activities readers relate their personal experiences, attitudes, values, relationships, and behaviors to general knowledge in psychology and sociology.

PRINCIPLE 1:
EXPLORING LIFE HISTORY

Every person's life history provides rich data that can explain "who the person is" in terms of crucial group memberships (racial, ethnic, religious, gender, social class); how the person's social development was and is shaped by experiences related to these memberships; the meanings the person attaches to these dimensions of social self; and the person's network of social interactions with other persons. Such exploration should balance the universal and the unique, the collective and the individual: Some life experiences are shared by all human beings, other experiences are particular to members of specific groups, and still other experiences are uniquely personal and idiosyncratic. Exploring their life histories, persons can come to recognize the reality and power of group differences and group affiliations in the formation of identity. By comparing and contrasting their own experiences with those of other inquirers, similar and different, persons come to formulate and reformulate their own socio-identities and their images of the socio-identities of others. Small and Birnbaum (1971) have delineated in detail the method and application of the "structured group interview," through which life histories are explored in the Clarification Group.

We consider the exploration of life history (conducted, preferably, in the company of others) to be of great significance. Therefore, we devote Chapter 4 in its entirety to this issue, presenting first a written account of a young woman's exploration of her ethnic and national identity, and following this account with specific guidelines that can be used by readers to explore their own life histories.

PRINCIPLE 2:
RECOGNIZING MULTIPLICITY OF SOCIO-IDENTITIES

Each person incorporates a complex profile of group identities. A white person has grown up as female or male, perhaps Roman Catholic or Jew, poverty-ridden or affluent, Italian-American or Swedish-American, southerner or Yankee. The proposed method of inquiry seeks to make persons aware of the multiplicity of socio-identities that they have internalized in the processes of their development. Each socio-identity exerts its unique influence on the person's social self, but the combination and interaction of these multiple identifications make for great internal complexity and heterogeneity.

"Pluralistic" solutions to inner heterogeneity require acceptance of the multiplicity of inner voices, acceptance of tensions and conflicts between "parts" of the person as normal and expected, and the ability to negotiate differences between the conflicting demands of various socio-identities. When one becomes more aware of this multiplicity in other people, one cannot deal with others through stereotypic, unidimensional, narrow notions.

PRINCIPLE 3:
BECOMING AWARE OF STEREOTYPES

Persons perceive others as members of groups and attribute to them what they hold to characterize these groups. These generalized attributes are stereotypes, and, like all generalizations, they have varying degrees of truth-value. Stereotypes exist because they are functional for people (see Chapter 5), and it is hard to imagine any person who does not use stereotypes at all. But many people are unaware of the stereotypes they hold and often quite resistant to such awareness.

It is important for people to become aware of their own stereotypes, to assess the validity of each stereotype, and to increase the flexibility of their systems of social perception. But awareness of stereotypes is important in a deeper way, since stereotypes are "behavioral" no less than "perceptual." Exchanges across intergroup lines often become ritualistic and stereotypic, or, to quote F. H. Bradley, a "ballet of categories."

An adequate method of inquiry into the social self helps inquirers to become aware of their own stereotypes and prejudices. Scientific knowledge concerning stereotypy and prejudice, as presented in Chapters 5 and 6, can facilitate awareness. But such knowledge needs to be personalized. Analysis of life history, especially of significant interactions with members of other groups, is one way of helping a person to locate and articulate some of the stereotypes he or she has learned in the process of growing up. Special exercises can further facilitate this process of attaining self-awareness. Babad et al. (1978) describe a variety of stereotypy exercises that are used in a C-Group laboratory. Many of the activities suggested in later parts of this book have been designed to help readers get in touch with their own stereotypes with regard to racial, ethnic, religious, national, gender, age, occupational, and ideological groups.

PRINCIPLE 4:
EXPERIENCING INTERGROUP CONFLICT AND RESOLUTION

Conflicts along intergroup lines occur when the existing balance between groups is disturbed. This may occur in a program for desegregation of schools that were previously all-white, all-black, or all-Hispanic; it may occur when members of a minority group are introduced into a work force from which they were previously excluded; and, of course, it may occur when minority group members attempt to change an existing balance that they find oppressive, asserting themselves and presenting demands to the majority group.

There are usually "realistic" differences of interest involved in such conflicts: competition for jobs, promotion, for recognition and prestige. Such realistic differences are potentially resolvable through rational negotiation and adjudication. But "realistic" differences of interest often become intertwined with "nonrealistic" elements—projections of fears, stereotypic and prejudicial ascriptions of undesirable motivations, and deeply rooted hostility and aggression. The opposing and polarized groups tend to depersonalize and dehumanize, even to demonize, each other, while group members "cling to their own." Such conflicts often become impervious to rational negotiation and adjudication.

Williams (1947) made this distinction between "realistic" and "nonrealistic" intergroup conflicts, while Deutsch (1973) made a similar distinction between "destructive" and "constructive" conflicts. Pluralistic strategies of conflict resolution aim at reducing and dissipating the nonrealistic and destructive elements of intergroup conflict and focusing attention on realistic and constructive elements.

In a laboratory or classroom situation, intergroup conflict may be simulated (Sherif & Sherif, 1953; Sherif, Harvey, White, Hood, & Sherif, 1961), so that learners may gain first-hand experience of their dynamics and intensity under controlled direction. Even when persons have become aware of their stereotypes and have developed some understanding and acceptance of persons who belong to groups markedly different from their own, such simulations nevertheless dramatically intensify the nonrealistic aspects of intergroup conflict, to the surprise (or rather, the dismay) of these enlightened persons. In addition to simulations, inquiry can focus on instances of intergroup conflict the learner has experienced as a participant or as a witness, analyzing the intensification of conflict, the emergence of destructive and nonrealistic elements, and the potential strategies of conflict resolution.

PRINCIPLE 5:
TRAINING IN EMPATHY

Effective communication between persons is possible only as persons are able to put themselves imaginatively into each other's shoes and view the situation from the other's as well as from their own perspective. This imaginative entry into another's perspective is called "empathy." It is relatively easy to empathize with those who are similar; it is more difficult to empathize with, or "enter the shoes" of, those who are different. Nevertheless, empathic understanding across lines of social cleavage is extremely important in achieving pluralistic solutions to intergroup problems.

Individuals differ in their abilities to empathize with others. But the empathic skills of all persons can be improved through training in the kinds of social inquiry already described—the comparison and contrast of the social influences that have shaped persons of markedly different group memberships, awareness of stereotypy and its limitations, and the sorting out of realistic and unrealistic elements in intergroup conflicts.

Special exercises may be designed to expand empathic understanding. Persons and groups in conflict may be asked to reverse roles, each arguing a conflicted issue from the standpoint of the opponent or trying to describe and analyze the situation from the other side's point of view. In these exercises, people discover how difficult it is to depart from their own perspectives, however objective they consider themselves to be.

PRINCIPLE 6:
"BACK-HOME" APPLICATION

An important part of the inquiry into the social self is the careful examination of "back-home" problems of heterogeneity and intergroup tensions that learners experience in classroom, work, civic, and other social situations. Learners can practice and experiment with strategies of applying their skills to situations in which they are involved outside the laboratory. Sessions of back-home application have always been considered a critical component of human relations training laboratories, and some activities in the following chapters were designed to facilitate such experimentation by interested readers. Learners must come to see themselves as "change agents" in their own worlds. That requires them to learn methods for diagnosing situations, to select situations that are accessible to their own influence, and to invent and test strategies of change for reducing intergroup tensions and conflicts.

PRINCIPLE 7:
LEARNING COLLABORATIVE INQUIRY

In most of the exercises recommended in this book, readers are advised to enlist the help of other readers. The use of others in self-inquiry is important for a number of reasons. Persons learn best about themselves by comparing and contrasting their own development of values, relationships, and action patterns with the experiences of others whose development has been different in some respects from their own. Persons also persist better in overcoming the obstacles to self-inquiry if they have the support of others engaged in a similar process. They can examine carefully how they interact with other learners, testing some of their ideas and notions about their social conduct.

Therefore, for the most effective process of inquiry, we suggest that readers form small learning groups. Two sometimes conflicting criteria operate in the formation of such a learning group: One criterion is that members should be able to talk about themselves to each other openly and freely; the other criterion is that the composition of the learning group will be heterogeneous enough along at least some dimensions of difference. We suggest that at other times readers enlist persons from their natural social environment (classmates, parents, relatives, colleagues, group peers, etc.) to aid them in generating relevant information and in making sense of particular events and processes.

3

OBSTACLES TO SELF-AWARENESS
AND SELF-INQUIRY

Knowledge and Its Application

It has already been emphasized that the aim of this book is to challenge and to support you in applying the knowledge it presents—drawn from social psychology, personality psychology, sociology, and social anthropology—to your own life situations. The application of knowledge involves persons in inquiry into themselves and their patterns of thought and action; their beliefs about themselves, about other people, and about their social environments; and their notions about appropriate and inappropriate, effective and ineffective, ways of behaving in the situations which confront them.

Each person has, so to speak, assembled throughout his or her lifetime a personal, unwritten "textbook" in social psychology. Persons have come to know about themselves and other people; they have learned ways of interpreting and evaluating their own motivations and those of other people; and they have acquired and tested a repertoire of behaviors. But personal knowledge of social-psychological phenomena does not always square with knowledge offered by scholars and researchers who specialize in the study of social behavior.

The vocabulary used in the two "books" is different, and the "chapter headings" in people's personal texts differ from those assigned by scholars and researchers in the books they write. The former are typically more oriented toward action; the latter, to the requirements of accurate observation, measurement, and scientific validity. The pages of some chapters in persons' texts are uncut, in the sense that people neither are always conscious of their cognitive assumptions or of their characteristic ways of classifying and interpreting social situations, nor can they clearly identify the noncognitive factors—needs, wishes, interests, feelings, values, *and* fears—that influence their social behavior.

The process of applying scientific knowledge to individuals' lives is very difficult when it is recognized that people already possess personal "knowledge" about self, others, and human situations and that they operate with varying degrees of awareness of their underlying theories and ways of "making sense." Obstacles to the application of knowledge from scholarship and research to self-inquiry and change exist in every person and every group.

We believe that the first step in managing the complexities of self-inquiry is to become aware of the obstacles that tend to block and complicate the process of inquiry. The obstacles discussed in this chapter are rooted in two psychological disciplines: one (derived from individual and personality psychology) is directed toward understanding the individual's internal dynamics and the emotional, sometimes unconscious forces that block effective utilization of knowledge; the other (derived from social psychology and sociology) is directed toward understanding social, attitudinal, cognitive, and behavioral obstacles to self-inquiry. In the remainder of this chapter we discuss and analyze the major groups of obstacles to inquiry into the social self.

Pains and Values
of Self-Awareness

The process of self-inquiry is intended to expand self-awareness. In the psychological literature, "awareness" refers most often to tracing and exploring nonconscious emotional forces as they operate within the individual, between persons, and in group interaction. In this book, "self-awareness" will be used to focus on the personal and social significance of socio-identities, on the influences of early life history and enculturation of the person as a member of particular groups (racial, ethnic, religious, social class, and so forth), and on the powerful effects of intergroup phenomena (such as stereotyping, prejudice, and group conflict) upon one's values, beliefs, and actions.

Freudian psychology has laid much emphasis on the nonconscious dimension of personality and on ways of helping persons become aware of the nonconscious bases of their own behavior. Some Freudians make a useful distinction between two areas of the nonconscious: the *unconscious* and the *preconscious*. The unconscious includes aspects of motivation, feeling, and fantasy that have been repressed. People invest considerable energy to keep unconscious feelings and thoughts out of consciousness and to prevent exposure of this material to themselves. Most unconscious material (aggressive fantasies, for example) may be quite threatening to a person if it reaches awareness; therefore, persons actively resist attempts by others to make them aware of their unconscious motivations and feelings.

The preconscious consists of ideas and images that are nonconscious at a particular moment but that could become conscious quite readily. According to some Freudians, the preconscious includes patterns of belief and value that have been built into persons in the process of their socialization, acquired without conscious attention or thought. In this view, the internalized cultural characteristics of groups to which persons belong are mostly preconscious.

Other Freudians view the socialization process as basically unconscious. In any event, many dynamic processes related to socialization and enculturation are resistant to awareness. These processes include, among others, the distorted perceptions of "different others" and the underlying aggression against "out-groups."

Nonconscious motivations and feelings are often in conflict with a person's conscious ideas and sentiments. In fact, the essence of a "dynamic" theory is that inner contradictory forces are in constant conflict with each other. The person is conscious only of part of them; therefore, the attainment of self-awareness involves accepting one's inner complexity and personal inconsistencies.

Self-awareness is sometimes attained through an experience of *insight*. Insight is a sudden experience of cognitive restructuring of a problem or a "field of behavior." It is a moment when everything "falls into place" and one is able to understand an entire pattern of behavior. Experiences of insight are relatively rare in daily life, but involvement in self-inquiry increases the chances of their emergence. Although insight involves cognitive closure, the experience of insight is emotionally charged—attaining insight is usually exciting and rewarding, even though the person becomes aware of something painful.

Absence of self-awareness can be explained both *cognitively* (that is, through limitations in people's information-processing and inference-making capacities) and *dynamically* (that is, through deep-seated emotional forces and powerful internal conflicts). The next two sections in this chapter explicate each approach. Both approaches share a central, underlying principle: that it is *more functional* for the person to be relatively unaware of particular contents and to distort somewhat the image of people and events in the person's social environment. Cognitive gains of unawareness and distortion include reduction of complexity and of informational overload, so that it is easier and less effortful for the person to act smoothly with sufficient accuracy in most situations. Dynamic gains include the avoidance of stress and conflict and maintenance of positive self-esteem.

Nisbett and Wilson (1977) provide a cognitive explanation for the commonplace lack of capacity for true introspection. According to Nisbett and Wilson, people cannot explain their behavior accurately, since they do not have direct access to their internal causes. When asked to explain why they acted in a particular way, they use their own "general psychological theories"—theories that provide plausible explanations of behavior. Thus, instead of being truly introspective, most explanations of behavior are mediated through these plausible psychological theories. The accuracy of a given explanation depends not on whether the person is truly introspective, but rather is a function of whether the appropriate and "correct" explanation is chosen by the person. If one chooses an inappropriate "theory," the explanation may be inaccurate. If one accepts this theory—and Nisbett and Wilson's notion of the lack of introspective ability has not remained unchallenged—the goal of "increasing self-awareness" should be rephrased as "teaching the best theories and providing criteria for selecting accurately among plausible explanations."

Cognitive and dynamic distortions are intertwined and often inseparable. Stereotypes, for example, are generalizations about the characteristics of a group that are indiscriminantly attributed to all members of the group, without regard to the range of individual differences among its members. Every person uses stereotypes, whether aware of it or not—about blacks and whites, men and women, children and old people, Protestants and Catholics, Italians and Jews, psychiatrists and teachers, Republicans and Democrats, New Yorkers and Californians. Thus, from the cognitive point of view, all stereotypes are distorted pictures of persons and groups. But there may be strong dynamic reasons that a person would hold *particular* stereotypes, especially those that are very negative or very positive. In general, believing that one "never uses any stereotypes" is, of course, an indication of lack of awareness.

The value of self-awareness is the value of knowledge—increasing flexibility, control, and the ability to make wise and informed choices. But self-awareness is valuable within limits. People may be more heavily defended against awareness and consciousness than they need to be, but this does *not* mean that they should not be defended at all. Processes of self-inquiry are useful as long as they are conducted within well-defined limits, without probing and pressing to surface deeply unconscious material that is heavily defended and without pushing inquirers to extreme and uncontrollable emotional states. We neither advocate nor encourage the practice of "parlor psychiatry" in the dormitory, residence, or classroom. We do advocate careful and well-planned self-inquiry to widen self-awareness and increase flexibility without increasing the person's level of anxiety too much.

Resistance to Self-Awareness

"Resistance" is a term used in psychological literature to refer to dynamic blocks to self-awareness. Resistance to self-awareness may be intentional but more often is nonconscious and without deliberate design. Persons may state (and sincerely believe) their intention to open themselves to learning about themselves while their behavior belies their words. Some people come to psychotherapy of their own initiative and free will, pay substantially for each session, and spend weeks or months resisting the therapist.

The main cause of resistance is the subjective feeling of *threat*. Awareness can expose undesirable parts of one's inner life, thereby threatening one's self-image and self-esteem, one's established attitudes and values, one's relationships with others, and one's sense of competence and general well-being. The cultural myth has it that paradise was the residence of the unknowledgeable, a fool's paradise. When Adam and Eve ate the forbidden fruit of the tree of knowledge, "their eyes opened to see that they were naked," and they were cast out of paradise into the cold, cruel world. This mythological idea is in essence an allegory of what the self-aware person might discover and of the "ignorance is bliss" notion.

Why do nearly all people assume that they will discover painful nakedness when their eyes are opened to see? It is because the negative and unwanted parts of the self have been pushed away from awareness and because a gap exists in every normal person between what one wishes to be ("ideal self") and what one actually is ("actual self"; see Rogers, 1951).

Resistance to self-awareness is manifested in three major ways: selective attention, distortion, and reversal.

SELECTIVE ATTENTION

Selective attention refers to persons' tendency to absorb only a portion of the stimuli potentially available to them. They choose to attend to and remember stimuli and information low in threat value, remaining unaware of more threatening instances. It is a commonplace that people remember and glorify the "good old days," forgetting the stress that was also a part of those days. Likewise, the adult's image of a child is often selectively idealized: Children are considered uniformly happy and carefree; adults forget how serious children's play actually is and how sensitive children are to disturbing events occurring around them. In viewing Archie Bunker's television family, those who identify with son-in-law Mike would probably remember most vividly Mike's good moments and forget his embarrassing moments. Jews seem to be more acutely aware than non-Jews of the high proportion of Jews among the recipients of the Nobel Award. Jews would also be more acutely aware of antisemitism than they would be of prejudice against blacks in South Africa or against secular leftists in Iran.

Defense mechanisms reflecting selective attention include denial, suppression, and repression. All three involve involuntary relegation of unpleasant information out of the field of conscious awareness: denial, the refusal to absorb threatening information from outside (for example, our failures to detect when others are angry at us, or neo-Nazis who deny today that Nazi Germany ever employed gas chambers to murder "inferior races"); repression, the transferral of ideation and psychological material from consciousness to unconsciousness, enabling one to "forget" it ("I'll never forget what's his name"); and suppression, the prevention of unpleasant material from surfacing into consciousness. But selective attention cannot filter out all unwanted information, and it is therefore supplemented by distortion and reversal.

DISTORTION

Threatening information can be distorted so that is becomes more pleasant and acceptable. People interpret events in a desirable light, sometimes in outright contradiction to their meaning as perceived by those less personally involved. The mechanisms of distortion include projection, displacement, and rationalization. The first two refer to changing the focus of the emotion; the third, to a distortion of meaning. In projection, one's own negative emotions are projected on the other, so that the other is perceived to own them ("Why does the teacher hate me?"). In displacement, the negative effect is diverted from one object to another object, more fitting to be victimized (angry at his father, the child kicks his dog). These mechanisms are apparent in the process of scapegoating, in which negative attributes are projected upon a victim, providing justification to be aggressive against that victim.

Rationalization refers to a seemingly logical process of self-explanation that actually masks distorted self-justification. Unpleasant facts are interpreted so that one's positive self-regard, rationality, and consistency are maintained: "Of course I am in favor of racial integration of the schools. My child attends the (private, all-white) school because she wanted to be in class with her friend Judy and because she is allergic to public buses." "I am not superstitious, but I refuse to live on the thirteenth floor because it may annoy other people." As Eliot Aronson (1976) put it, "Man is not a rational being; man is a rationalizing being."

REVERSAL

The third form of resistance is reversal of meaning, when an overt behavior or statement expresses the opposite of one's internal feelings. Reversals occur when people feel the threat of appearing stupid, weak, or aggressive and when it seems important to conceal from others how one really feels. Most people have had the unpleasant experience of being greeted with "how wonderful to see you" by someone who hates them, and every person pretends at times not to be hurt when he or she *is* hurt (after being insulted or having clumsily banged the doorpost, for example).

Anna Freud (1946) defined the reversal mechanism "reaction formation"—which is the tendency to manifest a trait or a behavioral pattern that is directly opposed to the unconscious impulse (for example, a child hugging and kissing excessively a hated or feared stepmother). Adults often show a more subtle form of reversal: "passive-aggressive behavior," where unaggressive, "nice" behavior substitutes for underlying aggressive feelings. Imagine the exhausted salesperson—after a customer has tried on 57 different pairs of shoes and not bought any—smiling sweetly and asking, "Would you like to try on another pair?"

Passive-aggressive behavior often characterizes the interaction between minority and majority groups. For minorities, fearing the repercussions of being aggressive, passive-aggressive behavior may be quite functional. It provides an outlet (albeit indirect) for aggressive feelings, at the same time guarding against negative outcomes. Students use passive-aggressive behavior with professors, defendants with judges, and citizens with government officials. In the intergroup context, the term "militancy" refers to the abandonment of passive-aggressive behavior and the expression of overt, explicit, and often exaggerated aggression. But passive-aggressive behavior is also functional for those of "majority status" (the teacher, the government official, or the white, Anglo-Saxon Protestant male). This behavior masks the use of power or prejudicial hostility, turning it into an expression of sweet acceptance ("Some of my best friends are . . .").

The term "counterdependence" describes another reversal phenomenon: the rejection of the inner need for dependence and the exhibition of hostile independence instead. Counterdependence, its conceptual kin "counterconformism," and most forms of reversal are detectable through their predictability: They almost always involve a consistent "anti," a demonstrative and excessive way of doing the opposite of what is expected. Hippies strongly rejected conformity to the the norms and values of the established adult society. In its place they created a new "establishment" of opposite norms, enforcing these new norms rather determinedly. A considerable degree of conformity was demanded by this "nonconformist" movement. In his treatment of "reactance," Brehm (1966) described to what lengths people will go to defend themselves, to distort, and often to make themselves look quite ridiculous, when their sense of freedom and free choice is threatened.

A final form of resistance is the *resistance to changeability*. Up to this point, we discussed forms of resistance to self-awareness, which precedes actual change. However, it has been observed that sometimes people who had actually changed might deny it! Personal needs to appear consistent and cultural pressures may account for the resistance to changeability—an admission of change implies that the person was bad, deficient, or in error beforehand.

Goethals and Reckman (1973) provided an interesting example of this process. They tested the hypothesis that when people change their attitudes, they distort their recall of their initial stand to make it consistent with the new attitude. They measured high school students' attitudes about 30 issues and formed small discussion groups. Each group consisted of three students, all of whom held the same position, for or against school busing. Each discussion group included a fourth student who, unbeknownst to the other three, was a confederate of the researchers. The confederate always argued convincingly against the group position. Most students were persuaded by the confederate, changing their opinion in a subsequent survey. Next, the researchers asked the students to recall the attitude they held at the time of the previous measurement, reminding them that their answers to the first questionnaire could be checked. Goethals and Reckman found that subjects distorted their recall, claiming that they had always held their present attitude.

Readiness to change and/or to admit that one has changed is enhanced when the group atmosphere and norms are favorable to changeability and when the person can identify external reasons justifying the change. An illustration of this point took place in 1977 when President Sadat of Egypt came on his first historical visit to Jerusalem. The visit made it socially acceptable for both Israelis and Egyptians to demonstrate a change in attitude toward each other, turning previous hostility into friendliness (see Babad, 1978).

Difficulties in Information Processing

Self-inquiry is hindered not only by deep-seated dynamic forces but also by *cognitive* shortcomings, limitations of the human information-processing system that result in various distortions. In efforts to cope with the complex nature of the social environment, persons develop consistent explanatory perspectives that enable them to act quite effectively with a relatively small investment of mental effort. They reduce the load and the complexity of the information they are called upon to process, so that they can more easily record what is happening, interpret events, and predict what will happen under given conditions.

This simplification is functional and economical, but people pay a price for its convenience. The price includes bias and distortion, generalizations that are inaccurate, crucial information that is misused or rejected, loss of logic and objectivity, and inflexible patterns of behavior based on preconceived notions. Jones and Gerard (1967) identified this phenomenon as the basic conflict between (a) developing cognitive schemata that serve to maintain a person's stable view of the world and to assimilate new information into preexisting concepts, and (b) the need to be flexible, to absorb new information, and to accommodate to new and changing conditions. While the first element requires stability and consistency of the cognitive system, the second calls for maximal fluidity and flexibility.

In recent years, social psychologists have focused their research on instances where the need for consistency and stability has taken precedence over the need for fluidity, leading to systematic biases and distortions. People attend to information selectively, giving salience to some stimuli over others. They attribute greater value and significance to information they have already internalized than to new information, and they repeatedly use information-processing and problem-solving strategies that worked for them in the past, without reexamining the present appropriateness of these strategies. People are prone to make a series of attribution errors in their explanation and prediction of social behavior of self and others (Ross, 1977), such as overestimating the influence of stable traits and underestimating the influence of situational conditions.

Stereotypes exemplify most of these processes. The process of stereotyping reflects the need for consistency and stability. Stereotypes are stable overgeneralizations about groups, characterizations that do not take into account the existing variability within any group. Stereotypes typically show great stability and perserverance in the face of disconfirming information. When people hold particular stereotypes (say, that Poles are dumb and redheads are hot-tempered) and they encounter representatives of these groups who do not fit the stereotypes, they tend to discount the disconfirming information by concluding that intelligent Poles or even-tempered redheads are the exceptions. In this way stability wins over fluidity: The stereotypes are maintained without scrutiny, and the disconfirming information has been filed away without disturbing the existing balance. On the other hand, instances that support the existing stereotypes are accepted and noted as proof of the validity of these stereotypes.

We believe that if psychological processes—even distortions and biases—persist, they must serve some adaptive function for the person. To understand further the adaptability of stereotyping and other distortions already mentioned, we conceptualize these phenomena as reflecting a conflict between *effort* and *accuracy*. Under ideal conditions, every person would wish to attain maximal accuracy while expending minimal or no effort. But high accuracy demands extreme flexibility and a great investment of effort, and most people are willing to "trade" some accuracy for a reduction of mental effort. To function well, however, the level of accuracy cannot drop below an optimal level. Thus, the various distortions and faulty information-processing strategies represent a nonconscious attempt to keep mental effort at a minimum while enjoying optimal accuracy.

The process of self-inquiry recommended in this book is meant to increase accuracy through the development of a more differentiated, more elaborate, richer, and more fluid set of social schemata. This requires cognitive effort, and the issue of cognitive resistance concerns the price to be paid in terms of effort expended for increased accuracy. In brief, a learner's subjective sense that overcoming biases in social judgment requires too much effort is a major obstacle to self-inquiry. As a result, self-inquiry is unlikely to be pursued.

This apprehension is well justified so far as the first stages of self-inquiry are concerned, but in later stages, higher accuracy can be maintained with minimal effort. This point is analogous to the process of learning to drive a car. In the beginning, the learner feels overwhelmed by the variety of stimuli to be interpreted and mechanisms to be operated all at once—the road, other cars, pedestrians, the wheel, the shift, the blinkers, the lights and wipers. The attention and effort required at an early stage of learning to drive is tremendous, while the accuracy of the beginning driver is minimal. Later, the accomplished, experienced driver can manage this complexity with ease, driving "automatically" with great accuracy and minimal effort. Analogously, for those who learn how to learn about themselves, accuracy can be much increased, while the needed effort can remain on a stable low level after the initial stages.

Dilemmas of Universal
Lawfulness and Individuality

People's beliefs about universality and uniqueness in explaining their own and others' behavior can influence the application of social-psychological knowledge and impede the process of self-inquiry. "Universal lawfulness" can be rather disturbing, as it violates the individual's sense of self-determination and freedom of choice. Social scientists have predicted people's behavior and explained their internal psychological processes even before they can choose to act in a particular way! People resent being "predicted" from universal laws. To accept that anyone can predict their behavior without knowing them personally or to recognize that they act according to universal laws they do not even know can be unpleasant and offensive. Even worse, sometimes the universal law negates and contradicts persons' own explanations of their behavior.

Nisbett and Wilson (1977) provide examples of subjects in psychological experiments being debriefed at the completion of an experiment, told about the covert experimental manipulations that were operated without their awareness, and subsequently asked to explain why they behaved as they did. They quote Aronson's subjects, who "typically said it was very plausible and that many subjects probably reasoned just that way, but not they themselves" (p. 238). Brehm's (1966) conception of reactance—people's strong reactions to apparent attempts to manipulate them and limit their freedom—probably helps to explain the resistance of the debriefed subjects.

Universal lawfulness is disturbing even when its content, the causal or predictive factor, can be acceptable in itself to the individual. But when the universal law exposes the person's faulty information processing, logical inconsistencies, or biases, the threat is greatly increased and resistance would certainly intensify. In other words, resistance to universal lawfulness reflects both the need to protect one's uniqueness and self-determination from being anonymously grouped and "predicted," and the need to avoid painful exposure of one's hidden drawbacks.

As persons advance in self-inquiry into their social selves, they discover a series of balances that are sobering to acknowledge yet more realistic than notions of unique individuality or of complete social determinism. They discover a balance between universality and individuality, between predictable influences that are beyond their control and instances when they can exercise free choice and self-determination, between the ways they are perceived and grouped by others and the way they experience their own uniqueness. In order to pursue self-inquiry, a person must make himself or herself an object of study, and this requires a degree of distancing of the person from him- or herself.

Up to this point, we have focused on the disturbing aspect of universality. But universality also has relieving aspects, and people sometimes find it desirable to assert the fact that they are like everyone else. When confronted with one's own negative attributes, "being in the same boat with others" as part of universal lawfulness is more relieving than remaining unique. On these occasions the acceptance of universality reduces personal responsibility, and people often use the excuse, "after all, I am only human," to explain away misdeeds and drawbacks that they cannot deny.

Universality can be relieving not only as an excuse and a strategy for reducing personal responsibility but also as a deep and authentic personal experience. Yalom (1975) presented universality as a major curative factor in group psychotherapy. Discovering that one is not alone and unique in one's pain and anxiety and that others encounter the same difficulties can be quite relieving.

Effects of Ideology
on Self-Inquiry

Ideology is the dimension of difference in heterogeneous society, discussed extensively in Chapter 13. Here we deal with "ideology" and ideological groups only as an obstacle to self-inquiry. To understand the effects of ideology on self-inquiry, it is necessary to distinguish between "values" and "ideology." Every person holds various values, and most people's values are organized in a meaningful value orientation (such as humanism or liberalism). We use the term "ideology" in this book to refer not only to a belief system but also to a socio-identity and a group of believers in which the person is a member. Thus, our working definition of ideology is in group terms, where values and beliefs are held with great intensity and with a strong commitment to the ideological group (communist, feminist, or Black Power, for example).

Ideology is functional for its followers and can benefit society in various ways. But it also obstructs the process of self-inquiry. Most ideologies are complete belief systems that provide an entire cognitive orientation, prescribe "right" and "wrong" answers to most issues, and demand—explicitly or implicitly—compliance with their norms and values. Ideological groups are not tolerant of members' "intellectual deviance" and overinquisitiveness, especially when in struggle with other groups; this state is common rather than exceptional for most ideological groups. Even if a particular ideological group encourages self-inquiry, that inquiry is often conducted in ways that are expected to foster more commitment to the group (for example, as in a feminist consciousness-raising group).

"Becoming ideological" in interpersonal conflicts is sometimes an indication of the escalation of conflict, unwillingness to come to terms with the other party, and the adoption of a righteous, moralistic stance. For instance, an argument between a wife and her husband about car pooling can escalate into a clash between a feminist representing oppressed women and a sexist. A dinnertable conversation can turn into a fight between "Marxists," "radicals," and "conservatives." Shifting into the ideological role in these occasions almost always ensures rigidity, aggression, and a lack of willingness to understand or accept the other side's point of view.

Relations Between
"Self" and "Other"

People are markedly different in the ways they perceive, explain, and evaluate their own motivations and behaviors and those of others, and gaps between "self" and "other" are obstacles not only to the process of inquiry but to the actual interactions between persons and groups.

People cluster other people into groups and attribute them the characteristics of these groups. In the first introduction to an unfamiliar person, people typically observe some of his or her group memberships (such as race and sex) and seek information about additional group memberships of the person: religion, nationality, profession, and so forth. But persons are apprehensive about being clustered by others, wishing to emphasize their sense of individuality and uniqueness. The stereotypic ways persons are perceived by others are seen as inaccurate and often felt as offensive. People are resistant to being "placed" in a group and stereotypically held there by others, yet they do the very same to others. There is pathos in statements such as (from a black) "Why don't the whites understand that they cannot see me simply as a black" or (from an adolescent) "Adults have such definite stereotypes about adolescents—they can never treat me as a unique person."

With regard to weaknesses, people tend to be more tolerant of their own weakness, viewing other people's weaknesses in a more critical and judgmental way: "I am a thrifty person—he is a miser."

Another gap between self and other is found in the explanation of behavior, where the behavior of others is explained as being determined by (or at least reflecting) universal laws of behavior, while one's own behavior is seen as reflecting a far greater degree of self-determination and free will. This distinction can be seen in the subtle difference of nuance between the terms "ambitious" and "driven," or between the terms "ideological" and "brainwashed."

Social-psychological research (Jones & Davis, 1965; Jones, Kanouse, Kelley, Nisbett, Valins, & Weiner, 1971; Nisbett, Caputo, Legant, & Maracek, 1973; Harvey, Ickes, & Kidd, 1976; Ross, 1977; Nisbett & Wilson, 1977) shows consistently that attributions of causes to behavior vary greatly between "actors" and "others." There is a strong tendency to explain other people's behavior in terms of fixed personality dispositions and stable traits, while one's own behavior is explained more flexibly in terms of situationally changing factors. People tend to see themselves as more flexible and changeable than they consider others to be. However, when they wish (as when explaining positive qualities or deeds), people can attribute stable traits to themselves and shifty situational causes to other. Summarized somewhat cynically, the underlying formula can take the following form: "When you are bad, it is your nature; when I am bad, it was caused by a particular passing situation. When I am good, it is my nature; when you are good, it was caused by a particular passing situation."

These gaps between self and other can be explained dynamically and cognitively. Dynamic factors would include unconscious defense against perceived threat, egocentricity, and maintenance of self-esteem. The cognitive explanation follows our earlier description of human information processing. People know that behavior is influenced by a variety of specific, situational factors, but they have no way of knowing the particular contingencies influencing the behavior of others. Therefore, they apply to others principles and generalizations that seem to be universal, canceling out the effect of specific situational influences about which they have no direct knowledge. In this way people maintain the above-mentioned balance between "minimal effort" and "optimal accuracy." As this pattern is learned and strengthened, people "forget" that a host of specific contingencies influence another's behavior.

These ideas further explain the particular difficulties in understanding those who are different. People's own sensations, attitudes, and thoughts are the best sources of psychological information they have. Since they cannot know for sure how others process *their* information, people have to rely on their own experience to explain behavior, assuming that their own processes are typical and that others operate in the same way. Therefore, persons tend to perceive others, interpret their behavior, and make value judgements about it not from the points of view of the other persons but from their own points of view.

When persons interact with others who are very different from themselves, it is harder to ignore the gaps between their own psychological processes and those of the others. Even then, people tend to rely on their own information and their own ways of processing it. Becoming aware of these gaps is distressing, since persons then sense the inadequacy of their own interpretations of those different others. Therefore, people prefer to seek the company of others who are similar to themselves, where the gaps between self and other are smaller and where they can more confidently and accurately assume that their own interpretive processes apply to the behavior of the other. Franklin Giddings's concept "consciousness of kind" is highly relevant here.

The differential treatment of self and other is a deterrent to effective self-inquiry and to the effective communication with those who are different. The ability to be enhanced is *empathy*—being able to put oneself into another person's shoes, to view the world and oneself from the other person's perspective. In a way, empathy is the emotional analogue of cognitive understanding, and "emotional understanding" of another person or group.

Skills for Self-Inquiry

Productive self-inquiry requires appropriate skills as well as good intentions. Some of the required skills do not develop "naturally" in normal socialization, but they can be learned in an educative environment with norms and conditions favorable to their development.

Some of the required skills are *cognitive*, others are *interpersonal*, and most of them integrate intellectual, emotional, and behavioral aspects. Among the cognitive skills are the enlargement of the sources of information about oneself and ones' characteristic responses to social situations. This means paying deliberate attention to information one ordinarily dismisses or ignores. Another skill involves the openness to absorb the responses of others to one's statements and actions and the careful examination of responses that contradict one's intentions. Another skill is to stay with ambiguous situations and reflect upon their meaning, rather than avoiding or escaping them because of their disturbing nature. Another skill is actually to make use of and apply one's universal social-psychological knowledge in explaining one's own behavior as well as the behavior of others. Interpersonal skills are involved in self-inquiry, since many aspects of the inquiry into the social self require the person to interact with others, similar and different. Self-inquiry requires a "laboratory," and other persons can provide such a laboratory. Needed interpersonal skills include deliberate cultivation of dialogue with others who differ from oneself in significant ways, listening to the responses of others even when these responses do not seem to make sense from one's own perspective, and clarity of communication in transmitting messages to and interacting with others.

The first preparatory stage for self-inquiry is *readiness:* the readiness "to look inside," the readiness to see oneself not only in the most positive terms, the readiness to recognize and cope with a series of obstacles and distortions. Beyond this readiness, self-inquiry must involve the development of appropriate investigative skills: One must learn how to analyze one's own life history, values, attitudes, and beliefs, and to identify their origins; one must be able to investigate one's typical behavioral patterns of reacting to different others and to stressful situations.

We believe that the major component of inquiry into stereotypes, prejudices, and intergroup processes is the development of *role-taking and empathic skills.* In individual psychology, empathy deals mostly with overcoming an egocentric outlook and being able to take another person's point of view. In the context of this book's inquiry, empathy is more demanding and difficult, requiring the person to empathize with people and groups who are basically different, whose commonalities and similarities are minimal. Moreover, one is often required to take the point of view of one's *opponents*—those who are not only different but also hostile to one's own group. It is rather difficult, for example, to empathize with and "feel" the processes involved in the formation and maintenance of "minority culture" when one's own experiences do not include such processes and when an element of that

---

Exercise 3.1

This concluding exercise is suggested as an attempt to facilitate a personal understanding of the various obstacles and blocks to self-inquiry discussed in this chapter and their applicability to you and your own life.

First, please list all the obstacles to self-inquiry and to application of knowledge that you can remember, without looking at the book. Second, leaf through the chapter and make a second list of obstacles that are discussed in the chapter but that you did not generate in the first list. Third, try to write a third list—of obstacles and blocks that have not been discussed in this chapter.

In the next stage of this exercise, please examine carefully all items on your lists, and mark those that are applicable and those that are inapplicable to you and your own life's experiences.

Working with a co-inquirer or in a study group, compare your lists and your markings to those of your co-inquirer(s) and focus your attention on the items that you find inapplicable to your own experiences.

culture is a tendency to attack one's group. Yet the process of inquiry cannot be effective if such skills of role taking and empathy are not developed.

The term "skills" as used in this section carries different meanings. Some of the skills we have discussed are "technical" in nature and may be acquired through training (for example, listening and learning to transmit clear messages). Other capacities are more "attitudinal" in nature and less readily acquired through training (tolerating ambiguity and ambivalence, for instance). But all are based on an initial readiness, and all require much attention, effort, and varied forms of practice to overcome the obstacles to self-inquiry.

4

EXPLORING LIFE HISTORY

Exploration of life history and socio-identities plays a central role in the inquiry into the social self. In Clarification Group laboratories, this exploration is conducted through Structured Group Interviews in which every group member is interviewed at length by the group (Small & Birnbaum, 1971; Birnbaum, 1975; Babad, Birnbaum, & Benne, 1978). But life history and socio-identities can also be investigated by the person alone or in interaction with one other person. This chapter illustrates the exploration of life history and provides guidelines to facilitate this process. Later chapters focus on specific dimensions of the social self (such as race, ethnicity, religion, gender, age, and ideology), presenting a more detailed analysis of their particular manifestations in society. We believe that an initial, global examination of your socio-identities will enable you to make meaning of your life history and explicate your personal order of salience of group memberships, roles, and life events.

In exploration of life history, one traces the meanings of one's central socio-identities as reflected in background, family, ideology, work, civic activities, and social relations. One explores how these socio-identities have acquired their meanings and how they shaped and were shaped by important life events. Socio-identities (such as being Mexican or being Moslem) determine and influence one's patterns of social relations, but at the same time they are also influenced and modified by the social experiences one accumulates.

In the following pages we present excerpts from a life-history account written by a young woman following participation in a C-Group laboratory in the mid-1970s. This woman, introduced under the false name "Susan Goldberg," explores in this report her life history, with a particular emphasis on her ethnic and national socio-identities. Following this account, we provide guidelines to serve the dual purpose of processing Susan's material and of helping you, the reader, to embark on the exploration of your own life history.

Exercise 4.1

Before you start reading the following account, please try to formulate some of
the anticipations and expectations evoked when you are told you are about to
read the life history of *Susan Goldberg, a graduate student in counseling in
Boston, born in Long Island, and in her mid-twenties.*

"Susan Goldberg's" Life History

I'd like to look at the theory of my own life and how it shaped itself in practice. At
this point in my life, such an approach might enhance my growth process.

I have a difficult time perceiving how my family origins have *directly* touched my
ethnic identity. Knowledge of the fact that my father's parents are from Poland and my
mother's from America is not directly relevant to my own life. However, I can see a
few outgrowths which might have come into play concerning the more "Jewishly
oriented" facets of my identity. Since my father was the only American-born child in
his family, he has been able to relay only vaguely and indirectly stories of his parents,
brother and two sisters in Poland during World War I. Apparently my grandfather,
whom I never met, had gone over to America to seek his fortune while the rest of the
family remained across the ocean. The stories seemed to connote the picture of a poor
Jewish family, living partly in the streets, and struggling to get by. My grandmother,
Bubby, was always depicted as a strong "Jewisha" figure whose shrewdness and desire for survival far surpassed, in strength, the hardships which were encountered.

As a kid, my conceptions of my father's side of the family are still quite vivid. They
were always poor, living in a two-family house in Brooklyn with the style of an
extended family—my father slept in the kitchen. It was in this same house that we
used to go visit Bubby. All I really knew about her was that she only spoke Yiddish,
couldn't seem to understand me when I talked to her, and seemed to enjoy giving me
plastic bags which were filled with cookies. As a little girl, the house struck me as
being old and rickety, conveying a slightly depressing hint of "Jewish suffering" to
my childish senses. Bubby was a different sort of character from any of my other
relatives. From her little gray bun to her heavy-as-lead matzah balls, she became a sort
of ethnic "myth" to me—unique in one kind of way and Jewish in another.

"Grandma and Grandpa," on the other hand, spoke English, gave me presents, and
showered me with lots of love. They were the epitome of grandma/grandpa symbols,
depicting more of a stereotypic middle-class image of America for me than my emotionally tinged picture of old and wrinkled Bubby. The fact that their parents were
from Hungary and Austria, respectively, had absolutely no bearing on anything.
Grandma never made "Knadelach" and never baked cookies—so how could she
seem Jewish?

Moving more directly into the realm of my immediate household, I was born in
Queens, New York, and moved to Long Island when I was 7. This is where I've lived
the major portion of my life and where my identity began to thrive. We joined a
Reform synagogue as soon as we moved there and, in second grade, I was enrolled in

Sunday school. That was just one of those boring things which Daddy made me do in addition to attending regular school.

Right around Christmas time, there were lots of beautiful Christmas lights and other assorted decorations. The houses on our block displayed lots of beautifully colored bulbs and the little kids who lived in them got the chance to sit on Santa's lap. There were also candy-filled stockings, elves, tinsels, and a helluva lot more presents sitting under that tree than the eight which I received on Chanukah. The people across the street used to invite us to see their tree—having a "Chanukah bush" in our house was just out of the question. Christmas meant pretty songs, lots of snow, no school, and jingle bells. It brought a more all-encompassing type of "spirit" along with its gifts. I mean, Chanukah was exciting, too, since it was the time when MY presents arrived but it meant something in a different sort of way. It wasn't as pervasive in feeling.

Thus, at this time of my life, my encounters with Judaism revolved around Sunday school, the Bible, Bubby, and Chanukah. My conception of non-Jews had an extremely Christmas-oriented tang to it. I suppose that my life had actually been tainted with a lot more ethnic variables than I had been aware of at the time. . . . I did not see a lot of them from an "ethnic" perspective. For example, Easter definitely existed for me but I was never aware of its religious origins. Grandma always sent me an Easter basket anyway—leave it to Grandma!!! Passover was another kind of occasion, one of those times that was associated with being very very hungry and having to wait for hours before getting any food into your mouth.

When I entered the fourth grade, Sunday school got to be an even bigger ordeal. Now, not only did I go on Sunday but also on Thursday. It was because I had both Jewish history and Hebrew. It was only in about fifth grade that the word "Catechism" began to make its appearance. I guessed that it was like my Sunday school. There were also a few kids who transferred from Catholic school to public school. In fact, on my block, I used to see kids all dressed up in uniforms, waiting for a special school bus in the morning. Boy, Catholic school must have been "strict" and it seemed strange to associate the name of a religion with a "normal" school. I took the freedom to conjure up pictures of being taught by mean nuns who made little girls wear ugly plaid green uniforms instead of pretty pink dresses. So, there were two different types of people—Jewish ones and Catholic ones. One group prayed in church and one in temple. One group went to Hebrew school and one to Catechism. One group celebrated Christmas and the other celebrated Chanukah.

When I entered the seventh grade, it was time to seriously prepare for bas mitzvah. The only problem was that, in my temple, two people had bas mitzvot at once and it so happened that my cohort was a girl who had some of the same friends I did. This was to be a big social happening and it got blown up into a "who's gonna go to whose" type of affair. What stands out most about this critical issue was an event revolving around Linda, one of the big bullies of my day. She started to pass around rumors that I was bragging about how my bas mitzvah was going to be more expensive than the other girl's—I believe the figure she construed was $15 a plate. Her reaction to the fact that my father could afford more, in connection with her devised fantasy about me bragging, left a very negative impression in my head. If I recall correctly, this was probably my first encounter with a negative association concerning my social class. All of a sudden, my father's upper-middle-class income began to acquire some meaning . . . hooked up to embarrassing connotations. In the long run, what ended up happening was that Bubby died and we had to postpone the affair to a later date.

Junior high school brings back good memories. We had a tremendous coed group of friends in those days and had oodles of fun together. Religion was never a factor in terms of our lifestyles or relationships. It was a mixed group (Catholics, Protestants . . .they were the same to me . . .and Jews). We were all white and of middle- to upper-middle-class backgrounds. I had little exposure to blacks and racial tensions were never directly experienced by me. High school followed similar suit and civil rights issues were really only alive in the far-off literature. It brought out in me emotions that favored the black position but, at the same time, I never had to deal directly with the issue in my immediate circumstances. There were a few blacks in my high school and they were generally accepted quite favorably—it was their very presence that made me aware of how sheltered I had been from them for my entire life. In my house, I was not exposed to any antiblack sentiment. I knew that most of the cleaning women were black but, then again, there were white ones also. In my eyes, they were not conde-scended towards, although the very occupation which I associated them with must have caused some impression to have been made on me.

Throughout high school my religious identity took on an almost rebellious qual-ity. Going to temple on Rosh Hashana and Yom Kippur seemed a farce, and I used to leave the service with a friend of mine. We used to talk about the phoniness and meaninglessness of it all. These were really the only two days of the year that the Reform congregation seemed to get off their asses to attend the services and it was gaudy, crowded, and stuffy. Jewishness really meant nothing, not a thing.

It was during my high school career that I began to do some traveling. My trip cross-country got me acquainted with the fact that I was a New Yorker. This was a new type of idea for me because, up until then, the most geographical ties I had in terms of titles was the fact that I was from a particular town in Long Island separated from its neighboring town by the railroad tracks. In California, I was an Easterner.

The following year, in Europe, I became attuned to some additional facts pertain-ing to my identity. In England, I spoke English in a funny American way (topped with New York, of course); in Amsterdam, I was a dark-haired American; in Italy, I was an American Girl, supposed to be "fast" all the way into the bedroom and beyond. This was all news to me. Even more importantly, my "country" became just what the word signifies, as opposed to my "world." My identity as an American became verified as a separate entity, whereas before it was a nonexistent aspect of my person—it just *was*. I was no longer just from New York—I was also from America. Heightened cultural awareness ensued and I became more realistically keyed into the fact that different cultures were going on at the same time my American culture was happening. There were people around who were incredibly diverse . . . much more so than going to church or temple or being from New York as opposed to California.

I was very much turned on by traveling and getting a feel for other sides of the world. I secured a job in a factory with the hope of extending my visits abroad. This work experience put me in touch with the life of a factory worker. Earning money was quite a burdensome and tiring occupation and, in folding disposable towels, the most territically refreshing thing was to learn a new fold. Second to that was to get your pile the highest in the least amount of time with a close third being to guess the time, *to the minute,* as read on the punch-in clock. Well, from all those endless piles of white absorbent towels, I finally reaped my reward—a trip to Israel.

Although the word "Israel" seemed incessantly to make its presence known in my prayerbooks of the past, my objective was nationally as opposed to religiously oriented. However, the group populace was of the Jewish youth group sort (a membership which I had always rejected as being "creepy"), and the leader of the trip was a rabbi. Consequently, Jewish elements did tend to siphon their way in, aside from the fact that the entire country of Israel was Jewish. Tradition came to life in the everyday sense of the word and even Hebrew language came alive from its place in the Torah and its stagnant position on the pages of the prayer book.

The absolute peak of my experience was the communal living at the Ben Shemen Youth Village, where I worked for a month. Here, I learned what it was like to "rough it" and live the life of a farmer. At three o'clock in the morning, I took the tractor out to the fields or else went to shovel the chicken shit, collect eggs, or milk the goats and cows. It was "togetherness," it was "spiritual," and it was incredibly and unexplainably "unique." We mixed well with the Israelis in the village and I began to see my Jewish education come alive as a lifestyle—from Sabbath prayers and celebration to Israeli dancing.

I began to feel some pressures, as a Jew, to provide answers as to why my life was in America and not in Israel. Responsibility, in the past, had only really been associated with "studentdom." For the first time, I was being asked to verify life decisions that I had really had no part in determining. The Jewish American tourist, although in actuality my very own reflection, was something to laugh at hysterically. The picture of the baggy Bermuda shorts and the Kodak hanging around the neck . . . the harsh sound of New York English asking silly questions and getting ripped off all over the place . . . bringing back enough presents for an army, as stacks of American Express travelers' checks quickly diminished . . . all this and more became symbolic of everything I disliked. I suppose that this was the second time my class roots popped up. The "rugged" life just seemed to be more "lavish" to me; so much more refreshingly filthy, sweaty, and close to nature. There was an all-encompassing spirit, like the Christmas of yesteryears, which was warm, heartfelt, and all-consuming . . . a sense of being bound to one's roots. Saying good-bye to all this made a lifelong impact on me, my heart as empty as it was full.

My return to the States was difficult and far more emotional than my return from Europe. I couldn't seem to provide a straight answer to the question, "How was the trip?." It could only be fully shared with someone who had experienced it with me. My air conditioner and two-car garage held a hint of repulsion for me. My individualism seemed blessed with something novel and stimulating while, at the same time, cursed with loneliness and isolation, stemming from a longing for brotherhood, spirit, and community. There was no question about it—I had to go back for more of this.

The High Holidays were different this year and I went to temple with my head held high. It is unclear as to whether this spiritual contact emerged from the seeds of Judaism or the seeds of Israel or, of course, both, if the two could not be separated. It would seem that the spirit of the nation was primary, but, since it was achieved through Jewish culture, Jewish history, and a sense of Jewish community, my religious identity was uncontrollably rekindled.

I got another part-time job, determined as ever to return. Injecting jelly into dough-nuts didn't seem so unbearable when I thought of the high-quality, succulent fruit that my labors would ultimately yield. I began to get more in touch with my feelings of missing the Sabbath, with its touch of something special and the sound of rich sing-ing. The seeds of Jewish tradition that had lain dormant inside me began to vibrate with a bit more life and we began to light the Shabbas candles in my house. (My parents' mouths were agape with wonderment.)

I decided that a good way for me to return to Israel would be to go there for my college education. This would enable me to live out my feelings in a deeper and more extensive way than I had originally had in mind. I felt that this would give me a chance to become a part of Israel which was removed from the American middle-class Jew, who was stepping off the tour bus with sunglasses perched on his long nose and bermudas (pinstriped) flapping in the breeze. My parents were not exactly delighted about my plan to study in the Mideast and voiced many objections to it. But I was determined and applied to Hebrew University of Jerusalem.

This experience differed from the first one. The emotional component continued to vibrate but, ultimately, accommodated itself to the feeling of every day. Interest-ingly enough, the first thing which I became attuned to was my American identity, which seemed to connote a different class of Jew. I was an American student in Israel and it was fascinating to see how many Israelis stereotyped the American Jew as being of the upper-middle grain. Thus my social class identity was manifesting itself in my newfounded national one. There were also English students, South African students, Scandinavian students, Russian students, etc., etc. . . . . The melting pot ap-peared to be, as of yet, a container of fairly separate ingredients. It's interesting how, once religion provides the framework for a nation, national identity moves to the fore as a base of differences. On the other hand, as in the case of America, when there is a strong national basis, religious distinctions become more apparent. It's paradoxical to think that, in the midst of a strong common bond which ties people together, splits inevitably come about as almost a necessary occurrence, to strengthen identity struc-ture through the creation of group differences.

In both the dorm and the school, nationality became a critical variable for identifi-cation. Our Jewishness was secondary and our "Americanship" primary. As Ameri-cans, we lived an "easy" life, we had money, and we did not have to be always con-cerned with our very own survival. As first-year students, we were young and inexperienced—we had never served in the army, we had lots of jeans, makeup, and toiletries . . . all of which were exceptionally expensive in Israel. Yet, the hearts of Israelis also reflected certain elements of materialism as they begged us for all these products from America.

Concurrently, I was being exposed to Jewish customs, in all their glory. I was constantly in the company of lots of observant Jews and was probably considered the "goy" of the bunch. However, I sensed the special quality of the holidays and was surrounded by different lifestyles, attitudes, traditions, morals, and concerns. Ameri-can Jewishness, in all its fussiness and "clumsily" blatant tradition, really stood out. For Israelis, it was more of a lifestyle than a religious tradition.

My ultimate decision to leave Israel was quite involved and difficult to arrive at, but I did land at Boston University. Here, all the upper-middle-class tourists whom I had grown accustomed to laughing at seemed to congregate in one place. It was terribly difficult to come to a place which was the epitome of all I wished to deny in myself. Coming from a culture whose people were concerned with the survival of a nation to one where the major concern was what type of pills to do Friday night was a major adjustment for me. The value systems were on totally different ends of the spectrum—I'm still not sure where mine, in actuality, fell at the time. It had definitely changed, though. I was presently one of the zillions of upper-middle-class Jewish kids from the New York/New Jersey area and I began to realize how much I had grown to enjoy my unique identity of being a foreigner in Israel, an overseas student, an American, a Jew, a potential immigrant. Here I was introduced to an empty identity, lacking in spirit and being smothered in an isolated microcosm of the world that was absolutely filled with little "MEs". Although the current "me" still felt slightly different from the others and remained, emotionally, a part of Israel, its religion, geographical location, and culture had a common outward appearance.

It took quite a while for me to assimilate into the BU society. Slowly I acquired a sense of where I was at, as a student, and began to feel some sense of direction as to where I wanted to go as a professional. Over the course of the years, I gradually slipped back into my old set of values, concerns, and aspirations. Although I never made a transition into the JAP (Jewish American Princess) sector of the community, I was an American Jew. Israel lived on, in the emotional sense, but I could feel the seeds of my future being established in American soil. My Jewish consciousness stayed ingrained in my character as a person. I felt that this was a part of me that I had attained through my own means as opposed to through the upbringing of my parents. And yet, they, too, had a similar sort of Jewish consciousness, which obviously had its roots in their own familial circumstances. I often wonder whether or not I would have eventually cultivated this portion of my identity, as I did, if I never had the experience of encountering Israel. Its lack of spark after Hebrew school might very well have remained constant.

My days at Boston University also gave me my major introduction to blacks. I noticed that, on campus, there were clear delineations between blacks and whites. Particularly in the dorms, racial tensions were quite blatant at times—differing cultural ways such as very very late parties and loud dancing caused a lot of disruptions centering on racial issues in the dorm. I feel that this did not play any major role in my attitudes toward blacks nor in my identity formation as a white. It did, however, introduce me to this new facet of my identity.

My emotional attachment to my experience in Israel remained strong and constant. I had to return. The summer of my junior year, I got a job as a group leader of 33 college students who were touring Israel and participating in an archaeological dig in the Negev. It was a free trip, in addition to being a field-related job, so I jumped at the chance. The experience itself was rather confusing, mixed with the "emotional" aspect as well as the "responsible leadership" component. I felt split in that I was entering a culture of which I was once so much a part and which I felt bound to like a home, with a group of American Jews who depicted all the qualities I would have most wanted to leave in America. As their group leader, I became the object of their frustrations and their blatant middle-class expectations. It was frustrating because I wanted them, so much, to enjoy the country instead of basing the whole experience on whether or not the hotels would have air conditioning or if there would be prime beef for dinner. Shoveling dirt for eight hours a day amidst swarms of flies and hot sun did not exactly complement the experience for them. I mean, there was no doubt about the fact that it was rough. I was, simultaneously, feeling badly because I felt that, for a first time in Israel, this particular trip was inappropriate and I really wanted them to get a keener sense of what the country was about spiritually. However, the trip did bring certain rewards and a few of the people definitely established emotional bonds, particularly toward the end. Many of them did have, previous to coming, strong Jewish identities . . . far stronger than mine had ever been. The experience itself, for me, was a totally different one and I answered a lot of my own questions. I made a decision that my place was currently in America because satisfaction of my more immediate needs was there. I wanted a good, old-fashioned middle-class education that was conveniently provided in English—I also felt a blooming desire to advance professionally, and the fact of the matter was that America provided a wider array of options for me in this regard.

At this time career goals started moving into first place in my life. I decided to join the rat race of applications and make an effort to pursue my master's. I entered the Counseling Program at Boston University in September. My placement site was a community agency and my supervisor-to-be a black woman. Prior to our initial meeting, I had been told that she had requested minority group (black) students for this year. Could you just fantasize her reaction upon seeing my Negroid-sounding name? . . . That "berg" must have looked like the root of all evil. She was also the type of woman who was very much into being "black" as well as very much into making you feel glowing "white." I felt my self-consciousness with regard to social class issues come into play again but, in addition, gained a heightened awareness of both my identity as a Jew and as a white. This latter category became more clearly focused this year because I was working with blacks. In addition to counseling black students, I also had the occasion to do some work at the YMCA, with students bussed in from Charlestown High. Being one of the only whites there, in the midst of several "hot" racial issues, I learned more about what it was like to be "on the outside" and more a part of a "minority" than a "majority." It proved to be a most interesting experience for me. In addition, my supervisor really used to "get off" on introducing us "naive upper-middles" to different aspects of black culture. As an isolated group, we were supposedly not in touch with the black sense of community, spirit, and the extended family. My objections were pretty strong to this aspect as, interestingly enough, I realized that she was talking about the Jews as well.

I feel that my present life of being a student brings out in me, more than ever, my upper-middle-class consciousness. It has made itself particularly apparent this year, after having come in contact with a great many more different individuals with diverse class backgrounds. I resent its assumed character, inscribing me with the qualities of being "spoiled," "rich," and "sheltered." I feel it's important that such general connotations be either eliminated or put into their appropriate contexts. However, the word "Jew," as a separate entity from social class, remains a strong identity for me and one I'm proud to accept. I find its stereotypic elements easier to joke about . . . expect being rich . . . the complaining, the Jewish mother, the yenta image, and the need to "struggle." . . .

Although each facet of my identity as a Jewish, upper-middle-class, white, American woman will become more fully crystallized with the flow of years, the seeds of their primary solidification probably go backwards to infinity. It has been most interesting to tune into their gradual formulation over the years and put into proper perspective some of the events that have touched them significantly. It also has made me wonder what additional changes, if any, the future may hold.

Analysis of Life History

"Susan Goldberg's" life history probably evokes different reactions among readers, depending on their level of similarity to or difference from her, their familiarity with the facets of Susan's life, their conflict with any of Susan's groups, and so on. As an illustration, this life-history account highlights quite vividly some aspects, while neglecting other aspects, of human experience.

We now proceed to provide guidelines that may help to focus your attention on specific issues in the analysis of life history. With regard to every issue we raise, we pose two kinds of questions. One asks you to analyze a specific aspect in Susan's life, and the other points the question directly at you and your own life.

DIMENSIONS OF SOCIAL SELF

Susan emphasized certain dimensions of her social self (ethnic, national, social class, and religious socio-identities) while neglecting others (such as her identity as a woman and as a professional). Can you describe the order of salience of these dimensions in Susan's social self? What are the significant dimensions in your social self and how would you define their order of salience?

INFLUENCES OF BACKGROUND AND EARLY LIFE HISTORY

Susan provided a rich account of the influences of group memberships she was "born into" and of early-life-history events that she recalled quite vividly. Try to delineate some of these influences and trace their impact on Susan's maturing social self. Can you identify salient background and early life-history factors in your own background? How did they influence the development of your social self?

SYMBOLIC INFLUENCES OF PARTICULAR PEOPLE AND EVENTS

People vividly remember specifically important events in their life histories and particular individuals that had a special impact on them. Such people and events often gain symbolic significance, remaining in memory as *repre-*

sentatives of inner experiences. As memories, these symbols are often more powerful than the original experiences. Susan's account provides several examples of people (like Bubby) and events (like the Bas Mitzvah) that have gained symbolic significance. In analyzing Susan's interview and your own life history, try to identify "symbolic" people and events, to trace what is it exactly that they symbolize, how and why have they gained symbolic qualities.

DEVELOPMENTAL SHIFTS IN THE FORMATION OF IDENTITY

Socio-identities are never fixed; they keep developing, growing, and changing. Their development in influenced by people and events, real and symbolic. In turn, they shape perceptions and judgments of new people and events. Susan's account of the development of her Jewish identity is quite engaging, and although some information is missing (such as her reasons for leaving the Israeli college), you may find it instructive to trace this developmental process and analyze its milestones. Please note that the same type of event or behavior can attain *different* symbolic properties, depending on the person's point of view at the time he or she experiences the event. Thus, for example, Susan found physical work loathsome when her goal was to save money for traveling, but shoveling chicken shit and collecting eggs at three o'clock in the morning was "spiritual," "unique," and reminiscent of "togetherness" at a different stage of her life. Can you identify similar stages and shifts in the development of your own social self?

ACTS OF CHOICE AND ACTS OF REBELLION

Many events in a person's life occur without choice, free will, or planning. But persons also plan and carry out acts of choice that can have profound influences on their lives. Acts of choice often yield unexpected outcomes. For example, Susan's first and third trips to Israel were planned with certain expectations in mind, and both yielded outcomes that were quite unexpected. Some acts of choice are actually acts of *rebellion*, directed against a certain person or group. Susan did not portray herself as a rebel, but some of her acts certainly seem rebellious. Try to identify acts of choice and acts of rebellion and trace their consequences in Susan's life. You are also invited to conduct the same inquiry with regard to your own acts and their influence on your own life.

UNIQUENESSES AND COMMONALITIES

Sometimes we need to belong and be like everyone else in a group, and sometimes we need to feel unique and distinguishable from others. A variety of factors determine which need will prevail at a given time. Try to identify when Susan makes one or the other choice (for example, to be a member of the Jewish group in Israel compared to a "citizen in the Boston University nation") and provide an explanation of why uniqueness or commonality prevails at that time. Examine your own life experiences and try to reach a formulation of the conditions under which you give preference to each of these needs.

STEREOTYPES

Identify some of the stereotypes expressed in this interview. At what groups were these stereotypes directed? You can distinguish between Susan's own stereotypes and the stereotypes she ascribes to others. You can also distinguish between the stereotypes of Susan's own groups (upper-middle-class, Jewish, and so on) and those of "other" groups (such as blacks and Israelis). How did these stereotypes influence Susan's thoughts, values, feelings, and behavior?

INTERACTIONS WITH "DIFFERENT OTHERS"

The individual can control what he or she includes in self-definition. But, through interaction with others, persons are also "defined," and new attributes are added to their self-definitions. Awareness of self is particularly sharpened by contrasts with others who are very different from oneself. Susan's account, and no doubt your own life experiences, provides numerous examples of interactions with different others and their consequences. Try to identify such interactions and trace their consequences.

EXPERIENCES OF MINORITY STATUS

Among life experiences playing major roles in shaping the social self are experiences of minority status. For many persons, the influence of minority experience is profound, overshadowing other life experiences and other socio-identities. Major experiences of minority status are noticeably lacking from Susan's life history, although some minor instances of that type can be traced. However, in your own life-history analysis it is important that you identify your experiences of minority status and trace their significance and impact on the development of your social self.

INTEGRATION OF THE SOCIAL SELF

The concluding issue is the "integration" of the social self. Acceptance and rejection of particular group memberships, the person's sense of "self," and the overall meaning of one's life are aspects of the integration of the social self. We offer the following questions to help you in examining Susan's—and your own—integration of the social self.

(1) The degree of *conflict and complementarity among the various socio-identities* is one indication of the integration of the social self. Are Susan's Jewish identity, American identity, and professional identity coordinated with each other? Do they create an integrated sense of self or are they partitioned as separate entities? How does Susan—and how do you—cope with conflicts between these parts?

(2) What are Susan's central *values* and how does she realize her values in her life? In what ways are her values reflective of specific socio-identities? Does she hold values that cannot be directly traced to a particular socio-identity?

(3) At crucial choice points, how does Susan make *life decisions?* In what ways do her decisions reflect specific socio-identities, and how do they, in turn, affect specific socio-identities?

(4) What is Susan's *future perspective?* What are her plans and aspirations, and in what ways are they directed toward "realizing" her social self and her values? Do Susan's present life and its future perspective give full expression to the salient dimensions of her social self? Is she happy? Is she frustrated? What prices does she seem to pay for specific choices and decisions? To what extent is Susan aware of these issues and conscious of various facets involved in the decisions that confront her?

PART II

THE SOCIAL PSYCHOLOGY OF INTERGROUP RELATIONS

5

THE PSYCHOLOGY OF STEREOTYPES

Recently we administered the Exercise 5.1 (p. 76) to a group of 120 teachers. Over 60 percent of these teachers claimed they held no stereotypes at all, treating every person as a unique human being without any preconception based on group membership. In fact, we were verbally attacked by several teachers who considered our assumption that they might hold and use stereotypes outrageous and degrading.

Like most (if not all) social psychologists, we believe that stereotypes are universal, used by every human being in processing information about the social environment. In our opinion, stereotypes are not only inevitable but also are usually quite functional for effective social interaction. The angry reactions of the teachers stemmed from widely held misconceptions about the nature of stereotypes, particularly from the confusion between stereotypes and prejudices. Many people hold this negative stereotype about stereotypes and are therefore apprehensive about recognizing and "owning" their own stereotypes.

Stereotypes are generalizations about social groups—characteristics that are attributed to all members of a given group, without regard to variations that must exist among members of that group. Stereotypes are not necessarily based on people's first-hand experiences with members of stereotyped groups. They may be learned from others or from the mass media. Stereotypes may be emotionally positive (for example, the Dutch are friendly, Latins are passionate), negative (Scots are misers), or neutral (Americans love hotdogs). The lack of regard for differences within a stereotyped group makes stereotypes into "over-generalizations," and as such they are always at least somewhat distorted. However, many stereotypes may have valid grounds and "a kernel of truth" to them.

"Prejudice" is a special category of stereotypes, characterized by a negative emotional tone and a hostile and aggressive nature. While stereotypes are mechanisms of cognitively organizing and simplifying the complexity of the social environment, prejudices are statements of superiority, hateful attitudes that pave the way for the practice of discrimination in the form of racism, sexism, nationalism, religious fanaticism, and the like. Later in this chapter we provide a more extensive comparison between stereotypes, prejudice, and discrimination.

Exercise 5.1

"Stereotype" is a generalization about the common attributes, traits, or characteristics of a defined *group* of people. "Using a stereotype" means attributing these general characteristics to any person known to belong in that group.

Please take a sheet of paper and list some stereotypes that you find more or less correct, stereotypes that you would tend to use yourself sometimes.

The Nature of Stereotypes

The term "stereotype" originated in Lippmann's (1922) work, *Public Opinion*. The famous quotation of Lippmann is that "stereotypes are pictures in our heads." He argued that people do not react directly to external reality—that their reactions are mediated through representations of the environment, which are, to a lesser or greater degree, made up or adopted by the perceiving individual him- or herself. Thus, according to Lippmann, stereotypes are cognitive structures that help people to process information about their social environments.

Lippmann's ideas are generally accepted today. Most psychologists agree that stereotypes can be defined as sets of generalizations and/or beliefs about the characteristics of particular social groups. Ashmore and Del Boca (1979) note four major points of agreement among social psychologists with regard to the definition of stereotypes:

(1) A stereotype is *cognitive* (a belief, judgment, view, perception, trait, attribution, assumption, expectation, and so on).
(2) A stereotype is a *set* of related beliefs rather than an isolated bit of information.
(3) Stereotypes describe the attributes, personalities, or characters of *differentiated groups*, such as men and women: that is, stereotypes compare groups and differentiate between them.
(4) These sets of beliefs are *shared* by individuals and groups holding them.

TYPES OF ATTRIBUTES IN STEREOTYPING

Stereotypes are generalized "pictures" of groups, containing different types of attributes. The first set is *identifying characteristics*—features by which a person's group membership is determined (Is the person a man or a woman? black or white? young or old? conservative or radical?). Identifying characteristics are mostly factual, so that this set of attributes is relatively noncontroversial. Some people would not even consider identifying characteristics as stereotypes.

The second group is that of *defining attributes*. If the first set helps to identify members and nonmembers of a particular group, this set defines the shared characteristics of its members. For example, to *identify* men and women, people typically do not look at their genital organs, yet the differences in genital organs and the reproductive system *define* male and female group membership. Likewise, people may *identify* a Jew by looks or by name, but *define* a Jew in terms of a particular faith and religious practice. Thus, different characteristics or attributes are used to identify group members and to define the parameters of their membership in a group.

The third, most problematic set is that of *ascribed attributes*—the psychological characteristics that are attributed to the members of a particular group (men's aggressiveness, blacks' musical rhythm, or Jews' shrewdness). The controversial nature of stereotypes and the apprehension of accepting and owning one's stereotypes relate most directly to the ascribed attributes contained in many stereotypes.

TYPES OF DIFFERENCES BETWEEN GROUPS

Groups differ from each other in a variety of ways. Stereotypes are intended to differentiate among groups, and as such, they document differences between groups and make them salient. However, stereotypes often distort the characterizations of groups by overemphasizing the differences between groups and underemphasizing the characteristics that groups have *in common*.

Allport (1954) described the following four types of differences between groups:

J-Curve. The first type of group differences is the J-curve, where a particular attribute is highly characteristic of one group but not characteristic of the other group. If the majority of American males play football but very few American females play football, there is a J-curve difference between American males and females with respect to football playing. If a majority of Japanese like to eat raw fish but most Europeans do not enjoy eating it, there is a J-curve difference between Japanese and Europeans with respect to raw fish eating. J-curve differences are the strongest and clearest type of group difference, and stereotypes based on real J-curve differences have a high probability of being "valid generalizations." (See Figure 5.1.)

Rare-Zero Differential. In this type, one group possesses a given attribute at a very low frequency, and the other group does not possess it at all. It is known, for example, that certain hereditary diseases (Tay-Sachs, for instance) are found in extremely low frequencies in particular groups (such as Jewish males from Eastern Europe) but not found at all in any other group. In spite of its near-zero frequency, the attribute is characteristic only of that group. (See Figure 5.2.)

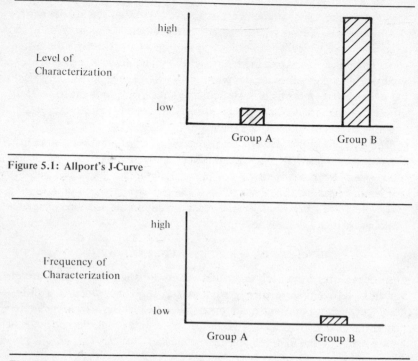

Figure 5.1: Allport's J-Curve

Figure 5.2: Allport's Rare-Zero Differential

Overlapping Normal Curves. This is probably the most common type of difference between groups. Both groups possess the attribute in question but possess it to different degrees, so that the mean of one group differs from the mean of the other. Thus, the groups "differ" from each other, but they also overlap with each other. However, the differences *within* each group (among individuals belonging to the same group) are usually *greater* than the differences *between* the groups. If group A in Figure 5.3 represented men, group B represented women, and the overlapping curves in that diagram described "emotionality," we could reach the following conclusions: There is a wide distribution of emotional behavior among men and a wide distribution of emotionality among women; the two distributions overlap, yet women's emotionality is, on the average, higher than men's; if we were to predict the level of emotionality of an unknown person, the predicted mean value would be higher if that person were a woman than if that person were a man; yet, *any* level of emotionality could characterize either a man or a woman.

Categorical Differences. This type is similar to the overlapping normal curves, except that it describes discontinuous variables, where a continuous normal curve cannot be drawn (for example, the frequency of blonds in a

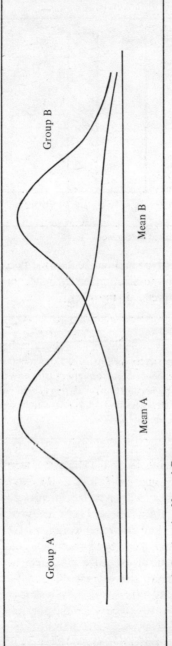

Figure 5.3: Allport's Overlapping Normal Curves

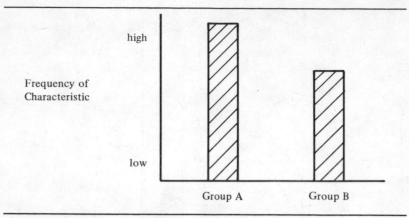

Figure 5.4: Allport's Categorical Differences

group). Like the previous type and unlike the first two, this type describes cases in which both groups possess a given attribute, but its frequency in one group differs from its frequency in the other.

Exercise 5.2

You can now examine the stereotypes you wrote down in the initial exercise in this chapter. In analyzing these stereotypes, check first how many of them were expressed (explicitly or by implication) as *differences between groups*. Next, examine each of these differences and determine which of Allport's four categories is reflected in that stereotype.

The major source of distortion in the process of stereotyping is the interpretation of one type of group differences as if it were another type. Most frequently, overlapping normal curves are interpreted as if they were J-curves, thus exaggerating the differences between groups and ignoring their often substantial overlap (Italians are temperamental, Englishmen are stiff, Americans are friendly, and so on). Such stereotypes transform what may be characteristic of a group into an exclusive characteristic.

This issue is crucial in sex stereotyping. Most differences between men and women (in emotionality, aggression, and physical strength, for example) are overlapping normal curves (type 3) or categorical differences (type 4), but they are interpreted and stereotyped as J-curve differences (type 1). Such stereotypes underestimate the differences *within* each group and overestimate the differences *between* the groups. Since stereotypes are accepted by their users as valid reflections of reality, people's expectations and behavior begin to follow such distorted "all or none" notions.

Acquisition, Validity, and Stability of Stereotypes

Before you continue reading this chapter, we suggest that you prepare lists of stereotypes in various domains by doing Exercise 5.3. These lists will be used in several analyses later, each illuminating a different aspect of the psychology of stereotyping.

Exercise 5.3

Please write several *lists* of stereotypes each focusing on another dimension of difference in society: racial and ethnic stereotypes, sex stereotypes, national stereotypes, religious stereotypes, professional stereotypes, and age stereotypes.

A "stereotype" may be simply defined here as a "commonly held belief" about a particular group (about blacks, whites, and Chinese-Americans; about men and women; about Americans, Japanese, and Israelis; about Catholics and Mormons; psychiatrists; politicians; old people; and so on). Please feel free to include in your lists stereotypes to which you do *not* subscribe personally. As long as you consider particular stereotypes to be commonly held by other people, even if you do not use these stereotypes yourself, they can appropriately appear in these lists.

THE ACQUISITION OF STEREOTYPES

What are the major mechanisms involved in the formation of stereotypes held and used by individuals? Apparently, only a few stereotypes are formed through the individual's direct learning and direct interaction with members of stereotyped groups. The majority of stereotypes are acquired as wholes by individuals. A central task in the process of "socialization" is that of organizing the world in a meaningful order and educating the person to find his or her "place" in that world. This "organization" not only creates stereotypes, but it forces the person to use them as well. Textbooks, folktales, literature and theater, and the television and the press, as well as the input from parents and teachers—these media "flood" the individual with stereotypic group images, many of which the individual absorbs and accepts uncritically. Thus, "getting educated" and "becoming socially adjusted" include an inevitable stipulation about the internalization and use of stereotypes.

But individuals do not accept and internalize indiscriminately all stereotypes to which they are exposed. (That would be impossible anyway—since every person is flooded with dissonant and often contradictory stereotypes.) People are *selective* and they choose among stereotypes according to various criteria of validity. They adopt stereotypes that seem to be most "helpful" to them in some way (in accuracy, consistency, or even wish-fulfillment). In addition, people's selection of stereotypes is influenced by their own groups of membership and the nature of their socio-identities.

Exercise 5.4

Choose several stereotypes from the lists you have prepared and analyze how these stereotypes have been acquired by you or by other people. Pay particular attention to the comparison between learning through personal experience and the acquisition of stereotypes as wholes.

VALID AND INVALID GENERALIZATIONS

The term "stereotypes" is commonly held to have a negative meaning. Many people tend to view all stereotypes as basically incorrect, distorted, and malicious. This stereotype about stereotypes is incorrect. By virtue of being overgeneralizations, stereotypes are distorted, but numerous stereotypes are quite correct, accurate, and free of malice, much as the process of stereotyping is psychologically functional.

If one accepts the inevitability and functionality of stereotypy, the issue shifts from "to have or not to have stereotypes" to "which stereotypes to have." In other words, the issue becomes one of examining the validity and the level of distortion of each specific stereotype on an ad hoc basis, of employing appropriate criteria for scrutinizing stereotypes and avoiding their blind use. Probably no stereotypic generalizations are "true" for all cases, nor would there be many stereotypes that are "false" all of the time. Most stereotypes probably have a kernel of truth to them, but they vary in their level of validity and accuracy. Thus, one must develop strategies for examining the validity of stereotypes. Empirical data for such examination are most often unavailable, but subjective scrutiny of held generalizations can be quite helpful. Effective strategies include the identification of the type of group difference involved, and the subjective assessment of the extent to which group differences are exaggerated in a given generalization. We found it useful over the years to employ a subjective "rule of thumb" for examining stereotypes: If a generalization can be said to be "true" in at least two-thirds of the cases (for example, Scandinavians have fair complexion, Italians are Catholic, or rush-hour New Yorkers on the subway are unfriendly), the stereotype can be considered to have some validity; if a generalization can be said to be "true" for less than one-third of the cases (for example, women are less intelligent than men or southerners are more racially prejudiced than Bostonians), the stereotype can be considered invalid.

Exercise 5.5

Choose several stereotypes from the lists you have prepared, and examine their validity and accuracy. Take a few minutes to reflect on the strategies you employ for this examination.

THE STABILITY OF STEREOTYPES

Once stereotypes are held, regardless of how they had been acquired, people seek instances that will confirm them. They attend selectively and seek confirming information and at the same time are highly resistant to disconfirming information. Jones and Gerard (1967) discussed the conflict, in the cognitive system, between the need for stability and consistency on the one hand, and the need for fluidity and flexibility on the other hand. In many areas of human conduct people act as fluid and flexible problem solvers. In the area of stereotyping the need for stability of the cognitive system is more dominant. The usefulness of stereotypes would be seriously impaired if they were too labile and easily changeable with every new bit of information. The value of stereotypes for their users lies in their stability and durability.

When a person encounters a bit of social information that disconfirms a held stereotype, the simplest form of resisting it is to refrain from absorbing the information (by negation, denial, suppression, or distortion). But it is also possible to absorb disconfirming information and yet hold on to the stereotypes. This is usually done through filing the disconfirming bits in a special category of "exceptions (that do not contradict the rule)." If the stereotype "Italians are cheats" is challenged by the person's acquaintance with an honest Italian, the person can conclude that "he is not like them." It is only after the person encounters more and more honest Italians that the stereotype might change, because it becomes less and less useful to hold on to a stereotype that is so frequently disconfirmed.

Resistance to disconfirming information is not limited to the area of stereotyping, and social psychologists view it as a generalized characteristic of human information processing. According to the theory of cognitive dissonance, people have a great investment in being consistent, and the absorption of disconfirming information may threaten this image. Therefore, in a variety of situations, people would rather distort and hold on to disconfirmed images than to absorb such information and appear inconsistent. "Don't confuse me with facts—I have made up my mind already" is the motto of this stance. Resistance to disconfirming information is particularly strong in the case of stereotypes because of their nature as generalizations about groups of people.

In a recent unpublished study we asked 600 people to grade a short composition written by a fourth-grader. Half of them were told that the child who wrote the composition was an excellent student, while the other half were told the child was a weak student. These stereotypes—"excellent" and "weak"—resulted in significantly different grades: The paper received a higher grade when believed to have been written by an excellent student. Next, we canceled the information about the ability of the student (either explaining that the experimenter had made an error or admitting a planned manipulation), and the subjects were told that the child was actually "an average student" and were asked to grade the paper again in light of the "corrected" information. Over 70 percent of the 600 subjects stuck to their original grades, maintaining (incorrectly, as the data indicate) that these grades were uninfluenced by the information about the student's excellence or weakness in school.

A very different aspect of the stability of stereotypes is the extent to which they would tend to change or to resist change with the passage of time and the accumulation of social changes and historical events in society. While the existence of stereotypes as a social phenomenon is an unchanging fact, it is logical to assume that the contents of particular stereotypes would change with time. A famous series of studies examined the stereotypes of various social and ethnic groups held by Princeton University students in the early 1930s (Katz & Braly, 1933), the 1950s (Gilbert, 1951), and the late 1960s (Karlins, Coffman, & Walters, 1969). These studies indicated that national and ethnic stereotypes maintained their overall high level of uniformity, although the contents of some stereotypes had changed over the years. Most noticeable was the growing tendency of Princeton students to reject previously held *negative* stereotypes of minority groups. Thus, for example, the level of agreement that being "superstitious" is characteristic of blacks dropped from 84 percent in 1933 to 13 percent in 1969; that blacks are "lazy," from 75 to 26 percent; and that Jews are "shrewd," from 79 to 30 percent; that Jews are "mercenary" from 49 to 15 percent; and that Chinese are "superstitious" from 34 to 8 percent. On the other hand, many other stereotypes remained unchanged throughout the four decades (for example, that the Chinese are tradition-loving and reserved, that Germans are industrious, that the Irish are quick-tempered and very religious, that Italians are passionate and talkative, and that Jews are intelligent and loyal to family ties).

Function of Stereotypes

As Lippmann suggested in 1922, the major function of stereotypes is to help people process information about their social environments. Every person is constantly bombarded with a barrage of social information and must

---

Exercise 5.6

Select several acceptable stereotypes from the lists you have prepared and examine their stability and change over time. How did your images of particular groups change, and how did you react in particular instances to disconfirming information?

---

find ways to ease the load and reduce the complexity of the social environment. Stereotypes are mechanisms that help people make their social worlds more manageable, functioning as "simplifiers" and "organizers" of social data. Much as behavioral habits are the simplifiers of the motoric system, enabling people to act more or less automatically and without premeditation, stereotypes act as simplifiers in people's thinking.

By organizing social stimuli in appropriate "groups," stereotypes act both to ease the informational load and to reduce its complexity. Consider the analogous example of a storekeeper. For maximum efficiency, the storekeeper applies principles of organization to the arrangement of goods in the store: All goods of the same type (say, soaps) are kept together; goods of the same type but of different brands are kept near each other; goods that are functionally related to each other, such as razors and shaving creams, are kept near each other; and goods unrelated to each other are separated.

If persons were to store in mind every person they encounter as a unique and different human being, they would need an unlimited mental capacity and would not know how to interact with new persons until they had collected large amounts of information about them. But if persons can create composite cells characterizing many persons who are similar to each other, they both reduce their mental load and make it possible for themselves to know what to expect and how to behave appropriately.

To understand the functionality of stereotypes, it must be accepted that *groups do indeed have shared characteristics* and that generalizations about groups *can* be made. Generalizations are partially inaccurate, but they can provide, more often than not, useful and relevant information about the groups they characterize. Thus, by knowing a person's relevant group memberships, we "know" something about the person without "knowing" the individual person.

In an earlier discussion of information processing (Chapter 3), we conceptualized the process of stereotyping as a balanced function of *effort* and *accuracy*. Generalizations can save effort, but their "price" is decreased accuracy. The most functional combination for the individual is to hold generalizations requiring *minimal effort* but producing *optimal accuracy*. To attain maximal accuracy, too much effort would be required. On the other hand, people cannot function effectively with less than optimal accuracy. They are willing to lose some accuracy in order to reduce effort. Thus, stereotypes are functional so long as they provide people with helpful generalizations about groups, generalizations that allow them to act appropriately in social situations without investing too much energy in collecting and evaluating information.

As we pointed out in Chapter 3, phenomena such as stereotyping and prejudice can be approached from a cognitive perspective and from a dynamic perspective. The cognitive approach focuses on the ways and methods people use in processing information. Cognitive social research examines the effectiveness of such methods, pointing out distortions in information processing. The dynamic approach focuses on emotions, latent motivation, defense mechanisms, hidden conflicts, and similar factors as constituting the bases of social phenomena such as stereotyping and prejudice.

To clarify this distinction, stereotypes must be separated from prejudice. Unfortunately, early writers (such as Lippmann or Allport) did not separate stereotypes from prejudice and thereby confused cognitive and dynamic elements. Prejudice involves more emotional dynamics and deep affect, while in stereotypy the role of cognitive factors is more pronounced.

In a book on cognition and social behavior (Carroll & Payne, 1976) and in later writings, Hamilton (1976, 1979, 1981) theorized about stereotypy in cognitive terms. He argued that the tendency to stereotype appears even with regard to hypothetical groups when no apparent "motivations" are involved. One example is a study by Hamilton and Gifford (1976), in which subjects read behavioral statements about members of hypothetical groups A and B. Members of B were mentioned twice as often as A members, and positive statements were made twice as often as negative statements, but each type of statement was divided in similar proportions between the A and B groups: For each group, one-third of the statements were negative and two-thirds were positive. Through a cognitive mechanism called "illusory correlation" (the tendency to relate two infrequent occurrences that are empirically unrelated to each other) group A was stereotyped more negatively and group B was stereotyped more positively, in spite of the proportional distributions of positive and negative statements. Hamilton argued that this is strong evidence for the creation of stereotypes in the absence of any "dynamic" factors, purely as a function of particular shortcomings of human information processing.

In the real world, stereotypes and prejudices *are* related to each other and cannot be separated as readily as they are in theory or in experimental research. Since stereotypes characterize real groups, not hypothetical As and Bs, people's perceptions of other groups are not as easily separable from their feelings about these groups. Thus, even when stereotypes are nonprejudicial, they may not be "cognitive" only.

Katz (1968) listed four major functions of stereotypes. In our opinion, his list summarizes well the theoretical aspects of the functionality of stereotyping.

(1) Value-Expressive Function. By holding and internalizing particular beliefs and stereotypes, the individual affirms his or her membership in particular social groups. Holding particular beliefs about other groups reaffirms not only the membership in particular groups, but also the views held by that group. Thus, the value-expressive function has little to do with the stereotyped group per se, but concerns the rewards to the *holders* and *users* of stereotypes. For example, to hold particular stereotypes of "communists" in the 1950s served for many Americans as a value-expressive function.

(2) Utilitarian Adjustive Function. This function deals with the cognitive gains of stereotyping in terms of reducing information overload and structuring the social environment in a manageable way. Our analysis of stereotypes as a function of optimal accuracy and minimal effort reflects the utilitarian adjustive function.

(3) Need for Cognitive Structure and Understanding. This function is related to the previous one, but it describes an internal human *need* rather than external usefulness. People need to structure their environments not only because it makes their social functioning more effective but also because ambiguity and disorder of stimuli are disturbing to them. The need to make sense would have an influence even when there are no external benefits to gain.

(4) Ego-Defensive Function. This function focuses on dynamic factors involved in the formation and maintenance of stereotypes, over and beyond the cognitive functions described above. Holding stereotypes about other groups affirms one's membership in one's own groups and clarifies one's images of self and others. By reducing ambiguity and prescribing expected patterns of behavior, stereotypes contribute to reduce anxiety and decrease the tension of internal conflict, at the same time justifying one's prejudice and aggression. Stereotypes can serve as tension relievers and as tension stimulants, depending on the person's underlying needs at a particular time. The highly charged and volatile process of intergroup conflict (see next chapters) is rooted in the stereotypic perceptions of own group and other groups, perceptions that can readily become self-fulfilling prophecies.

Change Goals for Stereotypes

CLARIFICATION OF TERMS: STEREOTYPES, PREJUDICE, AND DISCRIMINATION

The differentiations of persons and groups in heterogeneous society in terms of race, ethnicity, religion, and other dimensions are maintained and reinforced through the mechanisms of stereotypy, prejudice, and discrimination. Stereotypy may be perceived as creating the conditions in which prejudice is strengthened and reinforced, in turn paving the way for enacting discriminative behavior, "to keep lesser people in their place."

The working definition of stereotypes in this chapter emphasizes the cognitive role of stereotypic generalizations as simplifiers and organizers of the social environment. We stressed the functionality of stereotypes mostly in the area of information processing, arguing that stereotypes can be positive, negative, or emotionally neutral. In contrast, we join most writers in viewing prejudice as a particular, dynamic type of stereotype—characterized by a negative emotional tone, hostility, aggression, and judgmental nature. Prejudice is a statement of superiority: "We are better than they are!"

Some social scientists view all negative stereotypes as prejudices. We believe that a stereotype may be negative without being prejudicial. That happens when a negative stereotype has been learned as such by the person, but when it lacks emotional vehemence and is neither judgmental nor particularly aggressive. For example, holding the stereotype that Scots are misers or that Americans are phony may be prejudicial *or* nonprejudicial.

As to the distinction between prejudice and discrimination, we view prejudice as an attitudinal set and discrimination as a behavioral practice. One *holds* a prejudice, and one *acts* discriminately. The most common relationship between prejudice and discrimination is that persons holding prejudicial attitudes are more apt to manifest or support discriminatory practices.

But the relationship between prejudice and discrimination is sometimes more complex, since it is possible to identify nonprejudicial discrimination, much as prejudice need not be accompanied by discrimination. Nonprejudicial discrimination is typically the kind of discrimination that has been in existence for a long time, perpetuated without conscious planning or design. For example, the practice of all major religions involves a great number of discriminatory acts against women. However, this does not imply that every religious man who observes particular religious practices is prejudiced against women. On the other hand, people hold many prejudiced attitudes without ever expressing their prejudices in explicit acts of discrimination. Many politicians and many educators are probably prejudiced, but most of them are sufficiently well trained to prevent their prejudices from being expressed in actual practice.

WHAT CHANGES WOULD BE ATTAINABLE?

Many educators might support the demand to abolish stereotypes. People *should not* acquire and hold generalizations about groups; preexisting expectations are *bad*; and people should not "group" other persons in their minds, but rather treat every person as a unique human being.

In light of the inevitability and functionality of stereotypes, such an idea about how people should be is an unattainable goal. Stereotypes can be functional *or* dysfunctional, depending on the ways they are utilized. They are functional in reducing cognitive complexity, in enabling easier and smoother social action, and in making social interaction more effective. Stereotypes are dysfunctional when they become overly distorted and emotionally loaded, when they are believed to be totally valid truths, and when their holders use them rigidly and without awareness. Therefore, the goal should not be to abolish stereotypy but to find ways of making stereotypes *more* functional. This can be achieved by increasing people's flexibility in using stereotypes, including awareness of processes of stereotyping and of one's own stereotypes; continuous examination of one's generalizations about social groups—in terms of both the validity of one's stereotypes and the underlying dynamic needs that can affect stereotypy; caution that one's stereotypes should not be used judgmentally; openness to absorb new information—even if it disconfirms held stereotypes; and comprehension of the advantages and disadvantages of stereotyping other people.

Much as stereotypes are inevitable, "we are all prejudiced" (Aronson, 1976). As Wrightsman (1972) pointed out, a great deal of evidence leads to the conclusion that prejudice, in some form, has always existed and will continue to exist as long as differences between groups of people exist. Yet we believe that change goals for stereotypes should differ radically from change goals for prejudice. While we advocate "flexible use" for stereotypes, we strongly believe that educators should direct their efforts toward minimizing the intensity and destructiveness of prejudice. The various change strategies to be discussed in a later chapter should all be directed to fight prejudice and discrimination—through the socialization and education of individuals, legislation and public policies, and "reeducation" of adult citizens. Completely abolishing prejudice and discrimination may be unattainable, but these phenomena can undoubtedly be moderated in scope and intensity.

6

THEORIES OF PREJUDICE

Definitions

Examination of various definitions of prejudice in current books in social psychology shows a high level of agreement among authors. Goethals and Worchel (1981) define prejudice as "an unjustified negative attitude toward an individual, based solely on that individual's membership in a certain group." Gergen and Gergen (1981) provide an almost identical definition, adding that prejudice is an attitude as well as "readiness to respond." Wrightsman and Deaux (1981) add that this unfavorable attitude is intolerant and unfair, directed most often at members of racial and ethnic groups. Jones et al. (1979) further point out that prejudice is accompanied by beliefs that associate predominantly negative characteristics with the group and by behavioral tendencies to avoid or aggress against members of the group.

Going back almost three decades, to Allport's (1954) classic book "The Nature of Prejudice," we find two illuminating definitions of prejudice. Allport defined prejudice as "an avertive or hostile attitude toward a person who belongs to a group, simply because he belongs to that group, and is therefore presumed to have the objectionable qualities ascribed to the group." The briefest definition presented by Allport is that prejudice is "thinking ill of others without sufficient warrant."

Lexical definitions of prejudice consider both negative (thinking ill) and positive (thinking well) prejudgments of people. However, social psychologists and sociologists use the term "prejudice" to refer exclusively to the negative and hostile attitude, and we follow suit in this book.

Klineberg (1964) delineated three major groups of prejudices: (1) the prejudice of power and exploitation (such as slavery); (2) the prejudice of ideology, which is based on the sense of "monopoly on truth" (such as religious prejudice); and (3) the prejudice of racism (the notion of a superior race or Nazism, for example).

Personal and Societal Prejudice

This chapter deals with various aspects of prejudice, the relations between prejudice and intergroup processes in heterogeneous society, the psychological functionality of prejudice, personal traits related to being prejudiced, and factors that influence the emergence of prejudice in society. We treat prejudice in this chapter in a generalized way, leaving for later chapters the specific analyses of racial and ethnic prejudice, religious prejudice, sexism, and ideological prejudice.

The distinction between prejudice in society and the personal tendency to be prejudiced is important. Persons who are highly prejudiced are characterized by a particular personality syndrome ("authoritarianism"), and they typically direct their prejudice toward most or all groups who are different from themselves, rather than being prejudiced toward one group only. Authoritarian persons tend to be generally intolerant, bigoted, and righteous, perceiving and interpreting the world in extreme terms of good (ours) and bad (theirs). This theoretical approach ties together an authoritarian *personality*, a dogmatic *cognitive style*, prejudicial *attitudes*, and discriminatory *behavior*.

The societal approach focuses not on individuals who are prejudiced, but on the conditions and events in society-at-large that contribute to intensify prejudice and discrimination. These conditions include conflicts between racial, ethnic, religious, and ideological groups; political and economic competition between groups differing in power and status; tension due to the insufficiency of the available resources to satisfy fully each group's needs; scapegoating; and the short-range consequences of various acts of legislation and planned social change. In this approach, it is assumed that a particular social conflict or event would intensify the level of prejudice toward particular groups.

These two conceptions are complementary rather than contradictory. Even under the most relaxed and conflict-free societal conditions, some individuals are more prejudiced than others. On the other hand, particular intergroup tensions and conflicts intensify the overall level of prejudice in society, influencing the attitudes of nonauthoritarian as well as authoritarian persons.

Prejudice and Socio-Identity

Prejudice is basically an *intergroup* process. It is not what "the individual" thinks of members of another group, but what an individual member of a particular group thinks of members of another group. In other words, the relevant group membership and socio-identity of the *holder* of prejudice (in terms of that person's sense of belongingness in the group, identification with the group, self-esteem, and the like), together with the attitude and position of the holder's group toward the other group play a major role in determining the individual's prejudice. Prejudices are held and maintained by individuals in the framework of their own socio-identities. Even when prejudice is conceptualized in a personality perspective (where the tendency to be prejudiced is viewed as a generalized personality trait of the individual) the content and intensity of particular prejudices reflect specific socio-identities and group memberships.

Who Is Prejudiced?

There are great individual differences among persons in their tendencies to hold and use prejudice. Some people are very prejudiced, while others are relatively free of prejudice. Particular societal conditions intensify prejudice—but even then some people would remain less prejudiced than the normal level of prejudice of other people under relaxed conditions. Many people are unaware of their prejudice, employing various defense mechanisms to prevent painful knowledge of their prejudice to reach their consciousness. Thus, self-report of one's prejudices cannot be taken to reflect validly persons' underlying level of prejudice. Some research evidence (for example, Babad, 1979) points to the fact that persons who "allow" themselves to become aware of their prejudice—to own it and take responsibility for it—are usually those who are *not* extremely prejudiced. On the other hand, those who are most highly biased and prejudiced show a stronger tendency to deny it. Thus, one often finds an inverse relationship between the existence of prejudice "within" the person and the person's awareness of that prejudice. Minority group members often argue that only majority group members are prejudiced, while others argue that only authoritarian or dogmatic persons are prejudiced. We believe in the value of exploring how one relates to different groups and view it as the first step in lifting potential prejudices into awareness.

Exercise 6.1 was constructed by Max Birnbaum in the early 1970s for Boston University's C-Group Laboratory. The exercise focuses on desired levels of social distance from various racial, ethnic, and religious groups. "Social distance" is measured by the level of willingness to engage in different types of interactions with members of the various groups.

Before you begin Exercise 6.1, we would like to mention that its value depends on your willingness to be candid with yourself. Many people would prefer to maintain a facade of total acceptance of all different others rather than face any hint of prejudice in themselves.

Exercise 6.1 Are You Prejudiced?
A Suggested Exercise for Self-Inquiry
(created by Max Birnbaum for the Laboratory in Community Relations and Community Development, Boston University)

Instructions

Many of us do not consider ourselves prejudiced. But prejudice against persons or groups is almost universal, although the areas and intensity of prejudice

vary from person to person. The first step in dealing with prejudice is to identify the areas of prejudice and to recognize their varying degrees of intensity.

The following exercise is designed to let you examine your feelings toward
certain religious, geographical, ethnic, and racial groups and to determine the
level of *social distance* you wish to keep in interactions with members of each
group.

Using the scale of 1 to 5, write in each box on the next page the number of the
statement that agrees most closely with your feelings in each situation for each
group.

(1) I'd actively encourage it.
(2) It's alright with me.
(3) I'm neutral.
(4) I'd avoid it if I could.
(5) I'm strongly opposed to it.

Scoring: Add up all the numbers in the vertical columns in Totals (a). These
numbers summarize and allow you to compare the relative social distance
toward the different groups. A score of 39 indicates neutrality. A score of 52
indicates a wish for moderate distance, while a score of 65 would indicate
extreme social distance. A score of 26 would indicate acceptance of the group,
while a score of 13 would indicate a wish actively to seek out the group and
associate with its members.

While this analysis allows you to compare your feelings toward different groups,
the next analysis enables you to examine your relative sensitivity to particular
areas of social behavior. Add up the numbers horizontally in Totals (b). The
scores in each row may vary from 9 to 45, with 27 indicating neutrality. The
higher the score, the less comfortable you would feel in that type of situation with
members of other groups. The lower the score, the more comfortable you feel to
engage in that activity with those who are different. Comparisons of the values in
Totals (b) allow you to formulate your personal network of social distance.

It is recommended that you compare your data and discuss your conclusions
with another or several co-inquirers.

(1) I'd actively encourage it. (2) It's alright with me. (3) I'm neutral. (4) I'd avoid it if I could. (5) I'm strongly opposed to it.	WASPs	Catholics	Jews	Blacks	Irish-Americans	Italian-Americans	Polish-Americans	Hispanic-Americans	Southerners	Totals (b)
Be my friend										
Be my closest friend										
Work with me										
Work under me										

(continued)

	WASPs	Catholics	Jews	Blacks	Irish-Americans	Italian-Americans	Polish-Americans	Hispanic-Americans	Southerners	Totals (b)
(1) I'd actively encourage it. (2) It's alright with me. (3) I'm neutral. (4) I'd avoid it if I could. (5) I'm strongly opposed to it.										
Be my boss										
Live next door										
Visit my home										
Date me or a member of my family										
Marry me										
Go to school with my child										
Marry my child										
Talk about politics										
Have fun together										
Totals (a)										

The Prejudiced Personality

The focal work representing the personality-oriented conception of prejudice was summarized in the classic book *The Authoritarian Personality* by Adorno, Frenkel-Brunswick, Sanford, and Levinson (1950). The project was funded by the American Jewish Committee and was initially intended to investigate the dynamics of antisemitism, following the extreme manifestations of Fascism and genocide in World War II. The study of antisemitism quickly extended to include other prejudices, ending with a wide and deep personality structure, or "syndrome," labeled "authoritarianism."

Adorno and his associates were initially interested in investigating the variables that covary with holding a specific prejudice (antisemitism) against a particular group (Jews). Later, they found a strong relationship between the tendency to hold antisemitic prejudices and "ethnocentrism," that is, rejection of all unlike groups (blacks, "Japs," "Okies," and even "zootsuiters"). In the next stage, they discovered that antisemitism and ethnocentrism were related to the tendency to hold political and economic conservative (PEC) attitudes in areas other than contact with out-groups. Conservatism was defined as a belief in traditional values and in maintaining the status quo, and as resistance to social change. Thus, holding a specific prejudice, rejecting all unlike groups, and being politically conservative were all seen as aspects of the same phenomenon.

The next step went beyond prejudice and ideology, focusing on a personality style labeled Implicit Anti-Democratic Trends or Potentiality for Fascism (F) or Authoritarian. Holding prejudices was then seen as one characteristic of the authoritarian personality.

THE AUTHORITARIAN PERSONALITY STRUCTURE

The conceptualization of the authoritarian "personality type" was based on psychoanalytic theory. The authoritarian person was seen as having strong aggressive and sexual (id) impulses and an equally strong, punishing, strict, and rigid conscience (superego), while the ability to cope flexibly with external situations and compromise the internal conflict between drives and conscience (ego functions) was seen as relatively weak and undeveloped. As a result, Adorno et al. theorized, the authoritarian person experiences strong conflicts, yet lacks adaptive (ego) tools for coping with the ambivalence. The authoritarian person deals with his or her strong impulses and ambivalence by way of overdefensiveness, rigidity, externalization, and projection of all unpleasant ideation upon others, at the same time excessively glorifying self, family, and conventional values. Another component of this personality syndrome is the authoritarian's strong orientation toward and concern about authority and status. When the authoritarian discovers those who are *inferior* (by virtue of being members of out-groups and "having" the negative characteristics that are prejudicially projected on them), this inferiority justifies being aggressive toward them.

The authors of *The Authoritarian Personality* described nine major characteristics of this personality syndrome:

(1) Conventionalism. Rigid adherence to and overemphasis on conventional middle-class values, and conformity to social pressure (manners, treating relations and friends properly, and the like). A sample item from the F Scale reads: "Obedience and respect for authority are the most important virtues children should learn."

(2) Authoritarian Submission. An exaggerated emotional need to submit to the in-group authority; uncritical acceptance of strong leadership; idealization of authority (including God's authority). Typical item: "In our confused world, the only way really to know what is happening is to rely upon the leaders or trustworthy experts."

(3) Authoritarian Aggression. A tendency to prefer rejection, condemnation, strong discipline, and harsh punishment as the proper ways of dealing

with people and behaviors that deviate from the conventional values; aggression directed at weaker and subordinate people: "Sex crimes, such as rape and attacks on children, deserve more than mere imprisonment; such criminals ought to be publicly whipped or worse."

(4) Anti-intraception. A narrow range of consciousness and rejection of fantasies, emotions, impulses, and other "tender-minded" inner ideation; a preference for the practical: "When a person has a problem or a worry, it is best for him not to think about it, but to keep busy with more cheerful things," or "Nowadays more and more people are prying into matters that should remain personal and private."

(5) Superstition and Stereotypy. Thinking in rigid, oversimplified "black and white" categories, with no tolerance of ambiguity or "shades of gray"; shifting the responsibility to (mystical) powers beyond the individual's control: "Some day it will probably be shown that astrology can explain a lot of things," or "People are divided into two distinct classes: the weak and the strong."

(6) Power and Toughness. An excessive concern with issues of power and leadership, dominance-submission, strength and weakness; identifying with power figures, yet submitting to power figures; denial of weakness and assertion of toughness: "What our country needs is fewer laws and offices and more strong and loyal people that can be trusted."

(7) Destructiveness and Cynicism. A generalized hostility that is rationalized by its universal nature: "Human nature being what it is, there will always be war and conflict," or "Familiarity breeds contempt."

(8) Projectivity. The projection of all negative affect upon others, which leads to the belief that the most terrible things are happening "out there": "Nowadays, when so many different kinds of people move around and mix together so much, a person has to be especially careful."

(9) Sex. Excessive concern about sex and a harshly punitive attitude with regard to sexual "goings on": "Homosexuals are hardly better than criminals and ought to be severely punished," "Men are only interested in one thing."

Adorno and his associates, particularly Frenkel-Brunswick (1949), also characterized the cognitive style of the authoritarian personality. They defined two major dimensions:

(1) Rigidity. The authoritarian style tends to be rigid and field-dependent, with strict compartmentalization of stimuli, resistance to change, and overall lack of cognitive flexibility.

(2) Intolerance of Ambiguity. Much as the authoritarian's major emotional problem is dealing with ambivalence, the authoritarian is intolerant of ambiguity in cognitive style. The authoritarian typically polarizes and dichotomizes his or her reactions, forcing a sense of clarity, often by distorting the ambiguous.

In a study exemplifying these cognitive factors, Frenkel-Brunswick (1949) showed subjects a series of sixteen pictures depicting the gradual transformation of a dog into a cat. She found that high authoritarians tended to hold on longer than nonauthoritarians to their original interpretation (dog) before shifting to cat.

THE CONCEPTION OF DOGMATISM

In 1960 Rokeach introduced a new conceptualization of the authoritarian personality, which he labeled "dogmatism" or "closed-mindedness." Rokeach rejected the previous focus on right-wing, conservative ideology and the heavy reliance on Freudian formulations of personality dynamics. He viewed dogmatism as a mode of thought rather than a set of beliefs, a cognitive style characterized by rigidity and intolerance of ambiguity. Rokeach defined dogmatism as a cognitive organization of beliefs about reality that is relatively closed. It is organized around a central set of beliefs about absolute authority, which provides a framework for patterns of intolerance toward others.

Rokeach constructed a new scale that did not focus on a specific political ideology (as did the F Scale) but assessed the dogmatic style in a variety of content domains. Sample items from the dogmatism (D) scale read:

- The most important thing in a person's life is to want to achieve something important.
- The worst crime a person can commit is publicly to attack the people who share the person's views
- In human history there is probably only a very small number of truly great thinkers.
- There are only two kinds of people: those who are for the truth and those who are against it.
- Sometimes it is better to wait in voicing an opinion until one can hear the view of a respectable and authoritative person.

THE ATTITUDES OF THE AUTHORITARIAN/DOGMATIC

With regard to attitudes and political ideology, there is a break between the conception of authoritarianism and the conception of dogmatism. The former is quite explicit in identifying the authoritarian personality structure with antidemocratic, or fascistic, attitudes and with the right-wing ideology. The conception of dogmatism makes it possible to view this trait as a style of thinking independent of ideological content, meaning that there could be an "authoritarian of the left" as likely as there is an "authoritarian of the right." Eysenck (1954) followed the same line of reasoning as Rokeach. In his theory of politics, he formulated two orthogonal continuums, one (T) referring to *cognitive style* (tough-minded /tender-minded) and the other (R) related to the content of ideology (radical /conservative, or communist /fascist). Each ideology can then be located on a two-dimensional space: communist and fascist may be equally high in tough-mindedness but be on different positions along the R dimension; liberalism falls in the middle of the R dimension but high on tender-mindedness; and so on.

This view of dogmatism as a style of thinking independent of the content of ideology remains widely held even though the research evidence supporting it has not been very strong. Some studies confirm this hypothesis (such as Babad, 1979), while others do not (for example, Thompson & Michel, 1972). We believe that the content of ideology may well enter the picture after all, since right-wing conservatism declares its resistance to change, while communism and other left-wing ideologies declare their belief in social change. Thus, while some communists are definitely dogmatic, there may be good reason to expect to find a higher proportion of dogmatics among the conservatives.

RESEARCH FINDINGS ON
AUTHORITARIANISM AND DOGMATISM

Since the publication of *The Authoritarian Personality*, hundreds and thousands of studies have compared authoritarian or dogmatic people to nonauthoritarian or nondogmatic people. There is no way of summarizing concisely a body of research as large as that. The following list is an almost random sample of investigated correlates of authoritarianism and dogmatism:

- specific prejudices toward particular groups;
- political and social attitudes;
- rigidity in interpersonal perception;
- volunteering to be subjects in scientific research;
- selecting particular candidates in elections (for example, Goldwater)
- family ideology, child-rearing attitudes, and socialization practices;
- community participation;
- religious behavior;
- attitudes on specific world and national events (such as the war in Vietnam);
- conformity;
- supporting tough police forces;
- classroom behaviors of teachers;

- learning styles of children;
- viewing Archie Bunker as winning his arguments with son-in-law Mike;
- studies on the relationships between stereotypy and prejudice.

Almost all findings are in the predicted direction, showing high A-D subjects to be more rigid and tough-minded than low A-D subjects. Thus, there is a solid base for accepting the existence and validity of this personality syndrome.

DOGMATISM AND "PYGMALION IN THE CLASSROOM"

An interesting integration of stereotypy, prejudice, and dogmatism is found in the research on self-fulfilling teacher expectancies. In the well-known book *Pygmalion in the Classroom,* Rosenthal and Jacobson (1968) showed how teacher's expectations influenced students' performance. They chose children at random from class lists and told their teachers that these children were identified by a new and innovative diagnostic test to be "late bloomers," expected to show sudden and rapid intellectual progress. Rosenthal and Jacobson showed that for some teachers, these expectancies indeed led to substantially improved performance by some alleged "late bloomers." It seems that implicitly and without awareness, some teachers change their ways of relating to their students as a function of their expectations of these students (see Brophy & Good, 1970; Rosenthal, 1971; Rubovitz & Maehr, 1973).

More recently, Babad and his associates began to investigate the relationship between teachers' tendency to be influenced by stereotypes, their dogmatism, and the effects of their expectations on their own behavior and on their students' performance. In other words, Babad asked *who* would show preferential and discriminatory treatment of students and who would not. Biased and unbiased teachers were identified through the scores they gave to drawings allegedly made by a high-status and a low-status child—biased teachers giving the high-status child a much higher score than the low-status child (Babad, 1979). Biased individuals were found to describe themselves as more conventional and reasonable than did unbiased individuals (in line with the conception of authoritarianism) and to describe their political ideologies in more extreme terms than did unbiased individuals (in line with Rokeach's conception of the dogmatic style). Babad and Inbar (1981) reported that biased teachers treated their classes in a more authoritarian, rigid, and inflexible manner than did unbiased teachers. Babad, Inbar, and Rosenthal (1982b) examined how biased and unbiased teachers nominate "high" and "low" students. They found that unbiased teachers made nominations based only on ability, while the nominations made by biased teachers were "contaminated" by students' socioeconomic and cultural backgrounds, physical attractiveness, and quality of clothing.

Finally, Babad et al. (1982a) showed that unbiased teachers treated low- and high-expectancy students equitably, while biased teachers showed self-fulfilling expectancy effects in their behavior. They treated their low-expectancy students negatively, and the effects of these differential behaviors were reflected in the relatively lower subsequent performances of these students.

Exercise 6.2

You have probably encountered in your own life (at school, in your family or community) individuals who were highly authoritarian and dogmatic. Examine what you read about this personality type in light of your own experiences. What theoretical aspects stand out most strongly in your experience? What strategies did you and other people employ in dealing with these persons? How successful have these strategies been?

Social Determinants of Prejudice

A SOCIOLOGICAL CONCEPTION OF PREJUDICE

Individuals may differ in their personality-based tendencies to be dogmatic, but prejudice in society varies as a function of more global processes. While the personality approach seeks to understand the *variability* within the distribution of individual citizens, the sociological approach focuses on the changes in the *means* of distributions and the factors causing such changes.

Two basic human needs combine to produce prejudice in society: the need for belongingness and the need for power and status. Heterogeneous society is divided into distinct groups, with a great degree of similarity *within* each group and a great degree of difference *between* groups. Groups are determined by the dimensions of difference in society: race, ethnicity, religion, social class, nationality, sex, age, profession, geographic region, and numerous other partitions. People form socio- (or group) identities and seek need gratification through their groups. The conflict in heterogeneous society is the struggle between distinct groups (women and men, blacks and whites, labor and management), each vying to attain more power and status, better opportunities for its members, and more control over society's various resources.

For a group identity to be viable and meaningful, the group boundaries must be well defined, and there must be a recognizable "out-group," that is, those who do *not* belong in the group. Being just a member of "society-at-large" is too anonymous and lacking in meaning, and people seek more exclusive memberships that entail strong socio-identities and struggle with other observable groups.

The need for power and status is "relative" as much as it is "absolute." When a group lacks rights and privileges, its struggle is aimed at attaining equal rights and equal access to power and leadership positions. But having "high status" implies that some others must have lower status. Therefore, the struggle between groups is an eternal, continuous process in heterogeneous society.

Prejudice is an "instrument" in the struggle between groups, serving to *justify* the struggle itself, the aggression and hostility directed at other groups, and the practice of discrimination. In addition, prejudice also serves to assert the group's identity and strengthen it from within. Thus, in this conception prejudice is seen to be functional for the group holding and using it.

ECONOMIC AND POLITICAL COMPETITION

Economic and political competition between groups is a major antecedent of prejudice. Resources in society are always limited, and the "cake" is always too small fully to satisfy all the needs of all groups. Therefore, competition among interest groups over economic and political power is inevitable in modern society. To have a better shot at attaining power, individuals unite into groups pursuing common interests. The dominant group is in the best position to look after its own interests and to control the political structure so as to maintain its power.

The dominant group gains clear advantages from discrimination against minorities: It can monitor the distribution of jobs and other resources; it can provide fewer opportunities and lower compensation to minorities; it can direct minority group members to inferior jobs; it can reward its own members disproportionally; and, most important, it can legislate and establish policies that will maintain its advantageous status. Prejudicially believing that minorities are inferior and do not deserve (or wish, or are capable of handling) more resources is the best justification for continuing to engage in discriminatory practices while keeping a clear conscience.

If society were homogeneous in terms of race and ethnicity, interest groups would most probably be defined by social class criteria (occupational and educational level). But in our contemporary heterogeneous society, racial, ethnic, and religious groups have clearly become central interest groups (see Glazer & Moynihan, 1975; Dahrendorf, 1969). Given the distinctiveness and stable characteristics of racial, ethnic, and religious groups, and given that intergroup struggle strengthens socio-identities in addition to ascertaining the attainment of "goods," it is not surprising that the political and economic competition in modern society takes place among racial, ethnic, and religious groups.

Poor persons in Sicily, Greece, or Africa may wonder why the American Sicilians, Greeks, or blacks are involved in such bitter struggle, since relative to the rest of the world they are so affluent. Some conservative, rich, upper-class persons in America also like to argue that even the poor groups in America are much more affluent than the populations of most countries (and therefore—in their opinion—the American minorities are largely "ungrateful"). But deprivation is a *relative* concept, and people's frustration and anger are a function of how better off they perceive other groups in their own society to be. In that sense, the United States is a country of *gaping* differences, where, as a result of capitalistic ideology, consumerism, and television, the economic and political differences between racial and ethnic groups are extremely salient and painfully apparent. No wonder, then, that civil unrest in America so often follows racial and ethnic distinctions.

Political and economic competition is fierce enough even when society is affluent. The struggle becomes more bitter and desperate when the economic conditions get worse and/or when previous political attainments are erased by those in power. As Dollard (1937), Allport (1954), and numerous other authors have pointed out, intergroup struggle and racial and ethnic prejudice become explicit under conditions of uncertainty and "economic crunch" even if these processes were less discernible before.

The interplay between the process of economic and political competition, on the one hand, and prejudice and discrimination, on the other, can be explained on the basis of the theory of self-justification: Believing that some racial and ethnic groups are inferior provides a justification for taking advantage of those groups and discriminating against them. In turn, the inferiority that results from oppression further justifies prejudice and discrimination. Thus, prejudice begets prejudice.

Exercise 6.3

Can you remember instances of political or economic competition that were accompanied by increased intergroup hostility and prejudice? Try to trace at least one instance from your personal life history (in school, neighborhood, work, and so forth) and one instance of a more "societal" level (city, state, and the like). Examine the development of the conflict and the various manifestations of increased prejudice.

THE PHENOMENON OF SCAPEGOATING

The original ritual of "scapegoating" is described in the Bible:

And he [Aaron, the High Priest] shall take of the congregation of the children of Israel two he-goats for a sin-offering and one ram for a burnt-offering. . . .

And Aaron shall cast lots upon the two goats; one lot for the Lord, and the other lot for Azazel ["hell" in Hebrew]. . . . The goat on which the lot fell for Azazel shall be presented alive before the Lord, to make an atonement with him, and to let him go for Azazel into the wilderness. . . . And Aaron shall lay both his hands upon the head of the live goat, and confess over him all the iniquities of the children of Israel, and all their transgressions and all their sins, putting them upon the head of the goat, and shall send him away by the hand of a fit man into the wilderness. . . . And the goat shall bear upon him all their iniquities unto a land not inhabited, and he shall let go the goat in the wilderness. (Leviticus 17)

The "children of Israel" can be cleansed of all their sins; the scapegoat carries their sins and iniquities into the wilderness. In modern society, the scapegoat is hardly a goat, and the use of scapegoating is a nasty prejudicial practice. The victim of scapegoating is usually weak and helpless, projected as the *source* of a given problem and blamed for it.

Scapegoating is a form of displaced aggression, where an innocent but helpless victim or group of victims is blamed and punished for attributes or behaviors that are *projected* upon it. Scapegoating is more likely to emerge when groups cannot cope effectively with their problems and when a distinct and powerless victim for scapegoating is available. The Jews, the Gypsies, and other groups became scapegoats in Nazi Germany, much as the black people were scapegoated in the American South. Hovland and Sears (1940) recorded for a period of fifty years the price of cotton and the number of lynchings of blacks in the southern states of the United States. They found a significant and substantial negative correlation between these indices: The lower the price of cotton in a given year, the larger was the number of lynchings at that time. This dramatic finding is quoted by many writers as evidence of the societal process of scapegoating. Some politicians make cynical use of the principle of scapegoating: When there is tension and social problems seem insurmountable, find an innocent, weak, and distinctive group to blame and victimize!

Scapegoating is a major mechanism in the emergence of prejudice and discrimination in heterogeneous society, and it has played a similar role in the wars between nations throughout human history. Oppression and genocide usually involves scapegoating, allowing the aggressors to feel righteous and "cleansed." The psychological function of scapegoating thus derives from the fact that it not only provides full justification to the expression of aggression, but it also makes it possible for its users to preserve their advantageous position forcefully.

The use of scapegoating is not limited to majority groups. Minorities can displace their anger at the majority group by identifying and scapegoating a weaker group, of even lower status than themselves. Minorities can also use *reverse scapegoating* as a weapon in their struggle against the majority group. The images of police officers as "aggressive pigs" and of men as "male chauvinist pigs" probably reflect such instances of reverse scapegoating (or, more appropriately in these examples, "scapepigging"). In fact, people's reactions to "the government" often contain a tinge of reverse scapegoating. Some analysts follow a Freudian idea in arguing that "people elect leaders only to kill them later." The elected leadership is apt to be prejudicially perceived as inept, incompetent, self-serving, and often downright dangerous. Even if one initially voted for a particular leader, this attitude serves to strip the leader of some of his or her power, at least in fantasy.

Exercise 6.4

Can you remember an instance where you have used scapegoating? Can you remember the antecedents of that event? What were the affects of your scapegoating on the victim? Can you remember another instance where you have been the victim of scapegoating? What conclusions can you reach from the comparison of these two instances?

LEARNED PREJUDICE

We emphasized earlier that being a prejudiced person is not identical with holding a prejudice. Probably the majority of prejudices people hold are learned as wholes, simply accepted as reflecting the truth. If one is taught that communists are bad, hateful, nondemocratic people who should be fought against, why should one doubt that? If three-year-olds see on television every Saturday morning "bad guys" who are short, fat, ugly and speak with foreign accents, why should they not be prejudiced against short, fat, ugly people with foreign accents?

The distinction between holding a learned prejudice and being an authoritarian or prejudiced person is important. Numerous studies during the 1940s and 1950s showed southern whites to have a consistently higher preference than northern whites for discriminatory practices against blacks. But this may reflect no more than learned prejudice, since Pettigrew (1961) found *no* differences between northerners and southerners in responses to the F Scale. Aronson (1976) mentioned that famous English writers such as Christopher Marlowe (in *The Jew of Malta*) and William Shakespeare (in *The Merchant of Venice*) depicted Jews as conniving, money-grabbing, bloodthirsty cowards, even though Jews were expelled from England 300 years before these works were written, and Marlowe and Shakespeare therefore may never have encountered Jews at all!

"Religion" is probably the major source of learned prejudice in human history. Century after century, the world's religions spread and fostered highly prejudicial images of their nonadherents (out-groups). Prayerbooks of most religions provide great many instances of prejudice, and true believers have no recourse but to accept these learned prejudice. Furthermore, most long-standing religions (such as Fundamental Protestantism, Roman Catholicism, Judaism, and Islam) prohibit believers from even questioning some of their teachings if they wish to remain within the ranks of the group, demanding loyalty to the written word. As a result, some of these learned prejudices remain irrefutable and are taught from generation to generation.

Learned prejudice is strengthened through pressure for conformity that is brought to bear upon members, and this pressure increases in times of tension and conflict. Regardless of their personal tendency to be dogmatic or not, most people find it hard to resist such pressure to hold and maintain prejudice, particularly if society is characterized by tension, conflict, and a sense of impending crisis. Such pressure to conform was evident in Germany when the Nazis came to power, in the United States in the McCarthy era with regard to anticommunism, and in the Church for many generations with regard to prejudice against non-Christians. When membership in a meaningful group (see Chapter 7) entails conformity to prejudicial attitudes, many people accept the norm and internalize the prejudice. A chilling, if somewhat overdramatized, instance of this sort was recently described by Ron Jones (1976), a history teacher in a Palo Alto high school. In an attempt to demonstrate to his students how people can become Nazis, Jones applied strong pressure on his students to join an imaginary movement characterized by a highly prejudicial attitude and fascistic behavior. He reported how amazed he was to discover the students' enthusiastic conformity and their quickly emerging fascism.

Exercise 6.5

Please list 7 to 10 "learned prejudices" that you hold or held earlier in life (or learned prejudices held by other people you know). Analyze the sources of these learnings.

THE CONTRIBUTION OF PLURALISTIC
CHANGE TO PREJUDICE

Somewhat paradoxically, the early stages of pluralistic social change (for example, giving special rights to previously discriminated minorities through equal opportunity legislation or preferential treatment in allocation of public funds) intensify prejudice in society. When a change process is begun, intergroup tensions almost invariably increase. Planned change is the outcome of pluralistic struggle, in which minorities are assertive and militant, forcing those in power to institute acts of change (in housing, jobs, busing, and the like). The act of change adds to the preexisting tensions, since almost invariably the status quo is changed at the expense of the majority group. On the other hand, there are no immediate, apparent benefits of the change process that may reduce the intergroup tension. Thus, the early stages of planned change are characterized by high intergroup tensions—and this is the breeding ground for prejudice. Overassertiveness from one side always increases the prejudicial attitude of the other side, and each side can allow itself to be aggressively prejudicial if it feels "provoked" by the other side.

The clearest example of this process in recent years is the issue of busing. To achieve racial and ethnic integration of the schools, rulings in recent years have regulated the busing of children from one neighborhood to another. Thus far, unequivocal effects of busing, in terms of attitude change and improved scholastic achievement, have not been forthcoming. Some of the more observable short-range outcomes of busing have been quite alarming: white flight, riots, civil unrest, and intensified prejudice and intergroup conflict. Many white, middle-class parents feel that their children are victimized, suffering a decrease in the quality of their education and at the same time subjected to various hardships such as excessive travel, crime, and harassment. Busing has already led to substantial "white flight"; families have moved out of the cities and/or registered their children in private schools. Moreover, this situation has stirred explosive interracial tension, increased prejudice, and led to numerous acts of violence.

When pluralistic change is costly for those who are privileged, the short-range outcomes include an ideological regression, increased prejudice, and intergroup tension. Further examples of this process include "white flight," when minority families move into prestigious white residential areas (the earlier the white family moves out, the smaller its financial loss in property value); equal opportunity employment (when the less qualified minority candidate might be preferred over the more qualified white male); and profuse public spending on welfare payments to non-tax-paying minority group citizens.

Exercise 6.6

From your own experiences—in your town, school, or neighborhood—can you recall instances of increased tension and prejudice following the implementation of pluralistic change? Have you been personally involved in a process of that type? How did these processes develop over time?

7

INTERGROUP RELATIONS

This chapter deals with intergroup processes and their influences on the individual. We treat the individual in a *group* context in this chapter, showing the extent to which "groupness" has a profound influence on the individual's mental and emotional processes: judgments, sentiments, and behaviors. These influences are powerful both in a positive direction (a meaningful identity, a stable cognitive framework) and a negative direction (bias, distortion, intolerance, prejudice, and discrimination). We maintain that the meaning of a person's life cannot be understood without viewing the person in the contextual framework of his or her various group memberships. First we demonstrate how the creation of arbitrary, meaningless groups on the basis of irrelevant criteria produces powerful intergroup processes.

The Minimal Intergroup Situation

Imagine that you are taking ski instruction in upstate New York and you are assigned by an unknown researcher to one of two groups: one asked to wear green armbands and the other, blue armbands. You are informed neither of the "meaning" of being green or blue nor of the reason you were assigned to your group. You have no particular interaction with other individuals who wear the same color, and you are not segregated from those wearing the other color. After the ski instruction is over, you are asked to rate the performance of individual skiers wearing blue or green ribbons as they ski down the hill one at a time (from Downing & Monaco, 1979).

Imagine, again, that you participate in a social-psychological experiment in which you are assigned to one of two groups, supposedly on the basis of your preference for Paul Klee or another painter. This group membership is anonymous, you have no face-to-face interaction with any member of your own group or the other group, and the principle by which the groups are divided is totally unrelated to the task you are asked to perform. You are given a choice task of dividing a given sum of money between two other subjects, whose identities are indicated only by labels specifying their membership in your or the other group (from Tajfel, Billig, Bundy, & Flament, 1971).

Finally, imagine that you participate in a social-psychological experiment in which you are assigned to either a blue or a green group. You are not familiar with any of the other subjects. You are told that you will have no interaction at all with other subjects and that you were randomly assigned to a blue or a green group for the administrative convenience of the experimenter in obtaining first-impression ratings. The experimenter then flips a coin to determine whether your group or the other group will win a prize, so that your group becomes either a winner or a loser. You are then asked to rate members of your own group and the other group on a variety of rating scales including their traits, social characteristics, and your willingness to spend time with them (from Rabbie & Horwitz, 1969).

In these instances, there is a greater-than-chance probability that you will favor members of your own group over members of the other group—that you will like your own group better and prefer to be with them, allocating less money to the out-group and rating the skiing performance of individuals wearing your own color higher than that of other-color individuals, for example.

You may wish to argue that these processes might characterize *other* people, but not you. Indeed Downing and Monaco (1979) have shown that the bias effect in ratings of green or blue ski performance is stronger for individuals scoring high on the F Scale. However, a large body of research (Horwitz & Rabbie, 1982) shows the bias effect in the minimal intergroup situation to be a highly consistent and robust phenomenon.

According to Brewer (1979a), any categorization rule that provides a basis for classifying an individual as belonging to one social grouping as distinct from another can be sufficient to produce differentiation of attitude toward the two groups, in the absence of any initial competitive interdependence. The crucial point in understanding the significance of the in-group/out-group discrimination in the minimal intergroup situation is that these groups are not "real" groups: They are arbitrarily defined on the basis of an irrelevant principle of categorization, and the events taking place in them are minimal and of no central importance in the subjects' lives. But even in this minimal situation there is a consistent differentiation in social perception and social judgment between in-group and out-group.

Several explanations have been offered for this effect. Horwitz and Rabbie (1982) suggest that people feel better associating with others who share the same outcomes (or "fate"). Tajfel et al. (1971) thought that group members respond to a generic and implicit group norm that one ought to favor the in-group over the out-group. Tajfel (1979; Tajfel & Turner, 1979) and Turner (1979) suggested that persons treat group membership as a component of their personal identities and favor their in-groups because they desire to compare favorably with others. Most authors refer to Campbell's (1958) term "entitivity," which emphasizes the strength of the bonding within a group and its conception as a "dynamic whole" (following Kurt Lewin's terminology). These explanations are central in our conception of socio-identities (racial, ethnic, religious, and the like) in which powerful intergroup processes are tied to meaningful, lifelong group memberships.

Summarizing various findings on the minimal intergroup situation, Horwitz and Rabbie (1982) conclude that the tendency to favor the in-group over the out-group *increases:* when there is an explicit similarity within the in-group; when the out-group is perceived to be capable of controlling the outcomes ("fate") of the in-group; when there is a stronger perception of the in-group as an "entity"; when a spirit of competition between the groups is fostered; when the in-group experiences distinct success and/or failure; and when there is actual or anticipated interaction with other members of the in-group. Worchel, Lind, and Kaufman (1975) found that an anticipation of *continued* competition with the out-group tended to moderate somewhat the overevaluation of the in-group. Delineating the dimensions of the intergroup bias, Horwitz and Rabbie (1982) point out that it influences perception of self, that individuals identify with the success of other individuals in their in-group while individuals belonging in the out-group are "depersonalized," and that people hold an intuitive psychological theory (Nisbett & Wilson, 1977) that *others* would bias and discriminate along in-group/out-group lines as well.

In summarizing her review, Brewer (1979a) concluded: (1) that factors such as intergroup competition, similarity, and status differential affect in-group bias *indirectly,* by influencing the salience of distinctions between in-group and out-group; (2) that the degree of intergroup differentiation on a particular response dimension is a joint function of the relevance of inter-group distinctions and the favorableness of the in-group position on that dimension; and (3) that in-group bias is more a function of increased favoritism toward in-group members than to increased hostility toward out-group members.

Exercise 7.1

Try to recall a situation in your own life history that reflects the processes of the minimal intergroup situation. Analyze the conditions under which this situation emerged, and trace its development and its conclusion. We recommend you conduct this activity with (an)other learner(s), sharing and comparing your experiences.

Intergroup Conflict

FORMATION AND ESCALATION OF INTERGROUP CONFLICT

The classic field experiment on the formation and resolution of intergroup conflict was conducted by Sherif and his associates in the 1950s (Sherif, Harvey, White, Hood, & Sherif, 1961). Adaptations of Sherif's ideas transformed his design into training exercises with groups of adults (Blake & Mouton, 1961).

Sherif and his associates set up the "Robbers Cave Summer Camp for Boys" to investigate intergroup conflict, and the researchers took roles of camp counselors. The boys selected to participate in the camp had not known each other previously. The first few days of camp were spent in campwide activities that allowed the formation of friendships. The boys were then separated into two cabins, so that a boy's best friends were in the *other* cabin. Within a few days these initial friendships disintegrated, and new friends were almost exclusively in-group (in-cabin) choices.

Next, a pattern of inter-group conflict was established by increasing the competition between the groups and giving prizes to the winning group. Competition quickly led to increased tension, with greater solidarity within each group and growing hostility toward the other group. Out-group members were negatively stereotyped; plans for ambushes, raids, and other aggressive acts were designed; and the emerging leaders were those who were the more effective fighters.

The same process has been incited numerous times in exercises conducted in human relations laboratories. Participants are divided into groups according to some principle of categorization (women against men, New Yorkers against Bostonians, Jews against Christians, or the like), and a competition (say, for best speech) is set up between the groups. As the conflict escalates, ratings of self- and other-group are collected, and participants' behavior is carefully observed. Some predictable phenomena almost invariably emerge in these situations:

(1) There is an initial gap between evaluation of the in-group and the out-group, even if the evaluated product itself (such as speech) is not objectively superior to that of the other group.
(2) Evaluations of the in-group tend to become more positive as the tension of conflict mounts, while evaluations of the out-group become more negative. In other words, the gap between in-group and out-group increases with the mounting tension.
(3) Variability of evaluations decreases as the conflict escalates, indicating greater solidarity and intolerance of deviance within each group.
(4) Participants become more aggressive and abusive toward the out-group, while seeming increasingly to enjoy the company of their in-group members.

WITHIN-GROUP PROCESSES

The previous sections described processes of intergroup conflict that are fabricated in a laboratory setting under controlled conditions. In those studies, groups are arbitrarily defined on the basis of some, usually irrelevant,

---

Exercise 7.2

To make the following discussion more meaningful personally, we suggest that you select a situation of intergroup conflict with which you are familiar (in national politics, in race relations, in the local school system, and so forth). As you proceed to read the description of the various within-group and between-group processes, focus on your example and examine whether each process we describe took place at all, what form it took, and what contingencies affected it.

---

categorization principle. We now move on to describe processes of intergroup conflict in the real world, where group membership is not artificial and the struggle is a most essential part of group existence. The description in this section refers to conflicts between racial and ethnic groups, religious groups, ideological groups, national groups, age and sex groups—groups struggling with each other for power, status, and equal privileges in heterogeneous society.

When a group enters a conflict situation with another group, the central motive characterizing the phenomena taking place within the group is to *strengthen the group from within.* The following processes are aspects of this motive.

Group Cohesion and Solidarity. A group's strength lies in its unity. In order for a group to succeed in its struggle, members' solidarity and group cohesion must be strengthened. Members must stick together and be aware of out-groups' attempts to break their solidarity.

Politicians are aware that a sense of crisis leads to intensified cohesion and solidarity. For example, the Iranian hostage crisis in 1979 led to strong feelings of patriotism and cohesion in America, and this sense of common cause led Americans to give President Carter unprecedented support for a while. Some politicians design their campaigns to *create* an atmosphere of crisis, with the hope of reaping the fruits of enhanced cohesion and solidarity.

Mutual Support and Protection. Cohesion is fostered by the expectation that every member will be supported and protected by the group. The ancient Jewish proverb has it that "Israelis are responsible for each other," and every minority group establishes mechanisms for providing support and mutual protection.

In this process, violations of group cohesion and solidarity (such as crime or dissidence) may be chastised *within* the group, but when facing the outgroup, the group will present an all-protective, all-supportive common front.

Avoiding Competition Within the Group. Another way of maintaining group cohesion is by preventing friction and fragmentation in the group. The stronger the conflict with other groups and the more acute the crisis atmosphere, the more severe the punishments inflicted on competition and in-fighting within the group. But when the atmosphere of crisis subsides, fragmentation within the group is more permissible and more likely to take place.

Pressure Against Deviation. In times of crisis, members are demanded to conform strictly to the group norms, and deviations may be severely punished. "Deviations" are of two types: violations of the group's behavioral norms and violations of the group's membership boundaries. Thus, befriending out-group persons and crossing group boundaries (in dating, sexual relations, or sometimes even showing too much "understanding" of the out-group's point of view) are strongly stigmatized in times of intergroup crisis.

Strengthening the Need for Membership. In times of crisis, the group tries to recruit active and committed members from among all its passive, potential membership (for example, enlisting blacks into a black militant group), encouraging members to *demonstrate* their identification with the group. There is a strong emphasis on the *pride* involved in being a member, and the group's disadvantage (its race, poverty, poor education, and so on) becomes a source of pride in this process.

Separatism and Maintenance of Group Boundaries. The strengthened need for membership and the recruitment of members are complemented by mechanisms that make membership in the group seem special and exclusive. These mechanisms are meant to define the boundaries of the group, to make entrance into the group very hard, and to add to attractiveness of what takes place within the group.

Not every person can become a member of the group; candidates must pass various tests and initiation rites to prove their quality and loyalty, and even then they are not assured of entrance. As a rule, groups with exclusive boundaries and groups employing secret rituals gain disproportionate attention and attractiveness. The Masons provide a good historical example of these mechanisms, and one can understand in the same way the value of the increased separatism that accompanied the awakening of the Black Movement in the 1960s. In the Druze society (an Arab minority group, residing in Syria, Lebanon, and Northern Israel, which has its own, separate religion and which has been persecuted for centuries by Moslems), only proven and tested men of religious virtue can have access to the Druze holy books. Other individuals, and certainly non-Druzes, cannot ever see the writings of their religion.

The Use of Symbols. The boundaries of the group are maintained by salient *symbols* that indicate group membership. The symbols function to maintain and enhance group identity as well as serve to identify instantaneously who is a member and who is not. The most salient types of symbols include *uniforms* (collars, armbands, buttons, dress, and full uniforms), *insignia, physical appearance* (long hair, Afro hairdo), *normative behavior* (Black

Power salute), *gestures,* and *verbal expressions* (dialect, usage of particular phrases).

BETWEEN-GROUP PROCESSES

If cohesion is the major motive characterizing within-group processes in conflict situations, the central concept characterizing the interaction between groups is *power.* Conflict between groups is basically a power struggle, whether direct (regarding who will control the other) or indirect (who will determine the cultural norms). In the struggle, groups seek strategies that would increase their relative power vis-à-vis their opponents.

Prejudice. Prejudice is a *weapon* used by groups against each other in their struggle in ways we described in the previous chapter. For example, in the widely publicized confrontation at Ocean Hill, Brownsville, in New York in the late 1960s (see Berube & Gittell, 1969), where black residents and Jewish teachers fought over the controlling power in a school system, both groups became more and more prejudicial as the tension of conflict mounted. The blacks became more antisemitic and the Jews became more racist. These groups had been more amiable before, and they clearly used prejudice as a powerful social weapon.

Exclusivity. In our discussion of the within-group processes, we pointed out how exclusivity and secretiveness serve as instruments for strengthening the group from within. But exclusivity also serves as an instrument against other groups. There is something sinister and unsettling in a group being secretive and exclusive. The lack of information makes it impossible to have a clear picture of the group, and the fantasies about "plots hatched in secret chambers" are blown beyond proportion.

Minority groups, particularly militant ones, come to attain disproportionate power in this way, because they appear to be more powerful and dangerous. Even the American military draft is appropriately called "selective service."

Polarization. Polarization is a major aspect in the escalation of conflict. Attitudes and emotions become more and more extreme, and the two sides to a conflict polarize their positions beyond the possibility of compromising. Every person can recall dinnertable conversations that turned from friendly discussions into arguments and then into bitter fights in which people said irreversible things they were later to regret.

Group polarization is more intense and more dangerous than individual polarization, since members support each other in intensifying the polarization. The process reflects a "vicious cycle" in which polarization contributes to strengthen the group from within, in turn reinforcing the group to take a more militant position, and so on. Professionals specializing in labor relations are extremely wary of polarization effects in intergroup negotiations;

they know how easy it is to lead groups into sharp polarization and how difficult it is to cope with, and resolve, polarized conflicts.

Depersonalization. When groups are in conflict, perception of others becomes more and more stereotypic, narrowly limited to the dimensions directly relevant to the conflict. The out-group is viewed negatively, and its positive aspects are deliberately overlooked. Whites or males, for example, are just "oppressors" when their victims are fighting them; that they may also be cultured, gifted, or possess other qualities is not considered. In this process, negative characteristics of the out-group are overestimated and positive characteristics are underestimated. Thus, the out-group becomes depersonalized and dehumanized, in turn making it easier to fight its members and be aggressive toward them. LeVine and Campbell (1972) included in their list of orientations toward the out-group: seeing out-groups as contemptible, immoral, and inferior; seeing out-groups as weak, valueless, and hateful; and using out-groups as bad examples in training children.

This phenomenon is most evident in actual war situations. To enable soldiers to kill the enemy without hesitation and to boost morale and courage, the enemy is depicted not only as a cruel aggressor with no values and low motives, but also as *subhuman* (Huns, Japs, Commies, Gooks, or animals).

Militancy and Aggression. Militancy is a central component of pluralistic struggle, found in most racial and ethnic struggles. Militants often present their aggression as the inescapable outcome of their suffering and of oppression, so that the "other side" is made accountable for their militancy. However, in most cases militancy is a deliberate weapon rather than an uncontrollable impulse, connoting aggression, violence, and a deliberate lack of rationality. The militant can neither be reasoned with nor can he or she be stopped, even at the price of losing everything. The power of militancy is in its presumed desperation.

This, then, is the picture of intergroup conflict. It can escalate rapidly beyond reconciliation, since every group strengthens itself from within and sets itself in opposition to the out-group, becoming prejudicial, exclusive, and aggressive. Voices for moderation and for reason are lost quickly in pluralistic intergroup conflict, drowned in a vicious cycle of growing militancy, authoritarianism, and often ideological fanaticism. Witnessing how easy it is to evoke intergroup bias and experiencing a destructive and violent intergroup conflict, of which human history provides such an abundance of examples (racial conflict, war between nations, ideological persecution, and so on) is very painful, yet sobering.

Resolution of Intergroup Conflict

After Sherif and his associates (1961) incited intergroup conflict between the groups of boys in their summer camp, they applied themselves to the resolution of the conflict. They tried various techniques of tension reduction in an attempt to renew friendship and cooperation among the boys. Reduction of tension was achieved mainly through changing the nature of the functional relationship between the groups. Sherif and his associates systematically introduced "superordinate goals" that required cooperative interaction across group lines. They created emergency situations that demanded the combined and interdependent efforts of both groups, that is, crises with which none could deal effectively alone: The camp truck broke down and could be pulled only by all children together; the water supply was damaged and the children had to cooperate in finding and repairing it; and an expensive movie was rented by pooling funds contributed by both groups. These efforts led to a decrease in hostility and negative stereotyping, and after a few days the groups were again friendly to each other.

Sherif's work has been widely quoted over the years as a major theoretical framework for intergroup conflict resolution. Sherif's main factors—contact, cooperation, common goals, and interdependence— are still considered crucial elements in conflict resolution. Applied social psychologists (such as Blake & Mouton, 1961; Horwitz & Berkowitz, 1975, at Boston College; Amir, 1969, 1975, 1977, in Israel) have built on these principles in designing various types of interventions and experiential workshops for conflict resolution.

Another direction of work on conflict resolution is identified with Morton Deutsch (1973) and his colleagues at Columbia University's Teachers' College. Deutsch and his associates investigated competitive and cooperative forces in conflict resolution, working mostly with an experimental conflict situation known as Prisoners' Dilemma. Deutsch distinguished between "constructive" and "destructive" conflict and examined the workings of constructive processes that are functional in conflict resolution.

The laboratory situations studied by Deutsch and his associates did not constitute inter*group* conflict situations, but the various dimensions studied (such as trust, forms of communication, suspicion, and induced cooperation) and the techniques of conflict resolution that were developed (for example, bargaining techniques) were found effective for resolution of intergroup conflict. Group interventions related to Deutsch's ideas, focusing on structured negotiations of attitudes and political positions between groups in conflict, have been developed in recent years (see Brown, 1977; Cohen, Kelman, Miller, & Smith, 1977; Benjamin & Levi, 1979).

CONFLICT RESOLUTION THROUGH CONTACT

Following Sherif's work, most researchers and applied social psychologists working on intergroup conflict agree that *contact* is a major contributor to the reduction of intergroup prejudice. When groups are segregated from each other so that there is minimal or no contact between members across group lines, chances for conflict resolution are reduced. Indeed, major acts of planned social change—most notably desegregation of schools and busing of children to achieve an appropriate racial mix—have been based on the recognition of the value of contact in conflict resolution. But research shows that contact can reduce intergroup tensions only under particular conditions. When these conditions are not met, contact does not reduce conflict and may even *increase* tension and prejudice. In the following list of conditions, the first three are considered the major contributors of contact to tension reduction.

Equal Status. Numerous studies confirm the significance of equal-status contact in reducing intergroup tensions. When the parties in contact differ greatly in status, prejudice not only may remain unchanged, but may even increase. Unequal-status contact may increase derogation and "one-upmanship" as well as intensifying the anger and hostility of the low-status group.

But real groups in society differ greatly in social, economic, and educational status, and pluralistic struggle always takes place between groups differing in status. This is indeed the major source of the failure of forced contact (by legislation, court orders, and administrative fiat) to reduce intergroup tensions in society. However, in reviewing the literature on interethnic contact, Amir (1977) provided some encouraging answers to this problem. First, Amir argues, some research has shown that it is equal status *within the situation of contact* that makes the difference, and the groups may differ in status outside the contact situation or in their overall status. Second, it is sometimes argued that the crucial "status" is *relative* rather than absolute, expressed not in the direct comparison of the groups but in the gap between the stereotype of a group in the other group's eyes and how the stereotyped group is actually observed to act in the contact situation. If the group is perceived to be better than expected, the other group's prejudice may be reduced. Third, "equal status" must not be the average attribute of all group members. It is sufficient for majority group members to come in contact with *some* high-status members of the minority group for this contact to be effective in reducing prejudice.

Cooperation and Common Goals. Having common goals and needing intergroup cooperation to attain these goals contribute to the reduction of competition. Sherif et al. (1961) established superordinate goals that were shared and went beyond each group's interest. Numerous historical examples show how grave emergencies (as during natural disasters or when a nation is threatened by another nation) create superordinate goals that erase intergroup difference within society and motivate conflicting groups to cooperate with each other.

The combination of cooperation and common goals is important. Sometimes groups cooperate without sharing common goals, each group cooperating with the other only to forward its own interest. At other times groups have common goals but do not cooperate with each other.

Interdependence. The third major condition of effective intergroup contact follows and complements the first two. Interdependence means that neither group can attain its goals or satisfy its needs without the assistance of the other. Pooling of resources, the knowledge that the other side may have critical resources that one's group lacks, the common challenge, and the rewards that cannot be attained otherwise—all contribute to the constructive effects of interdependence.

Effective conflict resolution requires that all three factors operate together. The groups should have equal status, they should share common goals and cooperate with each other, and they must be interdependent on each other. Amir (1977) listed several additional factors contributing to conflict resolution through contact:

Opportunity for and Intensity of Contact. The extent to which the social context allows contact and the extent to which the contact is psychologically significant for the parties influence the effectiveness of the contact. "Opportunity for contact" includes the *amount* of contact, the possible *content* of the contact, the mutual significance attached to the contact, and the intensity of the contact. Interacting casually with out-groups in a gas station is different in quality from interaction at a cocktail party or a staff meeting.

Attitude Toward Contact. What are the attitudes of *both* sides toward the possibility of having contact with the other group? Amir (1977) argued that if the attitude toward the contact is positive, it can minimize the negative influences of unequal status and improve the outcomes of the contact. He further argued that it is sometimes easier to change the attitude toward the contact than to change directly the attitude toward the other side.

Control Over the Rewarding Outcomes of the Contact. The more pleasant and rewarding the contact is for its participants, the greater its potential for reducing conflict and prejudice. Rewards can be unrelated (or marginally related) to the issues of conflict between the groups yet maintain their effectiveness. Thus, even if conflicting groups do not resolve their differences, participating in mutually rewarding contact can affect attitudes about each other and about the conflict.

Normative and Institutional Support. If the contact is normative and receives "official" blessing and support (of the leaders or of the "group"), the outcomes of the contact will be more positive. Normative contact makes the initial attitudes of the parties more positive and rewards them for interpreting events that take place during the contact in a more favorable light.

Additional factors that may affect the outcomes of intergroup contact include specific situational conditions, events that take place in society-at-large at the time of the contact, the types of tasks facing the parties, and, of course, the personalities of the individuals involved in the contact situation.

Amir (1977) listed several factors that maintain the destructive nature of intergroup contact. These include competition; tense, unpleasant, and emotionally loaded contact; status or prestige being *decreased* due to the contact (for example, "stigma"); frustration; and conflicting norms of the two groups.

ACTUAL INTERGROUP CONFLICT RESOLUTION IN HETEROGENEOUS SOCIETY

The list of conditions necessary for conflict resolution is so extended and demanding that it leads almost automatically to the conclusion that actual conflicts between racial, ethnic, or religious groups are impossible to resolve. Moreover, the societal situations in which conflicts take place are usually far more complex than the controlled laboratory situations in which conflict resolution is studied. A variety of uncontrollable factors govern the course of real conflict in heterogeneous society. Lewicki and Alderfer (1973) wrote about the tension between research and intervention in intergroup conflict, and years before, Hovland (1959) wrote about "reconciling conflicting results derived from experimental and survey studies of attitude change." Real conflicting groups in heterogeneous society almost invariably *differ* in status, neither share common goals nor cooperate with each other, have conflicting interests, and have no wish at all to become interdependent on each other.

Numerous studies have investigated the outcomes of contact (mostly interracial and interethnic contact) on attitude change and reduction of prejudice in work settings, housing and residential settings, the military, and the educational system (see, for example, Amir, 1977; Carithers, 1970). In general, it turns out that in spite of the unfavorable conditions of most contact situations in society, contact does *not* intensify prejudice and often does lead to greater acceptance of the other side, to reduction of prejudice, or to a decrease in the importance attributed to racial or ethnic outlook. However, *forced contact* that leaves the parties no options or any degree of choice, particularly if that contact is not accompanied by additional conflict-resolution activities (such as those providing access of minority members to leadership positions in the military or implementing relevant educational interventions in integrated schools) does not contribute to reduction of prejudice and intergroup tension (see Coleman, Campbell, Hobson, McPartland, Mood, Weinfeld, & York, 1966; Minkowich, Davis, & Bashi, 1977; Chen, Levi, & Adler, 1978).

Ethnocentric Outlook

The concepts "ethnocentrism," "in-group," and "out-group" were coined by William Graham Sumner (1906, p. 13) in his book *Folkways:*

Ethnocentrism is the point of view in which one's group is the center of everything, and all others are scaled and rated with reference to it. Each group nour-
ishes its own pride and vanity, boasts itself superior, exalts its own divinities,
and looks with contempt on outsiders. The most important fact is that ethnocentrism leads a people to exaggerate and intensify everything in their own
folkways which is peculiar and which differentiates them from others.

Ethnocentrism is a "psychological stance," a consistent point of view directed indiscriminately at all or most out-groups. The analogue to ethnocentrism in individual psychology is "egocentrism." The egocentric child sees
himself or herself as the center of the universe, has only one (own) point of
view, and cannot readily take another person's point of view. One is reminded
of the story about a famous Hollywood actress who, after spending two hours
talking with a friend, said: "Enough said about me. Let's talk about *you*. Did
you see my latest movie?" Ethnocentrism is a similar point of view, only it
concerns groups rather than individuals.

It is important to distinguish between prejudice and ethnocentrism. The
term "prejudice" refers to negative stereotypes and a hostile attitude toward a
particular group (typically a minority group). Ethnocentrism is a wider concept, describing an attitude of rejection of *all* or most aliens and out-groups.
Despite the reference to ethnicity in the term "ethnocentrism," this concept is
not limited to relations between ethnic groups.

In this section we focus on the ethnocentric *outlook* and its role in intergroup relations—how persons view their social environment as group members and divide others into in-group (similar, "we") and out-groups (different, "them"), applying different criteria of social perception and evaluation to
each (LeVine & Campbell, 1972; Brewer, 1979b).

The essence of the ethnocentric outlook is, in Sumner's words, that "one's
own group is the center of everything, and all others are scaled and rated with
reference to it." A great variety of ethnic jokes make use of that ethnocentric
principle. For example, a well-known story tells about the French, German,
and Jewish scholars who spent a long time investigating the African elephant. At the conclusion of their project, the Frenchman wrote about "the
elephant's sex life," the German wrote a long monograph on "the elephant
and Immanuel Kant," and the Jew wrote an essay on "the elephant and the
Jewish problem."

Ample evidence of ethnocentric outlook is found in local news media
(newspapers, radio, and television) in America. Most of these media are characterized by *localism,* in which local events overshadow national and international news, reflecting the local public's "geocentric" hierarchy of interests. Similarly, a famous *New Yorker* poster draws the typical New Yorker's
"map of the world": close by (and therefore bigger in perspective) are Ninth
and Tenth avenues, next is a wide Hudson river, then comes a smaller New
Jersey, a tiny California, and finally a microscopic Japan.

Social events and behaviors are interpreted differently when attributed to the in-group or the out-group. This is felt most strongly when *identical* behaviors are interpreted in contrasting ways by different perceivers. Was the Soviet occupation of Hungary in 1956 an act of violent imperialism or an act of humanitarian and ideological concern? Are the members of the Palestinian Liberation Organization "freedom fighters" or "terrorists"? Was Wilt Chamberlain's scoring of 100 points in one NBA basketball game a show of superb ability (according to the Philadelphia press) or a show of extreme egotism and lack of team spirit (according to the Boston press)?

ETHNOCENTRIC STEREOTYPY

Perhaps the most interesting aspect of the ethnocentric outlook is ethnocentric stereotypy, the gaps between the stereotypes of the in-group and the out-group. In-group stereotypes tend to be positive, open-minded, tolerant, and permissive, while out-group stereotypes tend to be negative, judgmental, and punitive. Even when the in-group is viewed negatively, transgressions are tolerantly accepted, since "we are all only human."

Stereotypes of the in-group emphasize the group's *uniqueness* in the dual meaning of this word: "valuable" and "without like" (or, in other words, as better than others and as having a great range of individual differences within the group). By contrast, stereotypes of the out-group emphasize the common and nonunique elements. In Campbell's (1967) formulation, *we* are unique and individual, *they* are homogeneous. Examples of the value connotation of uniqueness is found in national and religious images such as "God's son," "the Chosen People," or "the People of Greatness."

Campbell (1967) also discussed the notion of *reciprocal stereotypes*—in which exactly the same image is projected on both groups, only it receives different connotations when attributed to self and or other groups. But each group projects the same image on the other: "We are loyal; they are clannish." "We are honest and peaceful; they are hostile and treacherous." Such stereotypes, often used by politicians when international tensions rise, do not necessarily characterize *any* group. In other words, they can characterize any group at wish.

MONOPOLY ON EXPERIENCE

One of the ethnocentric fantasies (and the egocentric fantasy on the personal level) is the "monopoly on experience"—the thought that our experiences are so unique and special that others could not experience them or even begin to grasp them. The bottom line of that thought is, "They cannot understand us."

The experience on which monopoly is taken is usually extreme, positive as well as negative. In both cases, taking monopoly on experience serves both within-group functions (of uniqueness, special identity, and the like) and between-group functions (exclusivity, one-upmanship, and so on). On the positive side, monopoly is taken on truth, love, spirituality, warmth, righteousness, responsibility, and the like: "Men can never experience the depth of the bond between two women." "Lay people can never grasp the joy of nuns and priests who devote their life to God and the service of humankind."

Taking monopoly on experience means denying that another group's experience may be comparable to "our" experience. In the case of negative experience—asserting the unique and special *suffering* of "our" group that others have not experienced and cannot even understand—the rewards for asserted uniqueness are quite apparent. A group is "entitled" to appropriate compensation if its uniqueness of suffering is established. The more extreme the uncomprehensible suffering, the more the group is entitled to receive in reparation. Blacks have argued that whites cannot understand their experiences with racism (and the television series *Roots* in the mid-1970s indeed served to assert this monopoly on experience); Jews have claimed that their suffering from persecution and genocide throughout the centuries is unprecedented; and women have claimed monopoly on the experience of sexist oppression.

A group's history and heritage ought to be respected, but we call attention to the point that claiming monopoly on experience reflects an ethnocentric outlook, serving as a strategy to exclude out-groups and gain power in intergroup situations. Except for very few instances (such as childbearing for women) there is *no* real monopoly on experience—almost the entire range of human experiences is universal and shared across group lines. There may well be unique *events* in a group's history, but an emotional experience of the same type and intensity can be caused by a great variety of different events. Particularly with pain and suffering, the "objective level" of an event bears no necessary relationship to the emotional experience of the suffering person or group.

It seems to us that the fantasies of monopoly on experience are extremely hard to give up. Accepting the universality of experience, believing that all

---

Exercise 7.3

Together with another co-inquirer, or, preferably, in a heterogeneous group of inquirers, try to generate and analyze life experiences reflecting ethnocentric outlook. Try also to identify examples from the folklore and history of your culture that reflect an ethnocentric outlook. Distinguish between instances reflecting your *own* ethnocentrism and that of *others*, and examine your reactions to each. Put a special emphasis on reciprocal stereotypes and monopoly on experience.

human beings are capable of experiencing the entire range of positive and negative experiences no less than one and one's group, and giving up the fantasy of experiential uniqueness (in other words, growing out of ethnocentrism) are extremely difficult and painful to do.

Positive Functions
of Group Belongingness

Our discussion of intergroup processes thus far has placed more emphasis on the negative manifestations of the relations between groups: prejudice and discrimination, bias and distortions, ethnocentrism, hostility, and destructive conflict. We conclude the chapter with a discussion of the positive psychological functions of group belongingness, an analysis of the value of socio-identities. The saying, "It is bad with [something]—but worse without it" is relevant to group belongingness: Having a meaningful group membership entails the negative and destructive intergroup processes we have discussed, but when people lack meaningful group memberships, they experience painful alienation.

As mentioned earlier, a group is characterized by a degree of similarity among its members along some dimension, and difference between members and nonmembers along that dimension. Both the within-group similarity and the between-group difference are crucial elements of this structural definition of groups.

Many writers have gone beyond this definition, emphasizing *dynamic* factors in addition to structural characteristics. Kurt Lewin (1948) wrote that *"a group is best defined as a dynamic whole based on interdependence rather than on similarity."* Horwitz and Rabbie (1982) defined a group as a social unit capable of acting to achieve outcomes for its members and not only as a social category based on similarity.

The groups to which persons belong are not arbitrarily defined, as is customary in the research on intergroup processes. They are meaningful groups; belonging to them and identifying with them are important aspects of a person's self-esteem and identity. These groups—racial, ethnic, religious, gender, national, professional, and ideological—are objects of membership, reference, *and* identification for their members. They satisfy various functions: cohesion, a common cause, shared interests, various rewards, and a common fate.

Kurt Lewin, a German Jewish social psychologist who left Germany when the Nazis came to power in 1933, wrote a series of papers on group belongingness and Jewish identity between 1933 and 1946 (collected in the 1948 volume *Resolving Social Conflicts,* which was published after Lewin's death). During that period six million Jews were killed by the Nazis in Europe. Lewin was concerned about the assimilation of Jews in America, the lack of self-esteem and positive sense of group belongingness he observed among American Jews. He felt that Jews should intensify their Jewish identity so they could enjoy the positive products of identification—cohesion, a common cause, higher self-esteem—and would be prepared to face the group's fate. Lewin's feelings were intensified by the fact that in Europe, even unidentified and totally assimilated Jews were labeled as Jews and persecuted to death.

Various authors have written in recent years about racial and ethnic identity, its value and rewards (Pettigrew, 1964; Isaacs, 1975a, 1975b; Glazer & Moynihan, 1975). They largely agree that "identity" involves strong images and emotions about affiliation with the group and carries a variety of symbolic meanings for the person. In his discussion of "basic group identity" Isaacs (1975b) stressed the two major elements mentioned above: sense of belongingness and self-esteem. Among the elements contributing to the formation of basic ethnic identity, Isaacs listed the shared characteristics of the group; the subjective "shared sameness" in the group; the group's history and its national, religious, geographical, or cultural origin; and the particular historical events and circumstances that have shaped the group's present.

Most authors agree that the salience of the group for its members and the strength of identification with the group increase when there is tension and conflict in society, particularly when the group has a "minority status" and is denied equal access to power, leadership, and societal resources. In other words, the positive functions of belongingness become more pronounced when tied to differentiation from others and ill treatment by out-groups.

Exercise 7.4
Intergroup Processes in Sports

Competitive sports provide an interesting area in which the various intergroup processes are reflected strongly and clearly. Since sports are socially acceptable, the intergroup phenomena are expressed in it without stigma and without embarrassment, and therefore they are more salient and pronounced. The world of sports serves as a *symbolic outlet* for various values, wishes, and needs in the personal and the intergroup domains. One can strongly identify, one can be ethnocentric and prejudicial, one can (as a spectator) "win" or "lose," gain honor or be humiliated, express the best and the worst in dignity, loyalty, self-sacrifice, and responsibility. Even after the most bitter loss, "this has been only a game."

Sports symbolizes and expresses intense intergroup processes in addition to the enjoyment of athletic ability. Evidence for that is the fact that people are fans of *particular teams,* "winning" or "losing" with their teams, often without regard to the athletic quality demonstrated by the competitors. Moreover, when

(continued)

watching a match between two teams about which the spectator feels neutral, most people would arbitrarily choose one team and root for it. Without identification with a team, the fun is limited!

We suggest that the following exercise be conducted as a group discussion. A "group" should include at least three persons, preferably two sports fans who support rival teams and a third person who is relatively uninterested in sports.

The exercise includes intellectual components (identifying phenomena from the chapters as they are reflected in sports, analysis of sports phenomena in intergroup terms) and experiential components (examining the experiences of self and others, follow-up of sports events and their accompanying emotions.)

I. Go quickly over the material presented in the last two chapters (prejudice and intergroup relations) and select the concepts and processes that in your opinion would be reflected most strongly in sports. Illustrate these processes by providing specific instances from your own experiences in sports (as participants and/or spectators). Examine the intensity of these experiences, how the intergroup processes have developed and how they reached their resolution (or end).

II. Try to identify and delineate various sports phenomena with which you are familiar, and analyze these phenomena in a psychological, intergroup perspective as provided in the last three chapters. Examples could include events such as success or failure of your college team; play-off battle between two professional teams; a player being traded to a rival team; reactions to the coach after the team has lost seventeen consecutive games; team success versus personal excellence; or reactions to referees.

(The difference between Part I and Part II of this exercise is the point of exit: Part I leads from the concepts to the examples; Part II leads from the examples to the conceptualization.)

8

PRINCIPLES OF SOCIAL CHANGE

Initial Distinctions

This chapter concludes the part of the book describing the social psychology of intergroup processes. Complementing the discussion of stereotypes, prejudice, ethnocentrism, and intergroup conflict, this chapter deals with social change, "personal" as well as "societal." First we present a typology of the central strategies of social change; then we discuss several issues in social change, such as the utilization of knowledge, political change, and the process of reeducation.

The term "social change" is somewhat ambiguous. We already distinguished between *personal change* (change in personal structure) and *societal change* (change in social structure). One domain deals with the psychology of the individual and his or her internal processes; the other, with the sociology of society, its institutions, and the forces operating in it.

Personal and societal change are tied to each other and influence each other in a spiral. On the personal level, the acquisition of knowledge leads the individual to a new awareness; awareness leads to internal change in values, attitudes and so on; and these internal changes lead to a change in conduct and social action. On the societal level, the emergence of social action changes social realities, leading to formal and informal, planned and unplanned acts of change. A "changed reality" ties back to the individual level, influencing the person's internal processes and leading to a new awareness. The internal processes of the individual are strongly influenced by the societal conditions he or she experiences (such as composition and heterogeneity of society, relative status and control of resources, and affluence), particularly by the conditions of the specific groups of which the individual is a member. But in spite of the interrelationship between personal and societal change, each is governed by different principles and entails different issues. Thus, for example, the goal of overcoming prejudice is a different issue on the personal and the societal levels, each involving a different set of strategies and change principles.

Further distinctions should be made within each of the two categories. With regard to personal change, it is significant to distinguish between *forced change* and *volitional change;* between change engendered for an *expected benefit* or advantage and change taken as the *lesser evil* compared to other alternatives; between a change process that *restricts* the individual and a process that *widens* the individual's options and choices. Probably the most important distinction within the category of personal change is that between *internal* and *external change*—change in attitudes, values, awareness, insight, and the acquisition of knowledge, on the one hand, and change in behavior, conduct, and actual practice, on the other hand.

With regard to societal change, the distinction between *forced* and *volitional* change is relevant as well. Additional distinctions include *prescriptive*, or active (as in legislation) versus *reactive* (as in court rulings) change; and *planned* (affirmative action, school desegregation, urban planning, and so on) versus *unplanned* change (migration of Mexican-Americans to Florida, changes in the ethnic composition of particular neighborhoods, growing popularity of Eastern religions or Marxist ideology). The following sections describe the major strategies of social change, and discuss some of the relationships between societal and personal change.

Exercise 8.1
Planning an Act of Social Change

This exercise is intended to increase your awareness of your underlying assumptions about principles of social change. Alone or (preferably) together with another learner, please select a social problem requiring some form of "social change." Relevant examples could include the harmful effects of cigarette smoking or drug use, the terrible statistics on traffic accidents, violence in an urban ghetto, and tension between white teachers and minority parents in a school system. Choose a problem with which you are sufficiently familiar, so that you can consider its various aspects.

Your task is to plan and design a program of social change that will have the highest probability of "solving" the problem. In designing the program, *assume that you have unlimited resources and sufficient administrative power to carry out your plan.*

When you generate suggestions and strategies, please rank them in terms of their potential effectiveness for the desired social change.

As you read the following section, you will be able to conceptually analyze your ideas and identify your underlying theory of social change.

Three Strategies of
Social Change

The central problem of social change is that people and groups, and indeed society-at-large, do not want to change. It is not that people are against change, but that individuals and groups are mostly in favor of *others* changing. It is easy to see and justify why (and how) others should change but much harder to recognize the need for self-change and to take steps in that direction. A variety of political, economic, intergroup, and social factors further block social change in society. Since the early formulations of theories of social change (Lewin, 1948; Allport, 1954) a major issue has been the relative effectiveness of the *law* compared to the effectiveness of *education* in changing people's values, attitudes, and conduct.

In *The Planning of Change* (Bennis, Benne, Chin, & Corey, 1976), Chin and Benne wrote an important chapter describing "general strategies for effecting changes in human systems." They defined three major clusters of change strategies, each based on a different conception of human learning and change: (1) empirical-rational, (2) power-coercive, and (3) normative-reeducative.

RATIONAL-EMPIRICAL STRATEGIES

Rational empirical strategies are based on the dissemination of *knowledge*. The underlying assumption is that people are rational and choose the most reasonable, empirically proven course of action to further their self-interests. People adopt proposed social changes if these changes can be reasonably justified and shown to be of value and utility to them. Therefore, the major method of effecting change is to provide relevant *knowledge*—empirical, scientific, valid, objective, rational knowledge. People seek knowledge in order to make the best decisions to direct their conduct. When the knowledge they have indicates that change is warranted, they get involved in a change process.

The central institution through which society implements rational empirical change is the school (high school, college, and university).Schooling is designed to provide knowledge and, it is assumed, *knowledge educates*.

This image reflects the belief system of Western Enlightenment. It is the most positive and favorable image of human learning and change. The underlying psychological model of the rational-empirical strategy is that knowledge shapes the person's attitudes, beliefs, values, feelings, and ideas, and that these, in turn, determine the person's behavior. The rational-empirical person *chooses* to behave in consonance with his or her values and attitudes; the rational-empirical person is *in control* of his or her psychological system.

The rational-empirical strategy rests on the value of universal, scientific knowledge. Scientific knowledge provides explanations and puts ideas in a proper perspective, forcing the person into an analytic, rational frame of mind. It reduces distortions and enables the person to consider issues and weigh options in the most effective way. The strategy of change derived from this perspective is simply that of providing people with the relevant and appropriate knowledge; it is assumed that the rest will follow. For instance, to deal with problems of heterogeneity in society, the rational-empirical approach would prescribe investigating the problems in depth and then teaching students, through courses (and educating the public-at-large through the media), the problems, their nature and various aspects, and the best course of action for their solution. Chin and Benne (1976, p. 24) wrote: "The strategy of encouraging basic knowledge building and of depending on general education to diffuse the results of research into the minds and thinking of men and women is still by far the most appealing strategy of change to most academic men of knowledge and to large segments of the American population as well."

The skeptics doubt the general applicability of this strategy. Do educated people stop smoking when they know its danger? Does knowledge about traffic fatalities affect driving habits? Does knowledge about prejudice reduce sexism and racism? The human capacity of acting in a rational-empirical way is beyond doubt, but there is a substantial chance that people act in nonrational and nonempirical ways and resist the educative value of knowledge. The limitations of the rational-empirical perspective include (1) that people are far more rational-empirical when relating to *others* than to themselves; (2) that the efficacy of the rational-empirical strategy declines as situations become more painful, more emotionally loaded, and more explosive; (3) that some of the processes involved in group membership, group identity, and intergroup conflict are basically nonrational; and (4) that particular human vices (such as smoking, adultery, negligence, stereotypy, and prejudice) are particularly resistant to rational-empirical inputs.

POWER-COERCIVE STRATEGIES

While the rational-empirical approach assumes that persons choose rationally how to behave and when to change on the basis of their thoughts and attitudes, the power-coercive strategy assumes that behavior must be directly changed first, *followed by* an internal change in values and attitudes. This strategy does not wait for the person to change out of choice; it forces the person to change. The social environment is monitored and behavior is controlled through laws, regulations, court orders, and administrative policies. Social change is implemented by "society" through its legitimate institutions (congresses; courts; federal, state, and local governments; and so on) using political power and legal authority in a coercive way. If the key symbol of the rational-empirical strategy is the school and its goal is to educate, the key symbol of the power-coercive strategy is the law and its goal is to govern.

Power-coercive change strategies seek to amass political and economic power behind the change goals that the planners of change find desirable. Examples of this strategy include the ban on television advertising of cigarettes and the regulation forcing cigarette companies to print a warning on every pack; equal opportunity legislation and the regulation of affirmative action; busing of children to achieve school integration; banning the use of IQ tests for classification of children; and providing funds for particular educational programs aimed at a restricted segment of the population.

The label "power-coercive" has a negative connotation and evokes an apprehensive reaction in most individuals. Nevertheless, "a power-coercive way of making decisions is accepted as in the nature of things. The use of such strategies by those in legitimate control of various social systems in our society is much more widespread than most of us might at first be willing or able to admit" (Chin & Benne, 1976, p. 40).

As Benne (1978) pointed out, the power-coercive strategy is directed at "societal changing" and it uses a model of "engineering." But like the rational-empirical strategy, it also has a basis in individual psychology. The (rational-empirical) theory that "attitudes influence behavior" is complemented by the (power-coercive) theory that "behavior influences attitudes." Bem (1967) argued that in order to effect attitude change, a behavioral change must be created first. He argued that people observe their own behaviors and the situational contexts in which they occur and *infer* their attitudes from their feelings and expectations while behaving in a particular way. Often we do not know what we think until we act, and our actions serve to provide us with attitude-building information. If one is happy and content in an integrated classroom, one probably has a pro-integration attitude. Thus, changing people's behavior or their social contexts may often lead to a change in attitude.

Bem's (1967) self-perception theory was presented as a rival to cognitive-dissonance theory, but dissonance theory explains why changed behavior can lead to attitude change: People have a strong need for maintaining the image of their consistency, and when their behavior is dissonant with their attitudes, they experience tension and a resultant need for self-justification. Attitudes are thus changed to make them consonant with behavior. In his discussion of "the psychology of inevitability," Aronson (1976) argued that this change process is particularly strong when forced behavioral change is unavoidable and inevitable. Aronson used attitudes about desegregation and race relations as his prime example of this process. This perspective—that "a person's *behavior* is educated" rather than "the *person* is educated"—is the cornerstone of the highly effective fields of behavior modification and behavior therapy in psychology.

In the long term, there is no doubt that actual practice and changed reality conditions eventually influence and change people's values and attitudes. Few people today would doubt women's competence to cast their votes; many did less than a century ago. The current young generation in America does not favor total racial separation, nor would present-day U.S. citizens advocate the right of one group to enslave members of another group. Laws about women's voting, racial desegregation, exploitation of young children in the work market, and the like create standards that eventually become generally accepted values. Living in a civilized society, people accept the legitimacy of power-coercive methods, although they demand that democratic checks and balances be maintained and they may strongly oppose *particular* power-coercive acts. Most people also believe that power-coercive laws and regulations should be implemented to guarantee the rights of underprivileged minorities and to improve their chances for better advancement in society.

In these ways power-coercive strategies can have positive effects. But in the short range, neither do power-coercive methods necessarily lead to the desired attitude change nor do people readily come to identify with practices that are forced upon them. Moreover, the apprehension about the negative connotation of "coercion" is hard to shake away. One is reminded how power-coercive methods were effectively exploited to incite racism in Nazi Germany, where a variety of anti-Jewish laws and regulations in the 1930s intensified anti-semitism and later justified genocide. The implication of being manipulated without exercising a sufficient degree of free choice is disturbing and creates "reactance" (Brehm, 1966).

NORMATIVE-REEDUCATIVE STRATEGIES

The third group of social change strategies is less common and more difficult to attain than rational-empirical education and power-coercive administration. Our approach in writing this book and guiding the inquiry into the social self is normative-reeducative.

The normative-reeducative approach bases the change process on the personal experiences of the individual and his or her interactions and negotiations with others in the social network. This approach emphasizes integration: It attempts to integrate motivations, feelings, thoughts, attitudes, values, and behavior *within* the person, and it attempts to integrate the change process within the person's social environment (emotional ties, group belongingness, interactions with similar and different others, and so forth). These attempted integrations differ from the more exclusive emphases of the previous strategies on cognitive rationality or actual behavioral change. As Kurt Lewin (1948); Lewin & Grabbe, 1945) envisioned the process of reeducation, changes in normative orientations would involve changes in attitudes, values, skills, and significant relationships, not just changes in knowledge, information, or intellectual rationales for action and practice.

In describing the normative-reeducative approach, Chin and Benne (1976, pp. 31-32) wrote:

Men are guided in their actions by socially funded and communicated meanings, norms, and institutions, in brief by a normative culture. At the personal level, men are guided by internalized meanings, habits, and values. Changes in

patterns of action or practice are, therefore, changes, not alone in rational informational equipment of men, but at the personal level, in habits and values as
well and, at the sociocultural level, changes are alterations in normative structures and in institutionalized roles and relationships, as well as in cognitive and
perceptual orientations.

Benne (1978, pp. 418-419) provided a further description of how normative-
reeducative strategies are utilized to effect change:

> Normative-reeducative strategies emphasize resolution of conflicts with re-
> spect to proposed changes through mutually reeducative transactions between
> parties to the conflict, often with the help of relatively disinterested and skilled
> third-parties. The goal is the collaborative development—in action-oriented
> study, dialogue, and research—of common commitments to goals and means
> for needed changes. This involves changes in attitudes, values, and significant
> relationships as well as changes in knowledge, information, and technological
> skills.

A major element in the normative-reeducative perspective is the personal
involvement and commitment of the person. One is not "taught" or "forced";
rather, one makes a free choice to learn from one's experience and to commit
oneself to a change ideology. One chooses to exercise one's commitment
directly in an experiential way, through community participation, sharing in
some project, donating money, time, and effort, and a commitment to self-
inquiry that may sometimes be painful.

If the prototype of the rational-empirical strategy is the conventional
school or the university and the prototype of the power-coercive strategy is
government and public administration, the prototype of the normative-
reeducative strategy is the human relations laboratory, where people learn
and change through their experiential interactions with others, making
meaning of their normative orientation, values, beliefs, norms, and behaviors.
In such "experience-based" learning situations, people must "learn how to
learn" from their experiences, so that change will be self-directed. This is
done through self-inquiry, group-inquiry, interactions with similar and different others, sensitization of self-awareness, and improved skills of empathy
and role taking.

There are numerous specific methodologies within the family of normative-reeducative strategies. They include clarification groups, sensitivity
training groups, study groups, encounter groups, confrontation groups, consciousness-raising groups, and many more. These methodologies of change
have common elements:

(1) The client (individual person or group) is responsible for his or her own learning and change.

(2) It is not assumed a priori that the client's problems can be met by more information and data. Although the need for knowledge is not denied, the foci of
problems are seen in attitudes, norms, and social values.
(3) Learning must be based on direct experience. The client's immediate experiences constitute the most crucial information for inquiry.
(4) Some nonconscious obstacles must be brought into consciousness and thor-
oughly examined.

Exercise 8.2

You can now reexamine the planning of an act of social change that you made
at the beginning of this section. Which strategy did you choose for the problem
on which you focused? How would solutions to the same problem based on the
other strategies of social change look?

Issues in Social Change

EDUCATION VERSUS ADMINISTRATION

The dilemma of "education versus administration" is a major issue of
social change. At one end one finds educators and social scientists who
believe in *individual, internal change* and search for ways and strategies to
educate persons toward social change. At the other end one finds legislators,
politicians, and experts in public administration who believe that the most
effective approach to social change is the appropriate *management of society.* Their approach to change is one of "societal changing" (Benne, 1978) as
opposed to "personal change."

Individual and societal change are complementary of, rather than contradictory to, each other, much as the rational-empirical and power-coercive
strategies do not negate each other even if based on opposite assumptions
about the nature of human change. Nevertheless, the individual and the societal emphases differ substantially from each other, especially in their images
of the individual person, their level of optimism or pessimism about the
potential of volitional social change initiated by well-meaning citizens, and
their beliefs about the significance of power politics in human society. In
fact, in the societal perspective, education is a planned social act, and
rational-empirical knowledge (about the value of the Salk vaccine or birth
control, for example) is disseminated by administrative decision. Furthermore, school is power-coercive and people are forced to attend it and be
"educated" regardless of their personal wishes and choices.

When an organization tries to change, it usually employs a combination of
all change strategies. Applied social psychologists specializing in organizational development search for an integration of methods to effect compre-

hensive changes (in policies, rules, and regulations), increased flexibility, dissemination of knowledge and information, experiential self-inquiry, and self-determined regulatory changes.

When societal issues of heterogeneity, pluralism, and intergroup conflict are concerned, the dilemma of education versus administration becomes sharper and more explosive. Education and administration often operate at cross purposes in these situations, although both may fall short of attaining the desired change. Planned social change in a pluralistic direction (for example, via the Equal Rights Amendment, civil rights legislation, or affirmative action) is almost invariably the outcome of a political struggle, and it minimizes the disadvantage of minority groups at the expense of the majority group. In other words, in most pluralistic changes, those in power *give up* some advantage when sufficient pressure and political power have been applied to force this process. Minority groups (and their ideological supporters among the majority group) search for leverage to force the hand of those in power, and the destructive intergroup processes described in the previous chapters (militancy, polarization, exclusivity, aggression, and so on) play a role in that struggle for leverage. In fact, many pluralistic societal changes have been brought about by such countereducational means. Education for tolerance and acceptance of others may simply not be very functional for minority group members seeking pluralistic change. Indeed, minority leaders often state that the "oppressors" should be educated for tolerance while members of their own groups should be trained to fight oppression.

When a loaded intergroup conflict threatens a group's existence or privileges, education and acquired tolerance and rational value orientation (applied so nicely before to other groups' conflicts) tend to disappear. Groups in serious conflict act in nonrational, countereducative ways—and it is functional for them to act that way. Education can at best minimize somewhat the role of nonrational, destructive forces. On the other hand, legislation and coercive acts are limited in the extent to which they can create internal changes in attitudes and value orientations. Forced changes often boomerang, especially in the short term. The segments of the population who lose from the change process may become more prejudicial and intolerant. The assumption that people change their attitudes and values to fit themselves to the inevitable social conditions forced upon them is not always confirmed. We are probably fortunate that this assumption is often wrong: decades of totalitarian coercion (say, in Eastern Europe) can control citizens' behaviors but not their value orientations.

In spite of these limitations, we believe that the combination of education and administration contributes to social change in modern, democratic society. Education alone may not have freed the slaves or provided blacks and other minorities equal access to prestigious jobs, nor might coercive administrative policies alone have changed attitudes and values. But when administrative acts reflect democratic and equalitarian values rather than arbitrary, unjust coercion, education and administration can combine in the long run to produce a lasting change in attitudes, values, and practice. Such changes have been recorded in America in racial and ethnic relations (attitudes about slavery, changes in ethnic stereotypes as recorded in the Princeton studies, for example), in intergender relations and attitudes about women (Cameron, 1977), and in other domains.

COERCION, EQUALITY, AND PLURALISTIC CHANGE

Legislated pluralistic change is usually the product of a political power struggle, a political compromise reflecting relative power positions. This type of compromise often falls short in terms of both social justice and its pluralistic efficacy. (One is reminded of the saying that a camel is a horse created as a compromise solution by a committee.) Such compromises are reflected in allocating funds to minorities in ways that do not really help them to improve their chances, in giving privileges selectively to militant minorities and ignoring other minorities that are not militant, and, generally, in superficial changes that result in destructive, unintended outcomes.

But some take issue not with the quality of changes that take place but with the basic principles that are reflected in legislation and court rulings dealing with the privileges of minority groups in American society. In a paper entitled "Ruminations on the Quality of Equality," Kurland (1979) attacked what he labeled "the egalitarian American revolution"—changes that institute societal equality among groups instead of equality of individuals. According to Kurland, "equality" means that no individual should be treated by a state differently from any other individual because of differences in skin color, gender, religion, and ethnic or national origin. However, the Supreme Court came to insist on a standard based on race when calling for "an appropriate racial mix" in the schools. Thus race, which was thought to have been abolished as a legitimate ground for governmental classification, was introduced by the Court as a coercive factor in later school cases.

Since in this "egalitarian" perspective the demand is for equality among groups, or classes, and not among individuals, the process leads to a quota system in which a person's gender, skin color, or origin becomes a factor determining his or her rights. Kurland admits that these rules are corrective, meant to treat minority *more* favorably. But, he argues, "invidious quotas that limit access to goods and positions on grounds of race, religion, gender, or national origin are replaced by benign quotas that assure access to goods and positions on grounds of race, religion, gender, or national origin."

We reject the notion of individuality in favor of the presumption of uniformity of all those within the once-condemned classifications. We treat groups, not persons. All blacks, all white, all Spanish-speaking, all males and females become fungible and their characteristics are assumed to be uniform. A black is treated as culturally deprived not because he is culturally deprived but because he is black. A white is treated as acculturated not because he is acculturated but because he is white. A black offspring of the middle class is to be treated the same as a black offspring of the impoverished, not because their upbringing or condition is the same but because their color is the same. Having joined all blacks and all whites, and all women, we then command equality of condition without reference to the merits of any of the individuals within the group. We have thus abolished discrimination, not only in the sense of racial, religious, or other irrational prejudices, but in the sense of recognition of real individual differences.... My principal personal complaint about the new egalitarianism is that its goal seems to be the homogenization of the human race, nay, that it already assumes homogeneity as the fact. (Kurland, 1979, pp. 19-20)

Exercise 8.3

We suggest that together with another co-inquirer (or alone, alternating between two roles) you role-play a dialogue between two views: one reflecting Kurland's "conservative" ideas and the other reflecting the ideas of a "liberal" person supporting such pluralistic power-coercive rulings.

Please remember that it sometimes is easiest to make a caricature out of every conservative, attributing bigotry, prejudice, and hostile intentions to all conservatives. Such mockery, however tempting, is not the most effective and beneficial way of dealing with differences of opinion.

REEDUCATION AND THE UTILIZATION OF KNOWLEDGE

"Education" is a central institution of civilized society. Individuals are educated how to "be" in the culture, are provided with appropriate values, knowledge, and skills to be "good citizens." A culture cannot develop without building some type of an educational system intended to promote its goals. In short, education is a culture's social instrument. But while education is largely formative, "reeducation" signifies a change process. In this book, we are particularly interested in the role of education and reeducation in dealing with intergroup issues in heterogeneous society.

With the great progress of modernized societies in this century, the issue of knowledge utilization has become one of central significance. A society's rate of progress is becoming more and more dependent on its capabilities of obtaining relevant knowledge and putting it to an effective use. Knowledge has become a marketable commodity, a resource of no less value than natural resources. (Japan provides a good example of this process: It has become a world power in spite of its lack of natural resources, mostly due to its efficacious knowledge utilization.)

Knowledge utilization is important in the social-moral-valuative domain no less than in the scientific and technological domain, although different types of "knowledge" are concerned. The moral power of a democratic society stems from the fact that its citizens are educated and become knowledgeable participants (albeit passive most of the time) in society's governance and progress, instead of ignorant subjects manipulated by totalitarian authorities. In a way, a government takes a "risk" in allowing citizens to become more educated and knowledgeable, because they develop value orientations and higher expectations, eventually turning to oppose the government with greater power and conviction. Although the U.S. race riots and feminist struggles have had destructive manifestations, their existence is also a sign of the moral power of the United States. By contrast, in countries like Poland or Czechoslovakia signs of moral dissent and pluralistic struggle have been forcefully extinguished by the so-called people's governments.

Teaching history, religion, anthropology, and social sciences is a means of providing individuals with rational-empirical knowledge that will "form" or "change" them. But individuals are also encouraged to make use of their "personal knowledge"—the more subjective and idiosyncratic knowledge they derive from their own life experiences and from what they witness in the social environment around them. Much as universal knowledge serves a variety of functions (see the foregoing discussion of rational-empirical strategies), personal (or self-) knowledge is also of educative value and serves positive functions: utilization of personal knowledge reduces anxiety, reduces biases and distortions, enables one to take responsibility and to conform less to external social pressure, and frees one to change at his own will and own pace. In other words, learning to utilize personal knowledge—especially in integration with universal knowledge—enables a person to employ regulatory self-control and to become an independent agent who realizes his or her own value system. But our argument throughout this book is that "having" personal knowledge is not sufficient; it is crucial to learn to *utilize* such knowledge, through the process Kurt Lewin labeled "reeducation" (Lewin & Grabbe, 1945; Lewin, 1948).

Lewin's conception of reeducation was one that would have incorporated all three groups of strategies discussed by Chin and Benne (1976), with special emphasis on normative-reeducative strategies and value-orientation. Lewin saw reeducation as a task of "acculturation" that must affect the person's cognitive system, value orientation, and motoric (behavioral) system. But these three systems are not governed by the same rules, and Lewin saw the interrelations between changes in one system and changes in another (for example, change in perceptual orientation and change in value orientation, between a change in behavior and a change in sentiment) as very complex: "Reeducation is frequently in danger of reaching only the official system of values, the level of verbal expression and not of conduct; it may result in merely heightening the discrepancy between the super ego (the way I ought to feel) and the ego (the way I really feel), and thus give the individual a bad conscience. Such a discrepancy leads to a state of high emotional tension but seldom to correct conduct. It may postpone transgressions but is likely to make transgressions more violent when they occur" (Lewin, 1948, p. 63).

This distinction between the cognitive, the affective, and the behavioral components has been widely held by social psychologists (McGuire, 1969; Oskamp, 1977). Most writers have seen all three components as aspects of attitudes, while Fishbein and Ajzen (1975) used the term "belief" to refer to the cognitive component, the term "attitude" to refer to the affective component, and the term "intention" to refer to the behavioral component. All theoretical formulations postulate the complexity of the relationships between the three components, assuming that change in one aspect is never sufficient.

But the volumnious social-psychological research on attitude change falls short of Lewin's conception of reeducation. Most of that research is highly theoretical and experimental, focusing on specific elements controllable in a laboratory setting and ignoring the multiple influences of numerous social factors that affect people's attitudes in "real life." Change has not been conceived according to the wide and integrative meaning used by Lewin but in a narrower and more restricted way. Furthermore, most writers and researchers ignored values and value orientations in their work, focusing on attitudes only. (Some of the most recent textbooks in social psychology do not even index "value" or "value orientation.") Rokeach (1968, 1973) is one of the few modern social psychologists who called attention to the central role played by values in social conduct.

Lewin's (1948; Lewin & Grabbe, 1945) ten principles of reeducation are presented next. Interested readers are referred to Benne's (1976) assessment and illumination of these principles in light of twenty-five years of reeducation.

Principle 1. The processes governing the acquisition of the normal and abnormal are fundamentally alike. (This principle, in Benne's assessment, served to break the wall of the traditional separation between "education" and "therapy.")

Principle 2. The reeducative process has to fulfill a task that is essentially equivalent to a change in culture. (Changes in individuals occur within cultural environments, and anchoring the person's conduct in something large and super-individual—the culture of the group—helps to mobilize the change process and stabilize the new beliefs.)

Principle 3. Even extensive first hand experience does not automatically create correct concepts (knowledge). (Restated in Chin and Benne's terms, this principle means that rational-empirical inquiry alone or experiential normative-reeducative inquiry alone is not sufficient for the attainment of meaningful personal change.)

Principle 4. Social action no less than physical action is steered by perception. (This principle emphasizes the critical significance of social perception. Changes in knowledge or changes in beliefs and value orientation will not result in changes in conduct unless the perceptions of self, others, and the social situation is changed as well.)

Principle 5. As a rule, the possession of correct knowledge does not suffice to rectify false perceptions (This principle focuses on the obstacles to the application of knowledge for self-inquiry and change, as explicated in Chapter 3.)

Principle 6. Incorrect stereotypes (prejudices) are functionally equivalent to wrong concepts (theories). (This principle refers to the resistance of the cognitive system to information that disconfirms preexisting notions and to the requirement that people learn to doubt their views and images and experiment with alternative ways of looking at social events.)

Principle 7. Changes in sentiments do not necessarily follow changes in cognitive structure. (Just as earlier principles clarified the relative independence of changes in cognition and changes in perception, this principle stresses the relative independence of processes of cognitive change and changes in sentiments, value orientation, and action ideology. Lewin was concerned about an externalized and intellectualized acceptance of an "official system of values," and he stressed the importance of involvement and personal commitment in the change process.)

Principle 8. A change in action ideology, a real acceptance of a changed set of facts and values, a change in the perceived social world—all three are but different expressions of the same process. By some, this process may be called a change in the culture of the individual; by others, a change of his or her superego. (Reeducation requires persons' involvement in new groups with norms that contrast previous norms. A reeducative "group" is one whose norms include a commitment to inquiry, willingness to face problems and to become involved in their solution, and willingness to put ideas to empirical test.)

Principle 9. Acceptance of the new set of values and beliefs cannot usually be brought about item by item. (The value system is indeed a system, and trying to convert one value at the time is to no avail. However, Lewin did see the importance of step-by-step methods in another aspect of reeducation: in the gradual change from the position of hostility to new values to the position of open-mindedness and friendliness to the new culture.)

Principle 10. The individual accepts the new system of values and beliefs by accepting belongingness to a group. (This principle stresses the indispensability of groups as media of effective reeducation. Attempts to influence persons individually—through television, books, and the like—and to bypass the group participation in the framework of which the change in conduct must occur are not very likely to be successful. Again, the "group" Lewin had in mind was not the racial or religious group, but the "reeducative" group—

those who share the willingness and commitment to inquiry, students and teachers, doctors and patients, children and parents.)

As Benne (1964, 1976) pointed out, Lewin's ideas on reeducation (and applied social psychology) are reflected in the development of the training movement, with which Lewin was involved close to his death. This movement rapidly developed from its beginnings in the late 1940s, became known by various names (including human relations training, sensitivity training, personal growth, group dynamics, encounter groups, and human potential), and is expressed today in fields such as group psychotherapy, organizational development, and experiential learning in school (such as Magic Circle). In the 1960s, Birnbaum and Benne developed the Clarification Group (Birnbaum, 1975; Babad, Birnbaum, & Benne, 1978), a method of experiential learning and self-inquiry most fitting with Lewin's ideas on reeducation in its emphasis on value orientation, group memberships and socio-identities, intergroup processes, and the integration of universal and personal knowledge. This book is our attempt to adapt that methodology to use by individuals and groups outside the training laboratory.

PART III

MAJOR DIMENSIONS OF THE SOCIAL SELF

9

RACE, ETHNICITY, AND RELIGION: CENTRAL DIMENSIONS OF IDENTITY AND CONFLICT

Sociologists speak of "ascribed status" as that confirmed by social characteristics, primarily race, religion, and ethnicity, acquired at birth and usually retained by the individual for better or worse throughout life. In a society where these social characteristics are of lifetime significance, such "birthmarks" contribute powerfully to the ease or difficulty of achieving a personally satisfying "advanced status," which reflects what sociologists have designated as the position one achieves on society's ladder of class, status, and power.

This chapter opens the part of the book dealing with specific dimensions of the social self and of heterogeneity in society. It deals with a group of dimensions that is perhaps the most critical and certainly the most pervasive in all modern societies, defining the major sources of the stratification of society. *Nationality* is a dimension of difference related to race and ethnicity, both in terms of intergroup processes (wars, international politics, sovercignty) and individual socio-identities (American, German, Russian, Israeli, and so on). In most societies, race, ethnicity, and religion are also tied to another dimension of difference: *social class*. The reality of most heterogeneous societies is one of overlap between these dimensions and social class: Particular racial, ethnic, and religious groups tend to occupy the lower levels of socioeconomic status, while other groups occupy the upper classes and enjoy the special advantages and privileges of power.

Race, ethnicity, and religion need not be tied to social class. Indeed, the essence of pluralism is that groups differing along these dimensions would share equitably in power and that an individual's social class standing will not be determined or predicted by that individual's racial, ethnic, or religious group membership.

In this and the following chapters we illuminate special phenomena characteristic of each major dimension of societal heterogeneity. The psychological processes described in the previous four chapters are applicable to all dimensions, and we focus on the special manifestations of each dimension. We treat each issue on both a societal and an individual level and suggest

activities of self-inquiry to integrate the present material with readers' own
life experiences.

Race and Racial Differences

In its original sense, race is a biological rather than a social term, reflecting basic genetic and physical differentiations. When physical anthropologists define racial groups, they emphasize skeletal characteristics and anatomical distinctions that are often not visible to the layperson. But people
tend to identify another's race, without using these primarily invisible characteristics. Instead, people commonly use more obvious but less accurate
indicators: degree of pigmentation ("color") and differences in features
which in the United States are contrasted with the typical Caucasian color
and facial structure. Thus, for "white" Americans, other races may have
slanty eyes, olive skin, and other distinguishing features that one would call
Oriental; a broad nose, thick lips, and dark pigmentation from black to light
brown that Caucasians would commonly perceive as Negroid; or the features
of American Indians, whose color would be more tawny and whose facial
structure would be significantly different.

The physical characteristics of racial groups were accompanied historically by territorial isolation, climatic differences, and stages of historical
development that created different cultures. Today, however, almost all racial
groups around the globe are genetically hybrid, and their composition does
not follow the biological definitions. Therefore, race must be discussed as
"social race" in terms defined and treated by social scientists. When one
speaks of race in the social sciences, one is talking about the perception of
racial difference that one group holds about another group. "Racism" relates
to particular negative perceptions of, and behaviors toward, the members of
one social race by members of another social race.

The conception of social race includes several elements: that membership
in a social race is determined at birth and endures for life; that membership in
a social race is usually highly visible and identifiable; that differences between sex groups, age groups, or social class groups are secondary to membership in the racial group; and that for social races of lower status, the racial
group membership is usually of subjective significance (of love or hate, acceptance or rejection).

Race is undoubtedly the most universal dimension of difference in the
perceptions of groups. There is not a country in the world in which racial
differences are not recognized as difference with considerable social significance and consequences. But since racial boundaries are no longer clear in
the biological sense, racial heterogeneity in many countries means distinguishing among groups that are culturally and socially, as well as physically,

different from each other. For example, two Kenyan tribes that for years fought and competed with each other, the Kikuyu and the Luo, are both Negroid. They are culturally and ethnically distinct, but these differences are rather minor, and the two tribes differ only somewhat physically. Nevertheless, their struggle has most often been characterized as a "racial" struggle.

Some people point at the situation in Brazil, where many dark-pigmented people of Negroid ancestry have entered into the upper social economic classes, as evidence that race may not necessarily be a significant dimension in itself. But Brazilian anthropologists point out that in spite of the unique racial composition of the country, racial differences continue to have powerful impact. Even in Brazil, they argue, there are private and social sanctions against intermarriage that prevail on both sides of the color barrier. In many other countries—the United States, South Africa, and numerous Asian and African countries—color consciousness and racial differences are extremely intense social barriers, in spite of education, legislation, and various acts of social change.

America has often been labeled a "racist society." Sociologists speak of its "institutional racism," meaning that invidious distinctions and social, economic, and political discrimination directed at socially inferior races have permeated all levels of society, to the extent that racism may often be perpetuated unconsciously by individuals who honestly view themselves as unprejudiced.

People are conscious of race in a variety of ways. Members of the dominant race most often do not define themselves in racial terms. When asked to define themselves, many American WASPs speak of other ascribed characteristics, such as religion or social class, or they provide information with regard to their professions, family status, interests, and the like. On the other hand, many American blacks define themselves first in racial terms.

In the South, prior to the 1954 Supreme Court decision that outlawed school segregation, whites, although the dominant group politically, socially, and economically, saw themselves as Whites, as contrasted to Blacks. It was not that the whites were not in the numerical majority, but there was a sufficiently large percentage of blacks to make whites aware of the racial distinction (in addition, of course, to the particular history of black-white relations in the South). This is contrasted to the North, where until the 1940s blacks were a relatively small minority compared to whites. (This changed with the waves of black immigration into the northern cities in the 1940s and onward.) Most northern whites at that time would not have included a racial designation in their self-descriptions. Today, following the events of the 1960s in America, racial consciousness is more keen on the part of blacks and whites alike, in the North as well as the South.

It is possible for persons born into a religion of relatively lower status in America (say, Baptist or Jewish) to pass into a religion of a higher status (say

Episcopalian or Presbyterian) in an attempt to change their ascribed status. It has often been possible for people of particular ethnic origins (Mediterranean, East European) to submerge this disadvantageous portion of their birthright. Race has been the most difficult to "pass;" but nevertheless, the extent of the racial passing phenomenon (by blacks of lighter complexion and less Negroid features) over the years has been substantial. The same phenomenon took place in America for many years with regard to the "Americanization" of people's names.

But the passing phenomenon is slowly passing away in America. The intensified black identity and the "black is beautiful" attitude pushed light-skinned blacks from a position of advantage to one of disadvantage within the black community. The awakening of racial and ethnic identity allows people to be proud of their heritage and their distinct racial and ethnic group memberships.

Ethnicity and Ethnic Groups

DEFINITION AND CONCEPTION OF ETHNICITY

Race is a rather visible dimension: Even if racial identification is not necessarily based on the most valid anatomical and skeletal distinctions, people easily identify others according to their race. Ethnicity is not always as salient and visible as race. The probability of successfully identifying a person's ethnic group is much lower than that of successfully identifying a person's race. Yet race and ethnicity act together in heterogeneous society to distinguish among groups, differentiating minority from majority, the powerful from the powerless, and those of high status from those of low status.

"Ethnic groups" are groups of individuals who share distinctive cultural characteristics separating them from others among whom they live. As "cultural groups," they are most often defined by *race* (black, white, oriental), *religion* (Moslem, Jewish, Protestant), *nationality* and *language* (Italian, Irish, Swedish), a particular historical conflict or struggle (Basques in Spain, Scots in Britain), or particular combinations of these factors. Ethnicity defines clear boundaries between in-group and out-group and is characterized by strong "consciousness of kind" and "consciousness of difference."

Persons are born into ethnic groups and therefore have no control over their membership in them. Some ethnic groups are distinguishable by pigmentation or other physical characteristics, but such distinctions may be erroneous, based on a restricted range of information. For example, the image that Italians are olive-skinned and have dark complexions excludes millions of Northern Italians who have a fair complexion. The American image of the Jew is limited geographically to those groups of Jews who immigrated to

America from Eastern Europe, and the unprepared American visitor to Israel is suprised to discover so many Jews of other origins "who do not look Jewish!" Many ethnic groups in European countries, for instance, do not possess distinguishing physical characteristics.

The phenomenon of "passing," which was discussed with regard to race, is relevant to ethnicity as well. Due to the relative lack of clearly distinguishing physical characteristics of ethnicity, people have often tried to "pass," to move upward on the social status ladder by changing names and eliminating cues to their ethnic group identifications. On the other hand, it has become more acceptable to be "ethnic" in recent years, and some people enjoy exaggerating their ethnic group characteristics, acting as "professional ethnics."

The major significance of ethnicity today in heterogeneous society lies in the differences between ethnic groups in the distribution of power and resources, leadership and social class. Social stratification in America and other societies has come to be based on ethnic group memberships. Glazer and Moynihan (1975) point out that the label "ethnic group" has become synonymous with a minority group status in society, whereas high-status, majority group members do not perceive themselves in ethnic terms. They argue that in a paradoxical way, the Civil Rights Act of 1964—which outlawed discrimination on the basis of race, color, religion, sex, and national origin—caused people to declare their group memberships, inadvertently *strengthening* ethnic identification.

Karl Marx viewed modern society as the "battleground" between social class groups and did not attach particular significance to ethnicity in his conception. Glazer and Moynihan (1975) and Dahrendorf (1969) view ethnic groups as "interest groups" struggling with each other. Thus, interethnic group struggle is a political and economic competition that incorporates cultural differences as well as social class differences.

An interesting illustration of these elements is found in the New York Police Department, in which every ethnic group, almost without exception, has its own "protective association" in addition to the overall union. The Black Guardian Society, the Jewish Shomrim Society, the Italian Columbian Society, and the Irish Shamrock Society are all "ethnic interest groups" within the larger interest group of NYPD membership.

ETHNICITY IN AMERICA

The United States is an immigration country, and the group that historically attained dominance in the American culture is the group labeled WASPs—white Anglo-Saxon Protestants. In effect, the ethnic composition of the WASP group has not remained Anglo-Saxon and Protestant over the years, although the white dimensions has remained constant. The WASP group incorporated over the years other white groups, including non-Anglo-

Saxons (such as Germans and Scandinavians) and non-Protestants. The WASP group today is not a clearly defined ethnic group but an amalgam of the dominant group in society.

Other groups that were absorbed into the American society over the years (blacks released from slavery and large groups of immigrants from numerous countries) have become "American ethnic groups" in this historical process. Most of them did not constitute "ethnic groups" in their countries of origin, since they had been part of the majority culture in these countries (Italy, Germany, Ireland, and so on). As we pointed out earlier, the majority group typically does not tend to perceive itself as an ethnic group. Upon reaching the shores of America, these immigrants became "ethnic," at the same time occupying a position of low status on the social class ladder and considered as "minority groups." Jews and Armenians were among the few groups that had previous experience as ethnic minorities in other countries, while most other groups had to experience the disadvantages and "learn the role" of an ethnic minority.

Although ethnicity has played a major role in the history of the United States, the denial of its importance has been very strong. Until recently, there has been a trend in middle-class white America against the recognition of ethnicity, perhaps an unconscious fear that if essential differences are recognized, society might fall apart. Many educators have stressed the importance of viewing all human beings as essentially the same, attributing individual identities to personality differences. The development of the melting pot ideology and its inherent belief in "Americanization" reflects strong wishes for uniformity and equalization. The yearning for a homogeneous, undifferentiated society is evident throughout American history and is exemplified in this repeated effort to "assimilate" immigrants. But ethnic heterogeneity continued to exist and could not be eliminated, especially since the dominant group did not wish to give away its excess power by implementing pluralistic solutions that would result in a more equitable division of power and resources among the different groups.

In recent years the situation has changed; racial and ethnic minorities have asserted themselves and demanded equitable access to power, increasingly conscious of prejudice, discrimination, and equality. It has become more acceptable to make one's ethnicity salient, and cultural uniqueness is often rewarded in present-day America.

The new awareness of ethnicity raises new issues. Some groups have become "American ethnics" of relatively low status and lacking an external reference. Such is the case, for example, with numerous Italian-Americans and Greek-Americans, who are identified in America as Italians or Greeks, but who cannot speak Italian or Greek, do not relate personally to Italian or Greek history and cannot identify emotionally with Italy or Greece. Traveling in Italy or Greece, they would be identified as Americans. But their socio-economic status in America is relatively low, and they find it hard to identify with American history and feel fully American. Thus, they have become a marginal, low-status group of "ethnics" in New York and other cities. Compared to them, the WASP group has great pride in its *American* history. The WASPs are not identified as English or Protestant, and they do not need any reference to England or its church. They perceive themselves as "the Americans."

But the new value placed on ethnicity and cultural uniqueness presents a problem for American WASPs, who lack a view of themselves as an ethnic group. In a humorous piece on the "New York WASP," Russell Baker (*New York Times*, July 18, 1978) complains that WASPs are "the only minority who cannot have any fun":

> Instead of marching down Fifth Avenue or eating wonderful old WASP food in an annual Central Park WASP Festival, WASPs have to sit around dim, musty clubs reading the Yale Alumni Bulletin and talking about their ancestors. . . .
>
> Members of all the other minority groups had mothers who had driven them, smothered them with love, worried about them, cherished ridiculous hopes for them, trained them in guilt and tyrannized them in emotional family relationships. In short, they had mothers. As a WASP, I was not permitted a mother. Attempts to prove that I had one were met with knowing glances passed surreptitiously among my listeners. What does a WASP know about mothers? An old lady wearing tweeds and pinstripes and telling Harvard jokes—call that a mother? (©1978 by The New York Times Company. Reprinted by permission.)

RACE, ETHNICITY, AND PLURALISM

What are the implications of these analyses of race and ethnicity to the conception of pluralism? We believe that it is crucial to recognize the great intensity of the need to differentiate groups from each other and to create recognizable distinctions and boundaries between groups. Establishing group cultures and distinguishing between groups is an extremely powerful social process, pervasive *and* functional both from the individual's point of view (satisfying needs for membership, reference, and identity) and from the societal point of view. If one accepts this assumption, one can readily see how race, ethnicity, and religion would constitute the most basic dimensions for the stratification of society into detectable groups. The apparent failure of the melting pot ideology gives more credence to these assumptions

"Pluralism" has different connotations in the sociopolitical domain and the individual domain. In the societal domain, pluralism involves the search for a delicate balance between the attainment of a national consensus and the creation of a national identity, on the one hand, and maintaining cultural differences and preventing melting pot uniformity, on the other. While such balance is more attainable when the nation is threatened from outside (as in the Pearl Harbor attack of 1941), it is very hard to maintain that balance when no such threat exists, particularly when the nation is not affluent enough to satisfy the needs of every group at the level it expects. Political pluralism aims at reducing the differences among groups in political power, social status, and access to leadership positions, at the same time preserving the cultural and psychological differences among groups, allowing groups to be unique and different without being victims of prejudice and discrimination.

In the individual domain, pluralism has to do with learning how to relate to those who are different—who live differently, who perceive, think, and reach conclusions differently, and whose value systems are different from one's own. Then the question is whether appropriate skills can be learned that would allow people to communicate across differences without eliminating them, to show empathy to those who are different without judging them. Given basic tendencies toward stereotypy and prejudice, such pluralistic goals involve, at best, a long and complex process of reeducation.

Minority, Majority, and Socio-Identity

The terms "minority" and "majority" describe the positions of groups in a society's political power structure. A minority group is a distinguishable group in society (in terms of race, ethnicity, sex and so on) that is—or perceives itself to be—relatively powerless, lacking in political influence, and victimized by the more powerful group(s). A majority group is a distinguishable group that is—or is perceived to be—more powerful and influential, in control of society's resources, and not victimized by other groups.

Minority status has little to do with numerical or statistical minority, nor does the majority group consist of the largest membership. The definition rests on power and status rather than sheer numbers. Some groups consider themselves of minority status, although they are *not* in the numerical minority (for example, women), and some minority groups (such as blacks in South Africa) constitute the absolute numerical majority yet clearly are of minority status.

Historically, "colonialism" was characterized by a small "majority" ruling a very large "minority." Colonial forces typically conquered weaker and more primitive countries, controlling them thereafter for centuries. In America, the WASP founding fathers *created* the dominant culture. The WASPs are no longer in the numerical majority, but they are considered by the various minorities as more powerful and in control, that is, the culture's "majority group."

Today, most distinguishable minority groups in America (except for women, who are considered by some as a minority) are racial and ethnic groups. We believe that this stems from the considerable overlap between having particular origins and being in the lower socioeconomic stratum in America. But not every ethnic group is of necessity a minority group, and the above trend would decrease as the overlap between ethnicity and social class is weakened. Moreover, some members of an ethnic group may perceive themselves as minority, while other members of the same group do not share this perception. Also, a group may consider itself a minority but viewed by other minorities as "majority," and vice versa.

In previous chapters we emphasized the functionality of the need to differentiate among people and partition them into distinguishable groups. In a heterogeneous society, differentiation along lines of race, ethnicity, social class, religion, sex, age, profession, and ideology is functional, since it defines meaningful similarities and differences in "group culture." Such differentiation is even more functional when some of these dimensions covary, or "go together," with each other. A basic principle we emphasized in earlier chapters is that a group label is effective as long as it differentiates between those who belong in the group and those who do not belong in it. A label is not functional if everybody belongs in the group.

An interesting example illustrates this point. Jews have been recognizable in most countries as a separate and unique religio-ethnic-cultural group. In Europe, Asia, or America, the label "Jew" was effective in differentiating Jews from non-Jews. (At times, this differentiation served as the basis for discrimination and persecution as well.) But in Tel Aviv, this label has no differentiating power, since everybody is Jewish. Thus, in Israel Jews are identified not as Jews, but as Moroccans, Poles, Americans, and so on. As one American immigrant to Israel put it: "In America, I was a Jew. In Israel, I am Anglo-Saxon!" Similarly, for two Americans in New York to identify themselves to each other as "Americans" or "New Yorkers" is meaningless. But if they meet in Nigeria, these labels may be of great value.

Group membership can be self-defined or defined by others. Self-defined group membership may reflect identification with the group or rejection of one's inevitable membership in it. Definitions by others are beyond one's control, and sometimes people are defined by others in ways they have not thought of themselves. In her life-history narrative (Chapter 4), "Susan Goldberg" wrote: "My trip cross-country got me acquainted with the fact that I was a New Yorker. . . . The following year, in Europe, I became attuned to some additional facts pertaining to my identity. . . . My identity as an American became verified as a separate entity, whereas before it was a nonexistent aspect of my person—it just *was*."

The concept of *racial and ethnic identity* has been discussed by many authors (Pettigrew, 1964; Campbell, 1972; Isaacs, 1975a; Bell, 1975; Horowitz, 1975; Parsons, 1975; Isaacs, 1975b). "Socio-identity" is more complex than "group membership." It includes strong images and emotions about affiliation to the group and carries a variety of symbolic meanings for the person. Socio-identity is not merely "belonging" in a group; it satisfies the person's *need of belongingness* and influences the person's self-esteem. Much of the person's "existence" as a member of society is tied to the person's racial and ethnic socio-identity, and many of the person's life experiences are influenced and colored by it.

Exercise 9.1
Examine Your Racial and/or Ethnic Identity

You may find it valuable to consider your own racial and/or ethnic identity. We suggest that you discuss the questions listed below with another person who is similar to you in racial and ethnic identity.

(1) Label your racial and/or ethnic socio-identity.
(2) What is the relative importance or salience of this identity among your other socio-identities?
(3) How important is this identity in determining the ways others perceive you and behave toward you?
(4) How would you describe this socio-identity and its meanings for you to another person who does not share your group membership?
(5) Can you identify and describe significant experiences in your life history that relate to your racial and/or ethnic identity?
(6) Are you satisfied with your racial and/or ethnic identity?
(7) To what extent are your thoughts and experiences with regard to your racial and/or ethnic identity similar to or different from those of other members of your family?

Racial and Ethnic
Intergroup Processes

Because of the great salience of race, ethnicity, and religion in modern society, we all experience many instances of racial, ethnic, and religious stereotypy and prejudice. Racial, ethnic, and religious groups struggle, sometimes desperately, with each other in heterogeneous society. To a large extent, racial and ethnic distinctions are not merely "cultural differences," since these dimensions have become highly politicized as explosive dimensions of conflict in society. Race and ethnicity have become more salient dimensions of struggle in recent decades, while religion was more salient in past centuries. If you, the reader, need an illustration of the impact of race and ethnicity in society today, we suggest that you scrutinize today's newspaper and identify the items that explicitly or implicitly reflect racial and ethnic issues. You will undoubtedly discover numerous instances of this type: in your own community, in your state, in the United States, and in news items from all over the world.

RACIAL ETHNIC, NATIONAL AND
RELIGIOUS STEREOTYPING

Exercise 9.2
Analysis of Stereotypes

In this activity it is crucial that you complete Part I *before* you read the instructions for Part II.

Part I. Please take a sheet and divide it as follows:

List of stereotypes

(1)

(2)

(3)

(4)

(5)

•

•

On each line please write a stereotype (commonly held belief) about some racial, ethnic, national, or religious group. Each stereotype should be short, usually taking the form: "Xs are _____." Please write as many racial, ethnic, national, and religious stereotypes as you can, using more than one sheet if necessary. Your list should *not* be limited to *your own* stereotypes. Rather, include in it any stereotype you think is held by any group.

Please do not read beyond this point until you have prepared the list of stereotypes!

Part II. Now that you have completed the list, you can proceed to analyze it. For this purpose, add column headings to the sheet on which you wrote the stereotypes, and proceed to characterize each stereotype as suggested.

List of Stereotypes	Positive (+) Negative (−) Neutral (N)	Prejudicial (P) or Nonprejudicial (NP)	About Self (S) or Other (O)	Valid (V) or Nonvalid (NV)	Who Holds?	About Whom?	Contact with Them

(1)

(2)

(3)

In these columns you will mark the stereotype as positive (+), negative (−), or neutral (N); as prejudicial (P) or nonprejudicial (NP) (remember that not every negative stereotype is prejudicial); as characterizing your own group (S) or a group to which you do not belong (O); as valid (V) or nonvalid (NV) on the

(continued)

basis of an arbitrary criterion such as we defined in Chapter 5 (correct in two-thirds of cases or in less than one-third of cases). You will also note who usually holds this stereotype about whom and the degree to which you are personally familiar with members of the stereotyped group and have contact with them.

At the bottom of the page you can summarize the proportions of the different markings. There are numerous ways of processing this material (for example, comparing groups according to level of distance, comparing levels of positivity and negativity, identifying likely sources of prejudice, identifying which groups are more heavily stereotyped), and we leave it open to you to decide how you wish to analyze these stereotypes. However, we strongly suggest that the analysis be conducted in a group of co-inquirers who have all completed Part I of this activity.

Most of the stereotypes we hold and use are racial, ethnic, national, and religious, reflecting the salience of these dimensions of difference in contemporary society. People perceive other people as members of racial ethnic and national groups, and their perceptions and images of these groups determine expectations and behavior. Barriers between groups become barriers between individuals, and these group memberships define people's experiences of similarity and difference in interactions with others. For example, if an American person describes an interaction with a person who is a "foreigner" (say, French or Russian), it is almost inevitable that one of the very first descriptors will be that person's nationality.

Cultural stereotypes find strong expression in humor. With the exception of sexual humor, probably the majority of jokes are racial, ethnic, national, and religious. Groups tell jokes about other groups and about themselves, making unique and presumably "typical" characteristics of self and others more salient and emphasized (Polish stupidity, Italian passion, and so forth), thereby sharpening the differences between groups. Humor is often aggressive, and ethnic humor almost invariably involves a prejudicial put-down of a defined group of others. In fact, some of the very same jokes are "mutually" told by rival groups with reversed punch lines (the rabbi outwitting the priest in the Jewish joke, the priest having the upper hand when Catholics tell the same joke). A tourist guide in Israel told us: "I use the same bunch of jokes with all groups of tourists—I only change the identities of the actors in the jokes depending on my clients' religion, nationality, and other group characteristics."

RACIAL, ETHNIC, NATIONAL, AND RELIGIOUS PREJUDICE

Prejudice against inferior races, ethnic minorities, national aliens, and members of various religions is as old as human civilization itself. The theory and research we presented in previous chapters with regard to prejudice, discrimination, and intergroup conflict applies directly to race, ethnicity, and religion (as well as to gender differences). Heterogeneous society is a battlefield where groups struggle for power and for respect for their cultural uniqueness. Prejudice is a powerful weapon used by groups against other groups. As we mentioned in Chapter 6, prejudice increases under conditions of political and economic competition, particularly when resources are too limited to satisfy fully the expressed needs of all groups in society. We also described in Chapter 6 the phenomena of scapegoating and learned prejudice.

The functions of prejudice for the majority group are quite obvious: Prejudice maintains occupational and economic status; prejudice maintains political power; prejudice maintains self-esteem through glorification of own group and images of its "cultural superiority"; prejudice strengthens the group identity and increases within-group cohesion; prejudice provides outlets for the expression of hostility and aggression; and it diverts attention away from a group's internal problems.

In a provocative book about the functions of prejudice, Levin (1975) argues that it is also functional for a racial or ethnic *minority* group to be the target of prejudice. According to Levin, prejudice may not carry "primary gains" for the minority group, but it can provide some "secondary gains" that cannot be discounted, particularly when a group is anyway in minority status. Therefore, minority groups may sometimes even have an interest in maintaining the majority's prejudices against them. The functions discussed by Levin include:

(1) *Reduction of competition.* Prejudice involves segregation, which leaves the internal market of the minority group in minority hands without competition with majority expertise.

(2) *Maintenance of identity.* Victimization acts as a strong factor that strengthens the minority group from within, increases its cohesion, solidarity, and pride, and provides the group with a "monopoly on experience."

(3) *Reduction of uncertainty.* Prejudice reduces the fluidity and ambiguity of the intercultural interaction, leaving clear norms and boundaries and making events predictable—even if nonadvantageous.

(4) *Reduction of responsibility for failure.*

(5) *Making gains through evoking guilt.* Guilt is a powerful social weapon, particularly effective when directed at highly educated, upper-class persons.

In America and other countries, this is the "age of minorities." The end of colonialism and the awakening of the Third World, growing concerns about equality and the witnessing in the recent past of racism in its most murderous form, the wish to share equitably in the growing wealth and potential possibilities opened up by modern technology, the greater participation of citizens in the political process, the dissemination of unprecedented amounts of knowledge and information to citizens through the mass media—all these factors contribute more than ever before to the growing assertiveness of minority groups in their struggle to attain rights and privileges. This is particularly true for the United States, a country noted not only for its great heterogeneity and for being a "new immigrant country," but also for its tradition of concern about democracy and freedom. But as we emphasized several times in earlier chapters, any development in a pluralistic direction involves a sharper and more painful awareness of existing prejudice and inequities, as well as intensified conflict that inevitably includes destructive manifestations.

RACIAL, ETHNIC, AND RELIGIOUS INTERGROUP CONFLICT

Because of the great intensity of racial, ethnic, and religious groupings, the most destructive intergroup conflicts in heterogeneous societies always took place among racial, ethnic, and religious groups. The term "minority" refers to low status and insufficient political power; thus, minority groups are rival "interest groups." The overlap between lower socioeconomic status and membership in particular racial and ethnic groups (the black minority in South Africa; black, Spanish-American, and Oriental-American minorities in the United States; "coloured" minorities in England; Asian and African ethnic minorities in Israel; Greek and Yugoslav "*Gästarbeiters*" in Germany) creates an interesting dynamic process: On the one hand, the struggle of the poor lower class against the affluent upper class (social class struggle) turns into an ethnic or racial struggle; on the other hand, the attempt of racial, ethnic, or religious groups to assert their identities and cultural uniqueness inadvertently becomes an economic and political struggle. It is easier to enlist membership and support for an economic struggle that may yield concrete outcomes (jobs, housing, better schools), yet an economically based conflict comes to attain special meaning when it is focused on a racial or ethnic identity. For instance, historians agree today that the Christian Crusades of the Middle Ages—ostensibly a noble attempt to protect Christianity and liberate the holy places—were motivated by a variety of economic and political interests of the participating European countries.

The majority culture aims at "acculturating" the minority groups, demanding conformity to its norms and standards—not only through obedience to the law but through the internalization of its values and ways of life as well. Minority groups accept many parts of the majority culture (consumerism, media, education, and so on) yet they resist the cultural coercion and struggle to maintain their unique cultures. They strive to feel *pride* in their identities and fight against the stereotypes that depict them as uncultured and inferior. They try to defy highly insulting prejudices that are deeply rooted in society, easily triggered by any conflict. They feel that even if society guarantees them formal equality, the fact of their birth into particular groups puts them a priori in an inferior position and limits their potential.

It is ironic that the best strategy for maintaining cultural uniqueness and a distinct socio-identity is to remain segregated from the majority culture. But remaining segregated comes at a high political, economic, and psychological price. By remaining in the European ghettos for hundreds of years, the Jews were able to maintain their unique religion and distinct culture and to avoid assimilation into Christian society. But the price of that distinctiveness was that the Jews became the most discriminated and persecuted minority in Europe. On the other hand, coming out of the ghetto can provide great political and economic advantages, but it creates difficulties in maintaining the group's unique identity. Indeed, the great problem of American Jewry today is assimilation and loss of Jewish identity.

The concrete objectives of racial and ethnic struggle in heterogeneous society are numerous: attaining civil rights, proper housing, and quality education; increasing job opportunities; preventing segregation and discrimination; receiving social services on an equal level as other groups; forcing society to invest resources that would enable minority group members to have an equal starting point in competition with others; and guaranteeing appropriate political representation of minority groups in the political system. Although the power of the law prevents blatant discrimination and protects every citizen's formal rights, a sense of desperation is prevalent in various racial and ethnic minorities in America—a sense that the minority person has a slim chance of "making it" in the existing system and that as a member of a minority group, one is never given a fair chance of competing on an equal footing with others. To understand the problem of interacial and interethnic issues in America means, above all, to understand this deep sense of desperation.

We pointed out several times that the early stages of pluralistic progress make an increase in the intensity of conflict, hostility, and level of minority demands. The first signs of forthcoming change foster hope, make the minority group more cohesive, and strengthen the group to fight for more change. Members of the majority group, who feel righteous for what they did and sacrificed for equal rights (indeed, most pluralistic changes are at the expense of the majority), becomes indignant about the ungratefulness of minorities. This marks the beginning of the backlash, a retreat into a more conservative stance. This cycle is quite universal and predictable, characterizing interethnic and interracial relations in most communities, cities, and countries. The rise of Ronald Reagan in the United States and Margaret Thatcher in England clearly reflect such conservative retreat in both countries, triggered by a combination of tight economic conditions, unrest among minorities, and a growing sense that public spending on liberal social causes is exaggerated.

We also pointed out several times the seemingly paradoxical fact that the intensification of intergroup conflict is part of a *positive* process of pluralistic progress, despite its enraging destructiveness, extremity, and nonrational-ity. The main problem facing leaders of all camps is how to maintain the "constructiveness" of the conflict (Deutsch, 1973) and prevent the destructive elements and "side effects" from attaining dominance that might destroy the potential progress. This presents a dilemma for the minority group, since part of its power in the conflict stems from its militancy and extremity. As a result, most pluralistic struggles in human history have been characterized by internal struggle between more moderate minority leaders (such as Gandhi and Martin Luther King) and more extreme and sometimes fanatic subgroups who wish to destroy society totally.

Prejudices of Minorities

One of us was involved as a consultant in a program entitled "Topics in Racism" that was conducted in a prestigious East Coast college in 1980. The turnout of black students to the program was extremely low. Explaining why he would not attend, one black student said: "I have nothing to do in this program. It's the whites' problem. It's the whites who are prejudiced!"

It is frequently (and conveniently) held that only the majority group is prejudiced, while minorities are free of prejudice. This position is rooted in the conception that prejudice is a weapon held by the majority to maintain its power to discriminate against the powerless minorities and to justify their acts. Minority group identity is based to a large extent on the experience of prejudice and discrimination, and it seems illogical that the victim of prejudice might be prejudiced as well.

The position that minorities cannot be prejudiced is, of course, fallacious. Persons of any group membership may be personally prejudiced, and some of the strategies used by racial, ethnic, and religious groups in their pluralistic struggles involve rather intense prejudice. We distinguish between several types of minority prejudice: reactive prejudice, directed as a weapon against majority groups; prejudice directed against groups of even lower status; and ethnocentric prejudice, directed at all unlike groups.

Reactive prejudice (or counterprejudice) is the minority's response to majority prejudice. It is defensive in nature, turned directly against the majority. "I am not inferior; *you* are inferior." Reactive prejudice increases or decreases as a function of the intensity of majority prejudice and the level of escalation of intergroup conflict. At the same time, reactive prejudice also serves to strengthen the minority group from within, in terms of pride, dignity, and moral superiority.

This description would seem to put the blame for minority prejudice on the majority group. Not only is the majority group made guilty of its own prejudice, but is is also made guilty of the minority's reactive prejudice! This impression is not accurate. Reactive prejudice is indeed a partial outcome of majority prejudice, but it is also functional for the struggling minority group, often used conveniently and deliberately by its leaders to reap particular benefits. Reactive prejudice sometimes continues to exist when its original antecedents no longer exist at the same intensity as they did before. For example, cries against "institutional racism" and "institutional sexism" have remained at the same pitch and level of intensity by some advocates over the years, in spite of the great many changes that have been attained in legislation, social policies, *and* people's attitudes.

Reactive prejudice is not the only type of minority prejudice. Every person has multiple group memberships, so that the minority group identity is but one of the person's socio-identities. A person may be relatively unprejudiced in one minority identity (say, as a woman), yet be prejudiced in another capacity (say, as a WASP); or a woman may be prejudiced against men but unprejudiced as a WASP. Thus, a complexity of multiple group memberships makes it impossible to determine simply that a person is "prejudiced" or "unprejudiced."

Another phenomenon relates to the notion of "relative minority status." Even if a group is of minority status compared to the group in power, other groups may be of even lower status and can become the targets of that group's prejudice. The group of the lowest status can serve as the scapegoat for the frustrations of groups with slightly higher status. A relevant joke that was popular in Israel in the early 1970s was the Moroccan Jews (who felt they were the most victimized minority) were the happiest about the decision of the Russian government to let Jews from Georgia (in Asian USSR) immigrate to Israel. Now, it was said, the Moroccans could pick on the Georgians.

Finally, prejudice is also conceived as reflecting a personality trait that is distributed more or less evenly in all groups in society. In every group, some individuals are more ethnocentric than others, expressing themselves in prejudices toward a variety of out-groups. The research on dogmatism and authoritarianism indicates that the incidence of that trait in lower-class and minority groups is not smaller than in the high echelons of society.

The history of early Christianity provides an interesting example of the shifts of majority and minority prejudices. The early Christians constituted a religious minority group within Jewish society, in a troubled era of domination by the Romans. The early Christians were subjected to rejection, prejudice, and discrimination. Generations later, Christianity prevailed, the Roman Empire collapsed, and the Jews were exiled, becoming a minority group in Christian countries. It was now the Jews' turn to be subjected to rejection, prejudice, and discrimination. Much as the early Christians had developed an anti-Jewish minority prejudice, the Jews developed an anti-Christian minority prejudice.

Exercise 9.3

Have you experienced or witnessed instances of minority prejudice? Have you experienced or witnessed it as a minority group member? as a majority group member? Of what "variety" (reactive, relative, and so forth) were those prejudices? Can you remember your reactions and the reactions of others in those instances? What are the conclusions you can reach from this examination?

Prejudiced Liberals

Much as minority group members do not readily accept that they, no less than majority group members, may be prejudiced, persons who subscribe to a liberal ideology often have difficulties in "owning" their prejudices. Minority members often ridicule the liberals as those who righteously *pretend* to be nonprejudiced so as to reduce their guilt feelings. The stereotype "liberals are really prejudiced" is, of course, prejudicial, but liberal persons are not free of prejudice.

We believe that the choice of a liberal ideology indicates the person's *wish* to be unprejudiced rather than an absolute lack of prejudice. Admitting to prejudice is socially undesirable in this culture, and liberals often persuade themselves that they are free of prejudice. For some, the label "liberal" symbolizes "lack of prejudice." This belief leads prejudiced liberals to unconscious distortions, where prejudice becomes more subtle and more refined. Liberal "do gooders" often appear smug, paternalistic, and superior, and minority group members are *extremely* sensitive to hidden messages of paternalistic superiority. Denial of prejudice is common in the American middle class, where guilt feelings seem to have transformed underlying prejudicial attitudes into self-righteousness. This phenomenon is particularly common among "helping professionals": teachers, social workers, psychologists, and various health professionals.

Several widely known phrases have come to identify, and to mock, the liberals.

Some of my best friends are . . . [Black, Jewish, etc.]." On one level this statement expresses liberalism, indicating that one does not keep social distance, respecting and liking minority group members enough to include them in one's circle of close friends. But this phrase has become the slogan of prejudiced liberalism, mocked as a righteous self-justification that reflects hidden prejudice. One may select "token" minority friends so as to be able to say, "Some of my best friends are . . ."; almost invariably it turns out that the selected best friends are really quite *similar* on a crucial dimension (the white surgeon's friend being a black surgeon) and are selected for their similarity but provide an additional benefit because they are racially or ethnically different. (One of us cannot forget how he was told by a southern WASP: "Some of my best friends are Jews, and I have attended many Jewish ceremonies, mostly funerals.") However, it is also true that often enough liberal persons choose friends without hidden agendas, and their choices *do* represent lack of prejudice.

"I accept and relate to every person as an equal human being." This phrase expresses the core of the liberal ideology, and it is genuinely held and believed by many liberals. However, it is pychologically impossible to relate equally to all people. Grouping people into meaningful groups and holding stereotypes about groups are inevitable, and differences between people simply cannot be overlooked or denied. Teachers do not relate to gifted and retarded children in the same way, nor would anyone treat the Pope or the President as one would treat a wino from skid row. Therefore, the foregoing statement is often interpreted to reflect the liberal's defensiveness, aimed at hiding the underlying prejudice. On the other hand, it should be accepted that this statement can reflect a genuine ideological goal: the *wish* to minimize prejudice by an equalitarian approach to people.

The statement about relating equally to all human beings can also be taken as initially limited to the dimensions of race, ethnicity, religion, social class, and sex without implying that one never groups people according to any dimension. In that case, the liberals do not deny their human tendency to group and to stereotype, but they express the ideological wish that these dimensions, so crucial to the quest for pluralism in heterogeneous society, would not affect their perception and their behavior.

"Bending over backwards." This phenomenon is the act of giving excess respect and consideration to members of particular minority groups, above and beyond the existing norms and standards. Minority students in college may receive higher grades than warranted by their papers, and the qualities of minority job applicants may be overestimated. The negative view of this phenomenon is that bending over backwards reflects the defense mechanism "reaction formation," where excessive goodness is evidence of underlying (and often unconscious) hostility (see Chapter 3). In such cases, minority students can both reap the benefits of the professor's bending over backwards and yet persist in viewing the professor as prejudiced. On the positive side, this phenomenon may be viewed as reflecting the liberal's genuine wish to compensate minorities for past inequities—respectfully and without a sense of superiority.

Liberalism and prejudice are relative terms, and both depend on particular conditions, especially when the "price" for liberalism becomes too high. "White flight" from particular residential areas (to escape a drop in the quality of education due to busing or to salvage the value of real estate when property values decrease due to an influx of minority residents) is not necessarily a reflection of pure prejudice. It is often the product of tough and painful internal conflicts of persons who wish to be liberals and yet do not want to feel "penalized" for their beliefs.

The issue of prejudiced liberalism stems, in part, from an erroneous dichotomy: that one can be *either liberal or prejudiced*. Persons can be well-meaning, liberal, *and* prejudiced! In our C-Groups, we encourage people to perceive liberalism as a *direction of change* rather than an *end state*. The test of liberalism need not be a total commitment to relinquish each and every privilege or give up all power differentials between minority and majority groups.

Exercise 9.4

Have you had personal experiences with "liberal prejudice"? Can you remember instances in which you acted as a prejudiced liberal? Can you remember instances in which someone else, interacting with you, acted as a prejudiced liberal? How do you think this phenomenon can be dealt with effectively?

10

SEX ROLES, SEX IDENTITY, AND THE STRUGGLE BETWEEN THE SEXES

Heterogeneity between men and women in a society is most obviously grounded in biological differences between men and women. While the anatomical and physiological differences between the sexes are more or less universal, the roles of men and women, the ways they are perceived, and the expectations with regard to what constitutes "appropriate behaviors" for each sex group vary greatly from culture to culture (see, for example, Mead, 1935; Barry, Bacon, & Child, 1972), and vary from one historical period to another within the same culture. In Western societies, the last century has been characterized by an emerging struggle for women's liberation, a struggle that has risen to a crescendo in America in the last two decades.

Although some women define themselves as members of a "minority group" and the struggle between the sexes is clearly a struggle for equality, the gender dimension is unique compared to other dimensions of heterogeneity in society, by which minority and majority status is defined. The unique characteristics of the gender dimension include the facts that (1) women are not in the numerical minority in society, as are many racial and ethnic minorities; (2) women are not segregated like other minorities, but are in continuous contact and direct interaction with men; (3) a woman and a man establish together a viable social unit ("family") that serves significant biological, emotional, social, and economic functions; and (4) attraction between the sexes is a biological reality that influences the patterns of interactions between them. In most racial and ethnic intergroup conflict situations, the variability in social status *within* the minority group is relatively small, while the power differential *between* majority and minority groups is large. The variability in social status among "women" is very large, and the power differential among women is much larger than the difference in power between any particular group of women and the men of the same social class.

Racial, ethnic, and religious minorities are often quite hesitant to recognize the disadvantaged status of women, particularly as it concerns rich, educated, upper-class women. This hesitancy reflects in part, the "monopoly on experience" factor discussed in an earlier chapter. Political expediency has sometimes dictated an alliance between women's groups and other struggling minority groups, but the latter have usually been quite apprehensive, suspecting that women's attainments would come at the expense of other minorities.

There is no doubt that women have legitimate cause for grievance concerning their status in modern society. Compared to men, women have less power and less access to leadership positions, and they are discriminated against in the work market and in certain aspects of the law. The stereotypic images of women in society often hold them inferior to men, and women's position in society has not changed, as is warranted by the technological advances.

Today, the social, economic, and political equality between women and men constitutes a societal issue of great significance, laden with ideology and emotion. Following the struggle of various minority groups, the U.S. Congress added gender groups (read women) to its list of protected groups— groups whose civil, political, and economic rights must be protected by the law and by the courts so that they are not discriminated against.

Socialist countries, especially the Soviet Union, have dealt directly with the gender issue not only via the declaration of equality in the law but also through the reorganization of societal institutions and the work market to facilitate such equality. Similarly, the kibbutz in Israel is a community that has been voluntarily planned and developed to fulfill ideals of equality. A section in this chapter describes how this planned equality between the sexes has fared under the tests of reality over a period of several decades. The current status of the gender issue in the kibbutz (and in Russia) indicates the complexity of this set of problems and the absence of simple, straightforward solutions to them.

Exercise 10.1 Images of Gender Reversal

To focus your awareness on this dimension of the social self, it is suggested that you engage in an exercise of your imagination. *Imagine that you have been born as a member of the opposite sex*, and fantasize about the differences this would have made in your life and your growing up. Hold constant your racial, ethnic, religious, and social class memberships—imagine that you were born into the same family and social setting, varying your gender only.

Please take notes and list the most significant things that you believe would have been different in your life had you been a member of the opposite sex.

Your reactions to this exercise will probably give you some insights into your own sexual identity, your opinions and attitudes about sexual differences, your expectations, and your relationships with members of the opposite sex.

A Continuum of Gender Issues

Gender problems are complex, and in the tension of conflict terms like "sexism," "sex roles," "feminism," "feminine," "gender," and "sex typing," are used indiscriminately. Defining the terms and organizing the issues in conceptual order may simplify the discussion somewhat. Figure 10.1 presents a continuum of gender issues, in increasing order of intensity.

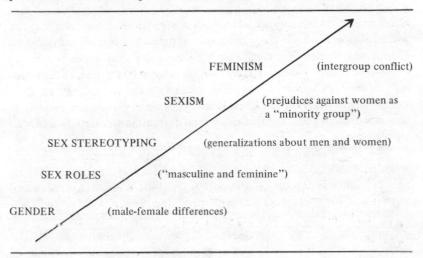

FEMINISM   (intergroup conflict)

SEXISM   (prejudices against women as
                            a "minority group")

SEX STEREOTYPING   (generalizations about men and women)

SEX ROLES   ("masculine and feminine")

GENDER   (male-female differences)

Figure 10.1:   A Continuum of Gender Issues

"Gender" is a biological characteristic, and almost all persons are born as male or female, clearly identifiable by physical attributes and gonadal, chromosomal, and hormonal characteristics. Males and females differ not only in sexual characteristics (genital organs, the reproductive system) but also in general body build and physical strength. Beyond these differences there are almost no other "pure" gender differences, and most differences between women and men in society are the products of cultural learning and sex-role socialization. Different writers provide somewhat different assessments of the extent of actual gender differences (Bardwick, 1971; Maccoby & Jacklin, 1974), but they all agree about the overwhelming impact of cultural sex-role socialization. Money and Ehrhardt (1972) argued that both men and women can show almost all conceivable behaviors, and the number of "biological imperatives" is extremely small.

The concept "sex role" differs from "gender," shifting attention from "male and female" to "masculine and feminine." Chafetz (1974) defined "sex role" as the set of behavioral, temperamental, emotional, intellectual, and attitudinal characteristics identified in a given culture at a given time as masculine or feminine. Sex role is the cluster of socially and culturally defined expectations that men and women are expected to fulfill.

While gender differences are more or less universal, sex roles vary from culture to culture. Most writers quote Margaret Mead (1935) and Barry et al. (1972) to show that in certain primitive societies feminine sex roles include behaviors and tasks that most contemporary Westerners would consider masculine, while men in these primitive cultures perform "feminine" tasks. D'Andrade (1966) pointed out that some behaviors that were considered feminine in our society fifty years ago are perceived as masculine today.

Sex stereotypes are generalizations about the nature and attributes of men and women. Sex stereotypes influence sex-role socialization, and they are powerful mechanisms in the maintenance of prevailing images and positions of men and women in society. Feminists view sex stereotypes as a major cause of sexism in Western society. But we believe it is a mistake automatically to view sex stereotypes as prejudicial and viciously tendentious. Like stereotypes in other domains, sex stereotypes describe what is commonly held in society, regulating expectations and determining culturally appropriate behavior.

"The 1970s added a new word to the language of prejudice: *sexism,* a prejudicial attitude or discriminatory behavior based on the presumed inferiority of women as a group" (Cameron, 1977, p. 340). When stereotypes attain a systematic judgmental connotation (specifying "better" and "worse", "superior" and "inferior") and when one group controls societal resources and dominates the other, the situation is one of prejudice and discrimination. The term "sexism" as it is used today refers to both the *prejudicial attitude* of viewing women as inferior and *discriminatory practices* against women.

"Feminists" are the persons who are committed to fight sexism, and "feminism" is the ideology that is committed to resolve gender-related problems in society. Both men and women can be sexist and both men and women can be feminist, but there are probably more sexist men and more feminist women in society.

Factors Contributing to
Gender Problems

A dimension of heterogeneity gains salience under particular historical, social, political, and economic conditions. These may include changes in the political power structure, changes in the economy and in utilization of workers in the work market, demographic changes, changes in ideology, growing gaps between groups, the emergence of competent advocacy and minority leadership, pluralistic progress made by other groups or other countries, and so on. With regard to the gender dimension, active pluralistic struggle in Western societies has been recorded in the last 150 years, with particularly strong waves of conflict early in this century and in the last 15 years. Several clusters of factors have contributed to the recent salience of gender problems.

TECHNOLOGY AND MODERNIZATION

In primitive societies, persons of each sex took upon themselves the social tasks they were better equipped biologically to perform, such as child care for women and hunting for men (D'Andrade, 1966). These distinctions have become obsolete in modern society, where more and more tasks are non-gender-related. Today, the number of tasks that members of one gender are better equipped to perform than members of the other is decreasing. Physical strength, one of the few biologically based differences between men and women, has a shrinking role in the work market as more tasks become mechanized and computerized. Women are no less equipped than men to succeed in business, engineering, or industrial management. As more facets of modern life become non-gender-related in the biological sense, the gap between socialized sex roles based on pretechnological images and the realities of modern society become more apparent.

The gender issue is related to another area of modernization. In the past, women had less control over their pregnancies and were strongly tied to the home and to the care of their young children. Today, women can exercise control in family planning; mothers can obtain a variety of goods and equipment to ease their workload in mothering; and social support systems such as day-care centers are available, freeing a portion of the mother's time from her traditional tasks.

CHANGES IN THE WORK MARKET

Traditional sex roles held for hundreds of years called for women to bear children and act as homemakers and for men to work outside and provide the family with a source of income. As Kreps and Clark (1975) phrased it, a man could expect to receive household services and child care from his wife in exchange for providing income for her. Women traded their domestic skills for claims on their husbands' incomes from market work.

This traditional sex-role differentiation has been changing rapidly in the twentieth century, and the participation of women in the work market (even through the period of child rearing) has become the norm rather than the exception. Kreps and Clark (1975) point out that women have moved in considerable numbers from the home to the work market; women comprise the majority of the working force in some occupations; women have shown the capacity to compete successfully with men in previously "all male" occupations; and, in particular periods (such as wartime), there is a great demand for women to move into previously all-male occupations. By virtue of playing a significant role in the work market, women have become a *political* force.

CHANGES IN THE STRUCTURE OF THE FAMILY

Changes in family structure have contributed to the erosion of traditional sex roles and to the need for more appropriate sex-role definitions. These changes include:

(1) The breakdown of the traditional family structure. Few people today live within an extended family structure. The patriarchal arrangement of men as heads of households and breadwinners, and women as homemakers, is eroding.

(2) The extremely high rate of divorce decreases the stability of the family, forcing women to seek both satisfaction and potential sources of income outside the family.

(3) The sexual revolution and the new attitudes toward sexuality, particularly the sexuality of women, influence the ways women perceive themselves and their interactions with men.

(4) The new possibilities for family planning and birth control provide women with more freedom of choice and enable them to plan and control their own lives so as to attain more satisfactions.

(5) The development of child-care technology (for example, ready-made food) and child-care support systems ease the burdens of motherhood, freeing women from household duties to pursue other interests.

THE DECLINE IN THE INFLUENCE OF ORGANIZED RELIGION

The leading religions in the world are largely male-dominated, reflecting in philosophy and in practice the submissive roles of women that characterized pretechnological society. Feminist writers (for example, Deckard, 1979) provide numerous illustrations of the sexist attitude in organized religion. The feminist movement is by and large a secular movement, and its growing intensity is associated with the decline in the power and influence of organized religion in Western societies.

THE INFLUENCE OF THE MASS MEDIA

We live in the age of the mass media, flooded with information coming through a variety of media and exposed in detail to events that would have been out of our scope only decades ago. The mass media provide extensive coverage of social issues, raising people's awareness and forcing them to consider these issues. Once people become aware of particular issues, they begin to see their relevance to their own lives, which enables them to act on and to attempt to resolve social dilemmas in their own conduct. The media's preference for providing more extensive coverage of extreme and dramatic events is well known; intergroup conflicts tend to escalate into tense, dramatic, and extreme confrontations.

THE EMERGENCE OF CONSCIOUS MINORITIES

Recent generations have been marked by the emergence of conscious minorities and of deep concerns about social justice, equality, and pluralism. The horrible manifestations of fascism and genocide in this century, the end of colonialism and the rise of the Third World, the relative affluence of Western societies, various technological advances, and many other factors have combined to create unprecedented concerns about issues of justice and equality. In the United States, issues of civil rights and group relations have been treated most seriously by the political and the judiciary system in recent decades, and no politician can ignore issues of heterogeneity and pluralism. Public awareness of dimensions of difference is heightened, and television series such as *Roots* and *Holocaust* have attracted unprecedented audiences.

Following the struggle of American ethnic minorities early in this century and the more recent racial conflicts regarding civil rights and desegregation, gender issues have gained high priority in the 1970s.

Inquiry Into Sex Identity

Chapters 3 and 4 defined and illustrated inquiry into socio-identity, providing guidelines for self-inquiry and analysis. However, "Susan Goldberg's" attention was focused on her ethnicity, religion, and social class, leaving out the treatment of her femininity and identity as a woman. In this section we provide excerpts from interviews with two women, a feminist and a nonfeminist. These interviews are preceded by suggestions for self-inquiry into sex identity that complement the guidelines provided in Chapter 4 by adding more specific considerations of gender-related issues.

The inquiry into sex identity can be conducted alone, in interaction with another person (of the same or opposite sex), or in a group interview. You may wish to consider conducting this inquiry before you continue your reading, after reading the two interviews in this section, or after completing the entire chapter.

The following questions complement the guidelines provided in the last section of Chapter 4.

- How would you define your sex identity? What does it mean for you to have a "sex identity" in addition to simply being a male or a female?

- How has your sex identity developed and changed over the years? What are the critical life experiences that shaped your sex identity?

- How central is your sex identity among your other socio-identities? How does it influence other socio-identities and how is it influenced by them?

- What are the central values inherent in your sex identity? Are you "ideological" with regard to your sex identity?

- What types of sex identities have you seen in other people? How have these experiences influenced the formation of your own sex identity? Did any person have a particularly strong influence on the formation of your sex identity?

- In what ways does your sex identity influence your social relations with others? How does it influence choices of friends? How does it influence your relations with your family?

- In what ways does your sex identity influence your daily behavior at home, work, and other settings?

- How did your sex identity influence your perceptions of your parents and your family, and how did (or will) it influence the creation of your own family?

- What problems and conflicts with others does your sex identity create?

- How is your sex identity related to your sexual behavior and dating?

- What is the influence of your sex identity on your life planning, your future? How does the current state of your sex identity compare to what you wish (and/ or expect) it to be in the future?

Excerpts from interviews with two women are presented next, to highlight particular aspects of sex identity and their relations to feminism and to the women's liberation movement. Please compare the two interviews and analyze their content, examining your own reactions to the two women and their attitudes. In what ways are you similar to or different from each woman? Are there instances in which you identify with one or the other?

AN INTERVIEW WITH DEBORAH, A FEMINIST

Deborah is 42 years old. She grew up in London and emigrated to Boston over twenty years ago. Deborah was trained as a social worker, and she holds a job in a mental health clinic. She has been married and divorced twice. Several years ago Deborah decided to have a child as an unmarried mother, and her daughter is now 4 years old. Deborah is active in the women's movement and defines herself "a radical feminist."

The area that interests me is the psychology of politics, that is, the psychology of change. I see myself as a politically aware person. The other thing is that I have a very clearly defined ideology. What I will do is to talk about myself and let the ideology about feminism come out in that process.

I come from a middle-class home in London. My parents were both very poor as children. My father was bright. So is my mother, but it took me years to discover that. We had a tailoring shop and were fairly comfortable (not in American terms, of course). I am an only child. I was different from most kids, because my father was a socialist. What you call an armchair socialist. There's the theory and then there is the practice and never the two shall meet! So I was given a wide humanitarian concept of social well-being.

I was very shy and scared as a child. I didn't have any contacts with kids until I went to school. I was with my mother and that was that.

There's another thing which is a sort of a personal thing. I was always very "old." At the age of 12 I knew Marx's philosophy and I didn't know children's stories. I didn't know how to talk to children. I knew how to talk to adults. That's because I was an only child. Also because I have had wide concepts presented to me but I didn't know that I was never supposed to live up to them. Things you believe in but you don't live by!

My first awareness of myself as a woman is related to a particular group of experiences: I was made aware that whenever I spoke to someone and I sounded "intelligent," the automatic reaction was "my dear, you've got a man's mind." You know, *now* I can laugh at it. I know how to answer it, but then I was in conflict. I knew I was being complimented, but somewhere, the woman in me sensed that there was something funny about it. Am I a pseudo-man? Am I a successful woman? What exactly were they saying about me? And it was a conflict I carried for many years. And this I found in consciousness-raising groups, talking to women, to be a very common thing. When I came into a room on social occasions the women were sitting in one corner and the men in another, and the men automatically talked about the things that interested me, politics, society, etc., while the women were talking about cooking, kids, and shopping. And I knew that I wasn't going to be like that. And I certainly remember feeling very aggravated. I'm like them but I don't like them! I don't like the way they are!

In high school it was the first time that I got close to some friends. Before, I was very isolated. I was 14 or 15 at the time. The school was a high-upper-middle-class public school, a day school. All my girl friends were sophisticated. Very much more into boys and makeup. And that created conflicts for me. I was 13 when mother got one of the neighbors' daughters who was 16 to take me to a party. She realized that I was too isolated. All the young men of 16 and 17 were there, and they kissed and they danced and they kissed. . . . And I wanted to talk to people, which was obviously my own personal thing, but also it wasn't expected of a girl that she should be interested in talking. And I found it very difficult, because I was also learning social skills at the time.

I saw that all girls kissed the boys, so I kissed a boy. And then I heard the comments of the boys, the guys, on "these girls." And I didn't know what to do. Obviously my home was very puritanical, but at the same time my father discussed with me the sex lives of the savages. I accepted that there were other ways of life and sexual relations, but he never suspected that I might consider these appropriate to me. So there were double messages all the time. It's nice to be open, warm, socialist but it was expected that until you are married to a nice boy you must be a virgin because this is how a woman should be. I am very proud of you that you can think, but don't use it too much. You know, my father wanted me to study (unlike many fathers at the time), but only so I would be a better woman fulfilling the normal tasks.

Today, as a therapist, when males talk about their difficulties about inviting a girl to dance, I understand the other side. But even today I am so aware of the experience of the girl sitting there, the whole row of girls sitting there, and the boys coming along, and looking sort of up and down, up and down, standing at the door as they come in and looking like this, and like parceling you out. And you have no say over it! It happens to you, and if you are chosen, you know you are worth while, and if you are not chosen, there must be something wrong with you. You cannot really show what you are worth. It is only if you have the right form, the right make-up, but it has nothing to do with your personality, your intellect, understanding, etc. On the contrary these are drawbacks! It is not only a sense of helplessness or incompetence. Because usually when you feel helpless or incompetent you have a frame of reference, you can understand why. But here you are in a situation when things happen to you, when you feel negated, negative, rejected, and you've no idea why. You may spend hours choosing the dress, and putting on the make-up, and fantasizing and not even daring to admit your fantasies, and then you are left sitting and you are not being asked to dance.

At that time I imagined that I was enormously fat. I probably weighed a couple of pounds more than I was supposed to weigh, but my self-image was that I couldn't get through a door. I used to feel bloated. Otherwise, I could not have understood. (Of course there were always a lot more women than men.) And it was a very simple matter. If I was not successful in exactly the very narrow terms in which success can be defined and made evident then I'm nothing. And I very much see it today. The one group in therapy that I really find painful are perfectly normal, competent, even attractive women, 25 and onwards, who got their B.A. or struggle to finish, or are doing a doctorate, who haven't got a boyfriend. And their sense of total worthlessness . . . as if all their intellectual apparatus is recognized on one level, but it is separated off from them. You know, you've got a good mind, but . . . how about you as a person? You're a woman who should be able to . . . have you got a man? Have you managed to achieve? It does not even matter what kind of man you were able to get!

When I was about 16 I read of two twins in the States who underwent an operation and became boys. And I was so envious of them. (And if anybody dare say this is penis envy I'll cut their throats.) It was just that as a man I could say, I could do, I wouldn't be told fifty times a week, "Yes, it's wrong for you to do this, but it's all right for a boy."

My feelings about work were also off the norm for girls. I wanted to work in carpentry, metal work, husbandry. Well, those areas were for men only. Men only! You know, you take a young guy and train him, but a woman couldn't be trained. It's not fair, especially since I was physically strong and knew that I could do better than many males if necessary.

In terms of ideology that is one of the basic differences between women's rights in the twenties, thirties, forties, fifties, sixties, and feminism. Because the goal for women's equality is to take a given world with given values evolved in terms of male needs, and say "we want entry." Feminism turns this on its head. That is, there are *human* values, *human* needs, we want YOU coming to our world. I want to be able to be a carpenter, I want you to be a kindergarten teacher. There's a very very great difference between these perspectives.

The whole thing begins with the "fact" that sex is something that the woman does not enjoy. You have children. That I learned from my mother. And as she has a bad heart, her sexual activity was very limited. A woman "enjoys" having children who are good, having a husband who is good to her, who provides for her, going away once a year to the seaside, having a wider family. These are not "enjoyment," this is BEING A WOMAN. I don't think my mother ever thought of it in terms of what does a woman enjoy, or what she is allowed to enjoy. This is what life is about. And I loathed my mother. I hated her. I hated her all the way through until I became a feminist in terms of awareness. Then I could see her in terms of the social setting. My father would not allow her to work. I talked with my father; we are very good friends now, and he is aware of all the different things that happened. And he said, "How could I let your mother work? A decent man did not allow his wife to work." It would be a sign of his failure to provide. So she sat at the home, with me, and the home, and me, and the home, and the arguments with this aunt and that aunt. In fact, quarrels gave interest to life. There wasn't anything else.

When they finally came after me to Boston, and she worked in the shop, she worked like mad day and night, and she was much better than he was. My father is a superb tailor, but a lousy businessman. And you could see all her frustrated intelligence. Only then could I begin to realize that she had a mind. She hardly went to school. She was afraid to write because she made mistakes, and she was very ashamed of her mistakes. As the years went on, and I decided to have a kid without having a husband, she could accept it (my father flipped, you know). She could accept it, and I could see that everything that I resented in her wasn't a question of her—it was that she had no choice other than becoming the very narrow, very limited, very grasping (in the emotional sense) woman that she was. And then I could love her.

The messages I got originally were that she wanted me very much to go out and be popular. This is how a girl gets a husband. She pushed me to go out with boys and wear makeup. My father didn't like it. And when I came and told her about the kissing games, you know, kissing with the tongue, I thought it was funny, and she slapped my face. Even before that, when I got my period, and I knew all about it, it was expected for a long time, first thing she did was slap me, and I burst into tears. Then she told me she had to slap me because this way you get rosy cheeks. But really the slap remained a lot longer than the explanation. But certainly with all my awareness and competitiveness and wanting to be the same as the men, I certainly see now that in my play with the man I was sweet, sort of played the fishing game, because there wasn't any other way to be, and still find a date on a Saturday night. I was aware enough to have an internal quarrel with myself.

So there develops a duality. There is the person, a human being, who is allowed to think, function, who is expected today to have a career, to develop potentials, to be able to earn her own living, and yet the woman must be prepared to serve. And, you know, the great satisfaction when a woman says, "Yes, my husband is very good, he helps me," not to talk about the many who say, "Yes, I am a liberated man, I help my wife." This terminology is very expressive, reflecting the state of mind.

Today I can be somewhat sympathetic with the man. After all, I am demanding of him incredible changes. . . . In the same way that I am demanding of myself to reevaluate myself and work and "be" in different terms, I am asking him to be in different terms, but in terms that detract from his self-worth. I'm saying we share power and he has to give up power. Intellectually to understand it is one thing, but to translate it into a new self-identity is more difficult. There is a difference between understanding the behavior of a friend that I can't take, and simply not being able to take it.

I see sometimes that men get frightened. For some time that was a problem for me. He cannot reconceive himself as having new roles more creative and satisfying. That there is something positive to replace this power which I demand that he give up.

I want a society of PEOPLE. With differences, but where the differences don't make them more valuable or less valuable, better or worse, more worthy or less worthy, more competent or less competent. Just differences. You have the man who loves being at home. Should be perfectly valid for him to bring up his children. And so for the woman. Social functions and roles should be divided in terms of the ability of the individual. And that should not be gender-related.

I have grave doubts about the family unit. Grave doubts about it being satisfying. Today it is essential, because of the alienation of the individual. I see a totally different form of social structure, very much more in terms of extended family, communes. I certainly believe in the value of one-to-one relationships. It's a very basic need. I know of a commune in Austria where one-to-one relationships are forbidden, and that is total nonsense. The need of the individual basically to relate, you could do to one, two, but certainly a very small unit. But there is a difference between that and the family. I also think that the property element in children is destructive. They are little people and don't belong to the parents. Exactly which way is not very clear yet to me.

AN INTERVIEW WITH MRS. D, A NONFEMINIST

Mrs. D is 71 years old. She was born in Holland and emigrated to America in 1932. Mrs. D has been married for 47 years, and her husband, now in his mid-eighties, is a retired scientist. Mrs. D teaches in a high school. She has four children, fifteen grandchildren, and one great-grandchild.

I hear and read what the young women argue about women's liberation, and I don't really understand what they are talking about. When I look back at my life it is very clear that I always achieved what I wanted, and I am definitely content and satisfied.

From a very young age I wanted to be a teacher, and indeed at the age of 18 I had become a certified teacher. Until this day I feel it was a good decision—that teaching is my role and goal in life. I have never perceived my profession as inferior or of low status. It is a difficult profession, with a lot of responsibility, challenge, and satisfaction. It is true that in my generation in Holland less women went to study, but those women who wanted it could get an education. A lot of my female friends (those who survived the years of the holocaust) have studied medicine or law, and those who wanted it could have a career. Nobody ever said that women cannot compete with men. I have always thought that a woman must have a profession and a satisfying job, and not only be a housewife and take care of the children. It seems to me that some women are lazy and wary of challenges, so they stay home and then complain that "society" made them stay home and be inferior.

My husband, who is now retired, was a scientist. Probably many people think that science is more important or prestigious than school teaching, but I never shared this idea. To teach generations of children and prepare them for adulthood is no less important than doing experiments in a laboratory or writing papers and books. In the final analysis, *only I determine the value of my work,* and I never felt that I had to conform to or accept what "society" says. Anyway "society" says many other things that are unacceptable!

I always tried to support my husband and provide him with the best opportunities to advance in his work, but I also demanded, and received, similar support from him. In retrospect, he might have advanced more than he did had I made myself and my life subservient to his career. But I never wanted to do that, neither was I expected to. My husband always took part in the family life and the education of the children, and did not see himself as "forced to help me." He washed dishes, shined shoes, cleaned the house, etc., etc., etc. In fact, it makes me angry when a woman perceives her husband's career to be more important than her own job, lowering herself and her needs and being subservient.

I have never seen myself, or other women, as less intelligent than or inferior to the men. On the contrary, I have met many inferior men, and it seems to me that the men could not handle our load of family, home, children, *and* work outside. Women who feel inferior really do that to themselves. I don't consider them too wise, and maybe they enjoy being miserable and complaining. It is true that in our religion the role of women in terms of the practice of religion is different (and maybe inferior) to that of the men. However, it is also clear that the *spiritual value* of the woman is very high, and the responsibility the woman receives in terms of shaping the next generation is tremendous. I do think that there is room for many changes in modern religion. Indeed, newer trends (to which I do *not* happen to belong) provide new and more varied opportunities for women in religion.

Generally, there are great biological and psychological differences between men and women, and these differences cannot be discarded. Some modern women maybe want men to bear children—but I do not want to give up this beautiful and rich experience, nor the role of mother. I raised four children, and when they were young I stopped working and stayed home. I saw that as my right and privilege. It was clear to me that it would be to my children's benefit that I could give them the maximal time and care. I do not particularly like doing housework, but it was a beautiful period in my life, and I have never been sorry nor felt that these years were wasted. Maybe my husband missed something! My husband participated as much as he could, and during these years I continued doing interesting things as much as I could. I continued studying, reading, singing in a choir, and doing some tutorial teaching. I knew that when the children would be old enough I would go back to my occupation. I attained an academic degree at an advanced age, and today I am happy to continue teaching and do not want to think of retirement.

Looking at my life in retrospect, I am quite satisfied. After 47 years of marriage our family life is wonderful, and my husband and I have the deepest affection and appreciation for each other. All the children have developed nicely and all have their own lives, careers, and families. I have never felt disadvantaged, inferior, or discriminated against. In my social group people are valued for their personality and cultural level, not for being male or female. Sure there are many things that I would have wanted to be different, but every man of my age would have wanted the same. I am sure that a sense of discrimination can exist only if you let yourself feel it. If I had to be born again—I would definitely choose to be a woman!

Sex Stereotypes

Exercise 10.2 Sex Stereotypes

Part I. Please take a few minutes to prepare two lists of *stereotypes*. One list will contain ten or twelve common *beliefs held by men about women,* and the other, ten or twelve common *beliefs held by women about men.* The items on your list do not have to represent your own views, nor should you be concerned whether these beliefs are correct or incorrect.

Part II. The lists of stereotypes about men and women that you prepared can now be analyzed. In your analysis, you may consider most of the theoretical issues discussed in Chapter 5. In addition, please pay special attention to the following questions:

(1) To what extent were your lists influenced by your own group membership?
(2) Can you identify cognitive and/or dynamic factors underlying specific items on your list?
(3) Which of the stereotypes on your lists would be shared by both men and women? Which would be shared within one group but contested by the other?
(4) What conclusions can you reach about the validity of specific stereotypes on your list? Did validity considerations affect the strength of your beliefs?
(5) Try to trace where you have acquired specific stereotypes on your lists.
(6) Which items on your lists would you wish to change or see changed?

EVIDENCE ON SEX STEREOTYPES

Sex stereotypes are the structured sets of beliefs and expectations about the attributes of women and men, or "the consensual beliefs about the differing characteristics of men and women in our society" (Rosenkrantz, Vogel, Bee, Broverman, & Broverman, 1968). The growing interest of social psychologists in social cognition in recent years has led to a renewed interest in stereotyping, and due to the great salience of the gender dimension in society today, much attention has been given to sex stereotypes.

Ashmore and Del Boca (1981) have counted the frequencies of published works on stereotyping in the *Psychological Abstracts* (the index of works published annually in all areas of psychology) over a span of fifty years, from 1927 to 1977. They report that less than one in 1000 works annually was focused on stereotypes in the 1930s, 1940s, and 1950s. In the late 1950s and the 1960s there was a slight increase in the frequency of publications on stereotypes (between 1 and 2 per 1000 published works annually). The 1970s brought a dramatic increase in stereotypy-related works: There have been more than 100 papers a year since 1975, and in 1977, 7.5 in every 1000 papers focused on stereotypes. This increase is almost completely attributable to studies of sex stereotypes, while in earlier years most studies of stereotypy focused on racial and ethnic stereotypes. In 1977, 78 percent of the stereotypy entries (159 of 203 works) concerned beliefs about women and men.

This lively interest in sex stereotypes is to a very limited extent a direct interest in stereotypes per se. A great number of these publications are political—written by feminists trying to demonstrate that women are victims of prejudice and discrimination. It is thus typical to read in one sweep that "women are different than men, less than men, and subordinate to men" (Cameron, 1977). We believe that the a priori assumption that all sex stereotypes (or rather, stereotypes of women) are prejudicial is misleading. Many sex stereotypes are certainly prejudicial, but neither are *all* sex stereotypes, nor is the phenomenon of sex stereotyping in itself, sexist. Differences between men and women have always existed, and definitions and redefinitions of sex roles throughout human history have had functional value. That contemporary society is in acute need of a redefinition of sex roles does not imply that previous definitions were outright oppressive and prejudicial.

It turns out that there are more claims made about sex stereotypes and how they spread than hard empirical data collected through comprehensive, high-quality research. Reviewing the research on sex stereotypes, Ashmore and Del Boca (1981) concluded: "Contrary to many discussions of this literature in secondary sources, we did not find a clear and consistent body of findings." Much of the "evidence" on sex stereotypes is either anecdotal or focused on the *spread* of sex stereotypes in the media and folklore (rather than in people's actual beliefs and conduct). Nevertheless, there is no doubt that sex stereotypes are held and used by people all the time and that women are, on the average, perceived more negatively than men.

The following list, quoted from Chafetz (1974), summarizes typical lists of stereotypes about men and women appearing in feminist literature:

(1) *Physical characteristics.* Virile, athletic, strong *versus* weak, nonathletic, worrying about appearance and aging, sensual, graceful.

(2) *Functional characteristics.* Breadwinner, provider *versus* domestic, maternal, involved with children, church-going.

(3) *Sexual characteristics.* Sexually aggressive, experienced, male "caught" by spouse *versus* virginal, inexperienced, double standard, must be married, passive, responsible for birth control, seductive, flirtatious.

(4) *Emotional characteristics.* Unemotional, stoic, don't cry *versus* emotional, sentimental, romantic, can cry, expressive, compassionate, nervous, insecure, fearful.

(5) *Intellectual characteristics.* Logical, intellectual, rational, objective, scientific,

practical, mechanical, contributor to society, dogmatic *versus* scatterbrained, frivolous, shallow, inconsistent, intuitive, impractical, perceptive, sensitive, "arty," idealistic, humanistic.

(6) *Interpersonal characteristics.* Leader, dominating, disciplinarian, free, independent, individualistic, demanding *versus* petty, flirty, coy, gossipy, catty, sneaky, fickle, dependent, overprotected, responsive, status-conscious, refined, adept in social graces, follower, submissive.

(7) *Other personal characteristics.* Aggressive, success-oriented, ambitious, proud, egotistical, confident, moral, trustworthy, decisive, competitive, uninhibited, adventurous *versus* self-conscious, easily intimidated, modest, shy, sweet, patient, vain, affectionate, gentle, tender, soft, not aggressive, quiet, passive, tardy, innocent, noncompetitive.

More rigorous researchers have employed sophisticated methodologies for the study of stereotypes (see Jones, 1977) and sex stereotypes. Rather than simply listing the attributes provided by groups of subjects, methods such as hierarchical clustering and multidimensional scaling trace underlying structures and clusters, which enables researchers to give systematic meaning and to conceptualize the great array of reported attributes. According to Ashmore and Del Boca (1981), the major distinction between men and women found in such studies falls along the dimension of "soft" versus "hard" traits. Women are perceived as softer (sentimental, naive, submissive, wavering) and men as harder (scientific, critical, stern, dominating, shrewd). This dimension is sometimes related to intellectual characteristics (scientific versus unscientific) and to "communion" (women are perceived as more generous and less selfish). Ashmore and Del Boca argue that many other dimensions do *not* yield systematic and consistent differences between males and females (such as sociable versus unsociable, active versus passive, ambitious versus unambitious, and intellectual ability).

Other researchers discuss "gender differences" rather than "sex stereotypes," focusing on *actually tested differences* between men and women rather than stereotypically *ascribed* attributes. In *The Psychology of Sex Differences,* Maccoby and Jacklin (1974) argue that actually tested sex differences were fairly well established only for four variables: visual spatial ability, mathematical ability, verbal ability, and aggressive behavior. Many writers (such as Block, 1976) take issue with Maccoby and Jacklin, arguing that men and women differ on a variety of additional psychological variables. However, the absence of tested differences only points to the seriousness and social significance of sex stereotypes that are so prevalent in society.

THE SPREAD OF SEX STEREOTYPES

Sex stereotypes are socialized from an early age and learned in the context of home, family, and school. Children absorb directly and indirectly the stereotypic images of their parents and teachers, much as they are *taught* the roles of men and women (what to wear, how to play, what to be concerned about, and the like) and are reinforced for having an "appropriate" sex-typed identity. Various sources continue to flood the growing and adult person with various sex stereotypes, many of which are prejudicial against women.

Children's Literature. Children's literature is a major source of sex stereotyping. Children's books, magazines, and toys are saturated with stereotypic images of males and females in our society. In their analysis, *Dick and Jane as Victims,* Women on Words and Images (1975b) reviewed a large number of elementary school readers and children's books, comparing the portrayed roles of boys and girls. Boys were found to be depicted as more clever, heroic, and adventurous than girls in a ratio of 4:1; girls were depicted as more passive, motherly, and domestic than boys in a ratio of 3:1; fathers were described as "fun," problem solvers, and adventure promoters, while mothers were mostly colorless, unimaginative, and concerned with cleaning, cooking, and scolding.

Mass Media. The mass media consistently portray women more negatively than men—as more domestic, passive, insecure, dependent, and less adventurous and attractive in character (though mostly attractive in physical appearance). In her review of the spreading of sex stereotypes through the media, Cameron (1977) showed the consistency of these portrayals. Additional writings include an analysis of television shows by Women on Words and Images (1975a), an analysis of television drama by Gerbner and Signorielli (1979), an analysis of jokes by Zimbardo and Meadow (1974), and Chafetz's (1974) analysis of popular songs, published print media such as *Time* and *Newsweek,* movies, and television programs and commercials.

In recent years there have been some noticeable changes in media images of women, evident in shows such as *Policewoman, Wonder Woman,* and *Bionic Woman.* In these instances, women are portrayed in more masculine and powerful roles without losing their femininity. However, it is extremely rare to find instances of males portraying feminine images in the media (English male butlers notwithstanding).

Daily Language. The images of men and women are so ingrained that the common language views men as markedly different from women. Typical examples include "all men are created equal" or words like "freshman," "chairman," "housewife," "midwife," and "manpower." In recent years, with the increased awareness of this issue, alternatives to the use of the masculine gender—such as the term "chairperson" or the replacement of the generic "he" by "he or she"—have become more common. Words representing sex bias through the use of gender-specific terminology are being eliminated in America through administrative rules and regulations and normative pressure.

People's reactions to these changes range from mild amusement to violent agreement. In the short range, such acts are mostly *symbolic*, a recognition of the legitimacy of feminist demands. Whether one uses "chairperson" or "chairman" has little to do with implicit sexism. However, in the long run, such changes may well have psychological significance, since people will not learn to use male-oriented language in the future.

Religion, History, Philosophy. The male orientation is prevalent in the ideology and practice of religion as well as in the writings of historians, philosophers, poets, and sociologists. The world's major religions are undoubtedly male-oriented; women traditionally play limited and secondary roles. The holders of central religious roles (bishops, rabbis, imams, priests, and ministers) are always men, and the women's roles are limited to childbearing, child rearing, maintaining the home, and supporting the men.

Analyses of historical and sociological writings also show a clear focus on men. Rosen (1971) wrote that sexism in historical writings is similar to sexism in daily life: Women are usually invisible, and if they are discussed, they appear in the domestic scenery behind the real male actors. In protest, authors such as Carroll (1976) wrote books to "liberate women's history," providing essays on the history of women (written mostly by female authors). Kirschner (1973) showed that only half of the sociology textbooks published between 1966 and 1971 indexed any references to women. Deckard (1979) provided rather extreme "sexist quotes" from Aristotle, Darwin, Schopenhauer, Spock, Boccaccio, Rousseau, Tennyson, and all major religions.

Social Science. "The writings of social scientists may be more influential on public opinion than literary writings because of people's belief in the objectivity and factuality of scientific findings. However, attitudes toward sex roles revealed by writers in the social sciences are characterized by androcentrism (i.e., focus on men), stereotyping, and a bipolar view of sex roles" (Cameron, 1977, pp. 345-346). Cameron and other authors (Weisstein, 1973) analyzed the sexist attitudes of psychologists and therapists, as well as the attitudes reflected in gynecology textbooks and family and marriage textbooks. Among psychologists the main culprit is, of course, Sigmund Freud, who wrote almost exclusively about male psychology and "doomed" women as motivated by "penis envy."

Sexism in Society

Sexism is a prejudice against women, a view of women as inferior to men which leads to different expectations of men and women and a differential treatment of women. In the following pages, we describe and summarize the domains claimed by feminists to be the major arenas of sexism in society.

FAMILY ROLE AND SEX ROLE SOCIALIZATION

Differential images of men and women are implanted in the process of socialization, and children learn and practice sex-typed identity: Boys train to become "men" (adventurous, active, and so forth) and girls train to become "women" (homemakers, dependent, and the like). These processes lead young persons—boys *and* girls—to become sexist.

The power of sex-role socialization, which is transmitted through a great variety of channels in the child's environment, is so strong that it often overcomes and defeats the role models provided by the child's parents. A 6-year old son of parents sympathetic to equality for women, who are both Ph.D.s and pursue independent careers, reacted to the election of Margaret Thatcher as Prime Minister of Great Britain with surprise: "How can a woman be prime minister?"

Most feminist writers are vehement in their discussion of family roles and sex-role socialization in early childhood and in school. They are particularly concerned (see, for example, Frazier & Sadker, 1973; Sadker & Sadker, 1980) about *latent* sexism: the hidden curriculum that they consider to be more dangerous and destructive because it is never stated explicitly and therefore cannot be directly challenged.

THE DOUBLE STANDARD

The same behavior might be interpreted and evaluated differently when it is attributed to a man or a woman. Typically men's behavior is viewed more favorably than women's behavior. For example, an anonymous source describes the difference between men and women businesspersons as follows:

> A businessman is aggressive; a businesswoman is pushy. He's good on details; she's picky. He loses his temper because he's so involved with his job; she's bitchy. He follows through; she doesn't know when to quit. His judgments are her prejudices. He is a man of the world; she's been around. He climbed the ladder of success; she slept her way to the top. He's a stern taskmaster; she's hard to work for.

The double standard is not limited to sexual behavior, although the most common examples usually describe a lax and permissive approach to men's philandering and a strict and punitive judgment of the same behavior in women. Feminists argue that this manifestation of sexism is particularly bothersome, "trapping" women in a prejudicial network. Whatever course they take is viewed negatively.

Exercise 10.3

Have you ever experienced a double standard with regard to your gender or any other socio-identity? Have you ever used a double standard in relating to others? Can you generate specific examples of sexual double standards?

ACCESS TO LEADERSHIP POSITIONS

Positions of power and influence in society are overwhelmingly held by men—in politics, government, industry, business, and numerous other areas. Feminists view this limited access to leadership positions as evidence of institutional sexism in society.

Chafetz (1974) analyzed the 1965 edition of *Who's Who*. She reported that only 4.5 percent of all listings were of women. Next, she selected a random sample of 100 men and 100 women listed in that edition and analyzed "the primary bases for elite membership." For women, the primary bases were education and the arts, while for men the prevalent base was business, followed by the "professions," administration, and education.

WOMEN IN THE WORK MARKET

Most feminist writers view the work market as one of the major arenas of the discrimination against women. The proportion of working women has been growing steadily throughout this century, particularly during the war years, when women's participation in the work market was of crucial importance. Various surveys and reports (such as Kreps, 1971; reports of the U.S. Bureau of the Census and manpower reports of the U.S. Department of Labor) indicate that of all women, the proportion of working women is extremely high, and women comprise almost 50 percent of all workers today. Kreps and Clark (1975) conclude that women have generally moved from the home to market work. Their work profiles reveal steady commitment to market work, with uninterrupted work participation through the childbearing and child rearing period rapidly becoming the norm. Women's earnings are considered in most families as an integral and critical part of the family income rather than "pin money" (Chafetz, 1974). In occupations allowing comparisons between male and female workers, the productivity of women is equal to men's, often even exceeding it.

One set of phenomena mentioned by most writers is the high concentration of women in particular occupations and their relative absence from other professions. According to Frazier and Sadker (1973) women comprise almost the entire work force of occupations such as bookkeeper, cashier, nurse, office machine operator, elementary school teacher, waitress, typist, secretary, telephone operator, and librarian. Some of these occupations (for example, nursing and teaching) may be perceived as historically gender-related, but others are not necessarily gender-related (operating telephones or office machines). Some of these occupations may be tied historically to periods when women's work was part-time and frequently interrupted, therefore involving less training and skill (waiting tables or practical nursing), but others (librarian) involve a long period of training. Frazier and Sadker (1973) argue that the common denominator of all these occupations is that they are low-echelon, low-prestige jobs.

Compared to the high frequency of female workers in low-echelon and nonprofessional occupations, women are relatively absent from high-prestige positions in academia (Kreps, 1971; Wasserman, Lewin, & Blei weiss, 1975); industry and business management (Deckard, 1979). Feminist writers argue that employers take advantage of female employees and discriminate against them—to the point that women's rights must be protected by the law and the courts. Women receive lower wages than men even when performing the same jobs, and their access to advanced on-the-job training and promotion is more limited than men's. Deckard (1979) presented a series of "pyramid effects," showing the decreasing proportions of women in the higher echelons of various professions, reflecting, in her words "the obstacle course of professional women."

Most feminist writers discuss another manifestation of sexism in the work market: the sexual harassment of lower-echelon female workers by their male superiors. No systematically valid data about the dimensions of this phenomenon are available, but there is no doubt that sexual harassment of women is not a rare phenomenon. In a recent survey of psychologists, 25 percent of recent female graduates reported having had sexual relations as students with their male educators and supervisors (Pope, Levenson, & Schover, 1979). The proportion of male students reporting similar events was less than one fifth of the proportion of female students.

Chafetz (1974) argues that a set of myths and half truths about women's work are persistently held despite evidence, serving as the basis upon which employers justify their preferential treatment of males in job considerations. Her list includes, among others, the notions that women do not need the income as much as the men; that women's participation in the work market lacks commitment and is often interrupted; that women shy away from the responsibility of high-status jobs; and that women lack skills or strength to be productive.

WOMEN AND THE LAW

The law is in a constant state of change with regard to minorities (including women) and their rights. In previous centuries, the law in the United

States and European countries did not provide women with legal rights equal to men's. English Common Law, upon which American property laws were based, viewed the woman as the "property" of her husband. Women's right to vote was granted in the United States only about sixty years ago. In other countries the legal status of women is not better than it is in America, and in many countries women are far worse off. The most widely quoted work on the legal status of women is Kanowitz's *Women and the Law* (1969).

The following list presents some of the more widely quoted issues of difference in legal status between men and women.

- By common law, women take the names of their husbands upon marriage. The laws with regard to property rights, domicile (the legal residence of the family), and support discriminate between men and women.
- Prostitution is defined in such a way that it is legally impossible for a male to be a prostitute. Moreover, only the prostitute, not her client, is held responsible and punishable by law.
- In some states, female criminals have been treated like minors, given indefinite sentences in "reforming" institutions. These terms were often much longer than formal jail sentences given to males for the same offenses.
- Until 1966 the rights of women to serve on juries were limited in several ways as compared to those of males.
- Until the draft was abolished in 1973, only males were liable to be drafted into the armed services.
- Divorce laws strongly reflect the double standard. In some states a wife's having had intercourse with another man *prior* to marriage was grounds for divorce, while similar behavior by the husband was not. A single act of adultery was grounds against the wife but not against the husband.
- Until the recent past, there have been numerous "protective laws" with regard to women's work. These laws established maximum hours, minimum wages, weight-lifting ceilings, and mandatory rest periods, and they prohibited certain types of nighttime work by women. The feminists argue that these laws "protected" women out of a number of well-paying jobs, overtime pay, and access to jobs requiring highly developed skills.

THE EQUAL RIGHTS AMENDMENT

Exercise 10.4

Did you hear about the Equal Rights Amendment? Do you know what the ERA states? Do you know what is the current legal status of the ERA? What, exactly, would the ERA change? Are you familiar with the major arguments for and against the ERA? What is your personal view and how do you justify your point of view?

On March 22, 1972, the U.S. Congress approved the Equal Rights Amendment (ERA). It states that "equality of rights under the law shall not be denied or abridged by the United States or by any state on account of sex." According to the U.S. Constitution, the ERA requires ratification by three-quarters of the states. After seven years, ratification by 38 states has not been achieved, and Congress extended the time limit for ratification by another three years. The Reagan platform in 1980 did *not* support the ERA, and it seems quite feasible that this amendment will not be ratified at all.

The ERA has become the focal issue of feminism in America, a highly symbolic and debatable piece of legislation. It is therefore important to examine the controversy around the ERA from both a legal and a psychological point of view.

If ratified, what will the ERA do? All state and federal laws, regulations, and practices that treat men and women unequally will be rendered unconstitutional. The ERA will remove any gender-based discrimination (or differentiation), making it as clearly unlawful as racial discrimination is today. What this means in actual practice and whether these rights are granted by existing constitutional amendments (particularly the Fifth and Fourteenth amendments, which guarantee equal protection under the law and the right of due process) are debatable issues.

In terms of the specific changes that a ratified ERA might bring about, the supporters of the amendment list the improvement in women's status in the work market (it will prohibit government and other employers from discriminating against women in employment and job training programs), the elimination of sex-segregated schools and universities, the greater benefits and rights women will receive from the social security system, and the fact that women will take responsibility equal with men's in marriage, family property, and child support. The supporters of the ERA are aware of the fact that the amendment will eliminate some advantages that women have today (in divorce law, alimony and child support, protective labor laws, and the like) but maintain that these advantages are "double-edged swords" that are harmful to women's equal status, so that their elimination is really for the better.

Opponents of the ERA argue that the existing Constitution and its amendments provide all necessary and/or desired civil rights, and there is no reasonable case of gender-based discrimination that cannot be litigated today without the ERA. They refer mostly to the extensive use of the Fourteenth Amendment in recent years in a variety of gender-based cases. ERA opponents argue that if the ERA were to be viewed flexibly, it would in any event not add much to the flexibility exercised in the present situation. If the ERA were to be viewed as an absolute bar to *any* gender-based classification it would eliminate differential treatment of men and women even when it is helpful and functional. All unigender colleges (such as Wellesley, and Bryn

Mawr) would be eliminated, separate-but-equal sports facilities and women's teams would be prohibited, separate prison facilities would be unlawful, and women would not only be drafted when necessary, but assigned equally to combat duties. (It might be added that desegregation of bathrooms would not be called for, since this collides with other constitutional amendments granting the right to privacy.)

Beyond the legal issues, the controversy around the ERA has symbolic and ideological facets. Feminists feel that ratification of the ERA would *declare* the equality of the sexes a national policy, showing the commitment of American society to the resolution of the inequality between the sexes. Much as the Supreme Court decision of 1954 with regard to racial segregation was a symbolic political landmark, the ratification of the ERA would give a symbolic boost to the value of social justice in America. Therefore, the ERA is of crucial importance even if it would not do much to change the existing legal situation. Ratification of the ERA would also be a political symbol of the *success* of the feminists in their struggle.

Opponents of the ERA feel that the mere use of "symbolic value" is a power manipulation that should not intimidate them. Advocates attach "symbolic value" to particular issues to attain their political goals, but no side has a monopoly on symbolism, and the issue must be examined factually and rationally. In other words, ERA opponents argue that symbolization is a manipulative attempt to "irrationalize" the issue. In addition, viewing the ERA as a symbolic issue almost inadvertently leads to stereotyping its opponents as reactionary, conservative, dogmatic, bigoted, and in favor of maintaining the oppression of women.

The Struggle Between the Sexes

The 1960s and 1970s were years of intense struggle for women's liberationists in America. Perceiving themselves as a minority group, feminist women (as well as feminist men) fought against prejudice and discrimination in the minds of people and in "the system," attempting to change the prevailing images, the rules and regulations, and the general "conduct" of society. All destructive manifestations of intense intergroup conflict were evident, and probably every family (particularly within the middle socioeconomic class) experienced aspects of this conflict in some way. This struggle has already yielded changes in the status and image of women in society, yet it fell short of attaining all its objectives (particularly to achieve ratification of the ERA).

During the late 1960s and the 1970s, the extreme manifestations of the conflict were so strong and the fanaticism of some feminists so intense that it was difficult to have a clear picture of the struggle between the sexes—what is feasible and what is not, what cause is more worth while, or what changes were actually taking place. In the last few years the fervor of this intergroup conflict has subsided somewhat, making it possible to form a more sober evaluation of the struggle and its outcomes.

OBJECTIVES OF THE STRUGGLE FOR WOMEN'S LIBERATION

The immediate objectives of feminist struggle encompass several domains: women's personal experiences of self and identity, women's roles in the family and at work, the images of women in society-at-large, and women's rights and privileges in the political and legal system. Most writers agree that serious progress has been made in these domains in recent years, especially with regard to stereotypes about and attitudes toward women (Chandler, 1972; Tavris, 1973; Roper, 1965; Cameron, 1977).

On the personal level, the major objective is to change the self-image and socio-identity of women (and thus of men as well)—to enable women to view themselves more positively, to widen women's perspectives on their options in their social roles and in their interactions with men, to decrease women's dependence and passivity and make them comfortable with being more assertive, and generally to improve their experiences as women. These objectives are pursued in a variety of ways, including consciousness-raising groups, college courses about the psychology of women, and advocacy through the media. However, there are some hidden paradoxes in this set of objectives, contrasting intents *not to be different* from men (or inferior to them), *to be different* from men (and unique), and to be *better than men*. Conflicting tendencies are evident: one leaning toward an ideal of uniformity of the sexes, the other a more pluralistic search for a unique feminine identity that is different from, yet equal to, that of men.

Beyond the change in socio-identity and self-image, another set of objectives concerns changes in women's actual conduct, defining new roles and liberating women from the limitations of their traditional roles. Through the creation of various types of support systems—day care for children, to free mothers to pursue careers; dissemination of information on various topics, including sex education, abortion, women's rights, and welfare; service centers for women (legal aid centers, divorce centers, rape centers, medical aid clinics, and counseling services); facilities for training women and improving their educational and occupational skills; and consciousness-raising groups and assertiveness training interventions—attempts are made to increase women's independence in the family and at work.

Another set of objectives concerns the image of women in the eyes of men and in society-at-large. These objectives include changing the existing stereotypes and establishing new means of sex-role socialization. To attain these objectives, feminists must struggle against the advertising industry, television and other media, and the educational system.

On the political level, the objectives of the struggle for women's liberation are numerous and varied. They include the protection of women through specific legislation and admistrative acts, the attainment of "society's" public commitment to women's rights through the ratification of the ERA, the activation of a political lobby that can bring pressure to bear upon various agencies and societal institutions, and the continuous litigation of women's issues in courts.

THE POLITICS OF THE STRUGGLE
FOR WOMEN'S LIBERATION

Like most intergroup struggles, the feminist movement consists of great many shades of groups and subgroups, from moderate feminists to fanatic, uncompromising extremists. As always happens in these instances, the most extreme subgroups have received most media and public attention—contributing not only to the image of the women's liberation movement as unrealistic, noncommunicable, and often downright ridiculous, but also to an extremely negative stereotype of feminists as hairy, single, homosexual women who neglect their physical appearance and hate men fanatically.

What distinguishes the struggle for women's liberation from other pluralistic struggles is that the great majority of the feminist fighters come from affluent, middle-class backgrounds. Other struggling minorities almost invariably originate from the lower socioeconomic classes. To escape this image of the feminist as an upper-middle-class woman, it has been necessary to enlist women from other walks of society and *men* in the movement. This has not been done easily, since lower-class and minority women show greater acceptance of traditional sex-role definitions and are not eager to join the feminist struggle, while the majority of feminist men are upper-class, liberal, and well educated. In spite of these limitations, the women's liberation movement has gained in popularity in recent years, and attitudes toward the movement, its causes, and its followers are gradually becoming more and more favorable (Tavris, 1973; Cameron, 1977).

In the last two decades we have witnessed all the classic phenomena of intergroup conflict take place with great intensity in the struggle between the sexes. This includes enmity and hostility, high levels of extremity, exaggeration of the oppression and victimization of women, monopoly on experience (directed even at blacks and other minorities), derogation of and prejudice against men, evolutionary rhetoric, and manipulation of guilt feelings, along with mechanisms of strengthening the group from within and making it more cohesive and intimate.

At the peak of radical feminism in the late 1960s and early 1970s (Roszak

& Roszak, 1969; Firestone, 1970; Weisstein, 1973), the polarization among women was almost as sharp as the conflict with men. Moderate women were excluded with at least the same vehemence as men. Radical feminists believed that the existing social order must be destroyed, to be replaced by a new society that would not differentiate in any way between the sexes (some may have wished that women would dominate men in the new society). It is this extreme view of the "end state" of women's liberation that allowed radical feminists to be so recklessly destructive; in their view there was no hope anyway of achieving their goals in the existing social order. Moderate feminists wanted to fight for changes within the existing social order—to attain equality and guarantee women's rights, to change the family to facilitate greater opportunities and new role definitions, and so on.

This conflict between moderate and radical feminists was clearly reflected in the different positions concerning women's sexual behavior. Some radical feminists adopted the stance of not needing, or even hating, men, advocating homosexuality among women. Deckard (1975) reports that in 1969, one radical feminist group in New York passed the resolution that at no time could more than one-third of the membership be living with a man. This new rule led a number of members to quit, leaving the group in the hands of the ultra-radical feminists. Kate Millett, one of the feminist leaders, was pressured by her followers to announce that she was bisexual. Denouncing heterosexuality was a strategy of extreme polarization that led to the reinforcement of negative and derogatory stereotypes of feminists, eventually reducing their potential impact for attaining social change. Moderate feminists felt that the chances of total rejection, guilt, and sex manipulations leading to permanent social change were minimal.

An interesting sequence of intergroup relations took place between feminists and blacks. Viewing themselves as an oppressed minority, feminist groups sought emotional and political alliance with other oppressed minorities, mostly blacks. Racial and ethnic groups are no less sexist than the white group, but radical feminists overlooked this fact in the service of political expediency. While specific alliances that were politically motivated were effective in reaping some benefits, the overall relationship between the feminists and the blacks was strained. The identity of most feminists as rich, educated middle- and upper-middle-class whites made it more difficult for blacks to empathize with the women's experiences as oppressed victims. Moreover, minority leaders were afraid that women's attainments would come at the expense of blacks and ethnic minorities and that white society would feel smug and righteous once they took care of their own women and granted them some privileges. Black women were particularly torn between loyalties to race and gender groups. With the rate of father-absent families in the black population approaching 50 percent, the disadvantages of black women are generally greater than those of white women. But black women were afraid that the attainments of white women would be at the expense of black men, and they were therefore particularly apprehensive about joining the women's liberation movement.

Exercise 10.5

From your own experience or the experiences of your friends and relatives, try to recall and list events reflecting intergender conflict. Discuss these events with a co-inquirer of the opposite sex, analyzing the emergence of these events, their course of development, and their conclusion—all in light of what you know about intergroup conflict and the struggle between the sexes.

Androgyny and Pluralism

ANDROGYNY: CONCEPT AND FINDINGS

Androgyny is a biological term that was adopted by feminists as an idealized end state of women's liberation. In biology, androgyny refers to species whose members have dual reproductive systems—male and female. Androgynous species are found among the lower animals (invertebrates, such as snails). They have both the male apparatus (sperm and so forth) and the female apparatus necessary for reproduction and can therefore reproduce themselves without coming in contact with other members of their species. At the early stages of human pregnancy, before the reproductive system reaches a level of differentiation, the human fetus also has a dual apparatus. Minor signs of this dual system remain after birth. Biologically normal human beings cannot be androgynous: they are either male or female.

In many cultures, the term "androgyny" is used derogatively, indicating that a person has no clear sexual identity at all. In the Middle East, "androgynous" is a grave insult. The concept of *psychological androgyny* that has been developed in recent years is the very opposite—a positive, even idealized psychological state of sexual identity.

> One consequence of the women's liberation movement has been a questioning of the traditional assumption that it is the masculine male and the feminine female who typify mental health. Rather, it is now the "androgynous" person, capable of incorporating both masculinity and femininity into his or her personality, who is emerging as a more appropriate sex role ideal for contemporary society. Theoretically, such a person would have no need to limit his or her behaviors to those traditionally defined as "sex appropriate" but would have the psychological freedom to engage in whatever behavior seemed most effective at the moment, irrespective of its stereotype as masculine or feminine. (Bem and Lenney, 1976, p. 48)

Constantinople (1973), Bem (1974), and others argued against the traditional conception of masculinity and femininity as two poles of a continuum, where femininity is viewed as the opposite (or worse, the absence) of masculinity. Bem claimed that masculinity and femininity are entities that are neither mutually exclusive nor opposites: A person can be high in one and low in the other. In Bem's (1974, 1977) formulation, an "androgynous type" is the person who endorses about equally high proportions of both masculine-typed and feminine-typed characteristics in a self-report questionnaire.

Bem (1974) argued that androgynous individuals are free of stereotypic sex-role constraints in their self-images, feeling equally comfortable in masculine and feminine activities. She saw them as more adaptable and able to enjoy a richer and fuller life. On the other hand, persons who internalize and impose conventional sex roles were conceived by Bem as more inhibited and unable to develop as wide a range of adaptive behaviors—women who are reluctant to appear independent, assertive, and ambitious, or men who are reluctant to appear soft, tender, and yielding.

Empirical reports on androgyny agree that androgyny is positive, healthy, and desirable, preferable to all other states of sexual identity. Bem (1975), Berzins (1975), and Kelly and Worell (1977) cite numerous studies indicating that androgynous persons are more flexible, creative, intellectually and socially competent, higher in self-esteem, and lower in anxiety than sex-typed persons.

CRITICAL EVALUATION OF ANDROGYNY

We have some apprehensions about the concept of androgyny and its implications. A few of our reservations focus on the methodology and measurement of androgyny, but our major concern is with the symbolic meaning of androgyny as a solution to the gender problem in society.

Bem's Sex Role Inventory is a self-report questionnaire, measuring androgyny in a highly transparent manner. Respondents can easily detect not only what is measured but also the desirable pattern. Androgyny studies have been conducted in particular cultural settings, and most if not all investigators of androgyny have clear ideological leanings. In the context of the American college of the 1970s it may well be that persons who endorse both masculine and feminine statements are indeed more flexible and adaptable, and Bem's inventory possibly measures social adaptability in this context. Research (see Babad, 1974, 1979; Babad & Inbar, 1981) has shown that responses to self-report questionnaires can have little or nothing to do with people's actual behavior or personalities. These patterns of results are restricted to their limited cultural contexts and would probably *not* be confirmed in an Indian village, a South American city, or numerous other non-college settings in America.

Androgyny research has been highly ideological since its beginning. The message—that it is good and desirable to be androgynous—is readily transmitted to subjects. We believe that ideological research should be treated cautiously, as it is prone to become a self-fulfilling prophecy.

But it is the intolerant prophecy of androgyny with which we are most concerned. In pluralistic society there is room for masculine and feminine persons, for sex-typed and sex-reversed persons, for androgynous and non-androgynous persons. But androgyny is "sold" today by its advocates as a single, uniform, and exclusive ideal, the only (or best) healthy, happy, well-adjusted, enlightened choice. Much as immigrants had to be quickly Americanized in the melting pot in a nonpluralistic way, persons may be required to be androgynized in the future. Pluralism means that differences are tolerated and respected, that being different does not entail loss of status or power. Especially with regard to gender, where biological, genetic, and possibly psychological differences between the sexes do exist, an "unisex" ideal that aims at eliminating differences is not desirable. As to the concept of androgyny itself, we find it a rather appealing addition to other types of sexual identities. It allows the androgynous person to integrate both masculine and feminine parts of his or her personality, behaving in a situationally appropriate manner in different contexts. Clearly there are many individuals who would welcome the legitimacy of this type of sexual identity.

A UTOPIAN SOLUTION
UNDER THE TEST OF REALITY

The Israeli kibbutz—a utopian collective community first established by young, idealistic Jewish pioneers close to eighty years ago—is an interesting site for testing how the planned equality between men and women has fared in real life. Most kibbutzes (*kibbutzim* in Hebrew) today have a three-generation membership and are economically viable communities that successfully realize their ideals of communal living, equality, productive work, and anti-materialism. Having rebelled against the traditional life and family roles of religious Jewish ghetto families in Europe, the kibbutz founders were particularly concerned about the equality of women and men. Institutions such as the children's houses, the collective kitchen, the laundry, and the other facilities, and the absence of economic problems facing the family were motivated to a large extent by the wish to free the woman from her traditional role as homemaker and allow her maximal flexibility in career and life choices.

In the early years, when the kibbutzim were extremely poor and extremely ideological, the predominant conception with regard to gender issues was that of *mechanical equality,* in which there are no differences at all between men and women (not unlike the ideal images of some radical feminists). In historical perspective, this desired uniformity had not been achieved: Many women did take on masculine roles and tasks, but few men took on feminine roles and tasks. Particular historical factors gave the masculine tasks (working the land, defending against enemies, and so on) special significance and value at that time.

As the kibbutz grew more affluent and multigenerational, the mechanical equality ideology was gradually replaced by the ideology of *organic equality*, a more realistic—and pluralistic—perspective. This view respects the relative advantages of each gender, encouraging each group to specialize in its domains and reach the highest level of competence. No field or speciality is perceived as "more important" than another, and high competence is valued regardless of its field.

Today, Kibbutz women have essentially drifted back into the more feminine roles (working in the service and educational sectors), but the status of their occupations in the kibbutz is not much lower than that of men's occupations in the productive sector. The level of training and professional standards in all sectors are equally high. Moreover, the kibbutzim are highly tolerant of individual choices that are androgynous or sex-reversed, and women take an active part in the governance of the community. Thus, under ideal conditions, most kibbutz women opt for a clearly "feminine" identity, making far more traditional choices than most feminists would care to accept. To us, this indicates the great complexity of both pluralism and the gender dimension.

11

AGE: A DIMENSION OF SOCIAL HETEROGENEITY

> To everything there is a season, and a time to every purpose under the heaven; A time to be born, and a time to die; A time to plant and a time to pluck up that which is planted; A time to break down, and a time to build up; A time to mourn, and a time to dance; A time to get, and a time to lose; A time to keep, and a time to cast away; A time to keep silent, and a time to speak; A time to love, and a time to hate; A time of war, and a time of peace. (Ecclesiates 3:1-8)

Age is a dimension of difference and heterogeneity in every human society. From a sociological point of view, society is *age-stratified,* divided into age groups differing in interests and political power. From a psychological point of view, identity changes as persons advance in age. Despite the consistency and continuity of the individual's personality throughout life, members of any given age group share particular concerns, values, and life perspectives in a way that makes them similar to each other and different from other age groups.

People are expected to act according to their age, "to be" in an age-appropriate way: We often hear people exhorted to "act your age!" or described as "precocious," "acting like an old man," or "falling behind." Most people develop and maintain appropriate and functional age identities, shifting successfully from one age identity to another as they advance in age.

A person is similar in many ways to other persons of the same age, sharing roles and tasks, duties and privileges, major concerns and ways of dealing with life issues, salient values, and the ways the age group is perceived and stereotyped by others. The person is different from persons of other ages and also different from what he or she was like at a younger age.

As a dimension of societal heterogeneity, age is as salient as race, ethnicity, religion, gender, and social class. But age is different from all other dimensions in that it is *transient*: Every person moves from one age identity to another and cannot remain in any age group for long. (Attempts to "stay" in a particular age group are not viewed favorably in society). All other dimensions of the social self have a high level of constancy: Some cannot be changed at all (race, gender). Others (religion, profession) are changeable (usually for not more than one change), yet they remain constant for most people. Throughout their lifetimes, persons experience a wide range of age identities. However, there is another kind of constancy in age shifts: the entire membership of an age group shifts *together* from one age to another. Thus, transiency of age identity is accompanied by a constancy of age group membership.

When sociologists discuss age stratification in society (Riley, Johnson, & Foner, 1972), they refer to the unequal distribution of power and wealth among age strata; some age groups (typically in the upper-middle age range) are wealthier and more powerful, controlling and influencing other age groups. They also refer to the fact that many societal customs and institutions are "age-segregated," limited to particular age groups (the school, the military, retirement age, voting age, age of legal dependence on parents, and so on).

Sociologists distinguish between the terms "age group" and "cohort" (or generation). "Cohort" identifies not only people's age, but also the historical period in which they lived. Being in the 20-year-old age group during the depression of the 1930s was quite different from being in the 20-year-old group during the Vietnam era in the 1960s. Riley et al. (1972) argue that the sociological investigation of age stratification should integrate age group analysis and cohort analysis.

Exercise 11.1

To acquire a more personal meaning of the age-cohort distinction, compare your experiences as a 16-year-old with those of today's 16-year-olds. You will probably discover both age similarities and cohort dissimilarities

---

Age differences and age stratification have always existed in human societies, but particular factors have made age-related problems more pointed and complex in contemporary society (Mead, 1970). Earlier generations dealt with age in a more institutionalized and orderly manner. Their society was based on "tradition" that explicitly determined the normative patterns for age-appropriate behavior. The structure of traditional society provided the elders with more wisdom and more influence. The structure of the extended family, the clan, and the tribe further strengthened the base of age authority. The passages from one age stratum to another (from childhood to adulthood, for example) were ritualized and given high significance as symbolic "marker events" (initiation rites or rites of passage) in people's lives.

Modern society has largely lost this institutionalized order in its treatment of age. There has been a dramatic decline in the power of tradition, and patterns of age socialization have ceased to be as clear and explicit. Age authority has largely disappeared. American society is by and large a "youth culture" that appreciates youthfulness and ignores the old. The media, particularly television, rarely portray the old as carrying authority and wisdom (although this has begun to change in recent years.)

Swift technological development often leaves older persons rather obsolete, lacking up-to-date knowledge and skills, while the young become more knowledgeable and competent. At the same time, societal affluence and the great advances in medicine have reduced the rate of mortality, leaving society with growing proportions of older citizens.

The traditional family structure is breaking in modern society, and socialization is no longer carried out in a multigenerational context. Watered-down versions of initiation rites (commencement, bar mitzvah, confirmation) are still performed as traditional rituals, but they are not perceived and experienced as crucial life events that mark significant transitions.

Benne (1976) discussed the breaking down of age authority. The future has become highly ambiguous and unpredictable, and adults cannot lean on their past experiences as a basis for authority. The future must, in a way, be invented, and young people must participate in determining the future. In fact, they are better equipped than their elders to shape the future. Therefore, authority and power shift into the hands of the younger generation, forming the political structure of the "youth culture."

Age Identity and Psychological Development in Adult Life

Psychological theorizing about adult life development has become prevalent in recent years. In the past, most psychological formulations of developmental life stages (such as those of Freud, Sullivan, and Piaget) were limited to childhood and youth, with "adulthood" being the *last* stage. Nobody argued that adults do *not* change or develop, but the underlying assumption was that changes in adulthood are idiosyncratic and do not follow a systematic developmental scheme. In recent years—when the large boom of post-World War II psychologists have reached middle and late adulthood—systematic psychological theorizing about development in adult life has begun to emerge.

Today, the prevalent conception in the psychology of age is that people pass through a life cycle consisting of normal and expectable stages from childhood through various phases of adulthood and old age. These stages and substages are delineated quite accurately, showing relatively low variability among people as to when they emerge and what issues they present. Persons do differ from each other in how they resolve the inherent problems of each stage (getting divorced or remaining married, making or not making career shifts, and so on). This general conception is shared today by philosophers, sociologists, and psychologists (Erickson, 1950, 1959, 1965, 1968; Pressey & Kuhlen, 1957; Ortega Y Gasset, 1958; Clausen, 1972; Parsons & Platt, 1972; Neugarten, 1973; Sheehy, 1976; Levinson, Darrow, Klein, Levinson & McKee, 1978).

The central idea in this conception is that persons *change* as they pass from stage to stage. Despite the continuity in personal history, personality, abilities, and one's general life framework, one is not "the same person" in different stages. Those who perceive the person from outside may observe mostly the continuities, thinking that the person has not really changed. But the inner experience of most people is one of profound change in perspective, ways of thinking, concerns, and values. Sometimes one is not even capable of specifying how, exactly, one has changed, but one does feel strongly that one is not the same person one used to be.

CENTRAL CONCEPTS IN THE PSYCHOLOGY OF ADULT LIFE

In their influential book, *The Seasons of a Man's Life,* Levinson et al. (1978) developed the concept of *life structure*. We find this concept quite helpful in inquiry into age identity. Levinson et al. defined life structure as "the underlying pattern or design of a person's life at a given time." Each stage in adult life has its unique life structure, and a "transitional period" is a time when one life structure is terminated and the possibility for a new life structure is created. Life structure is a complex construct, integrating the internal experience of the self for that particular period with the experiences of one's interactions and transactions with the outer world. In self-inquiry, the life structure must be considered from three perspectives:

(1) *The person's sociocultural world.* The place the person occupies in the world and in the social context, in terms of social class, religion, ethnicity, family, polity, and occupational structure. Not all of these domains are relevant for a particular life structure, but some are always relevant. New life structures that the person will create may change the relative relevance of these domains.

(2) *Salient aspects of the self.* Central values, ideals, conflicts, traits and talents, and modes of feeling, thought, and action.

(3) *The person's participation in the world.* Transactions with the social environment that the person carried out through taking particular roles (citizen, worker, boss, friend, lover, rebel, and so forth).

The life structure can be described and analyzed through *choices* the person makes and through their consequences for the person. "The important choices in adult life have to do with work, family, friendships and love relationships of various kinds, where to live, leisure, involvement in religious, political and community life, immediate and long term goals" (Levinson et al., 1978, p. 43). In every life structure, particular components gain salience, and these reflect the values that are most significant to the person at that time.

The life structure is satisfactory to the person to the extent that it is suitable and rewarding, advancing the person in his or her "life enterprise." This can be best understood by introducing the concept of *developmental tasks*. In each period, the person faces specific tasks that establish the patterns of salience mentioned above. The life structure is centered on successfully completing these tasks, and the transition from one life structure to another is related to the emergence of new developmental tasks. The overall developmental task is to build and modify a life structure and realize it in a satisfactory way. In early adulthood, some of the major developmental tasks are to form and modify a "dream," to form and modify an occupation, to form an ideology and value orientation, to form mentoring relationships, to form mutual friendships, and to deal with the issues of love-marriage-family. In late adulthood, the overriding developmental task is to become "individuated," that is, to integrate internal polarities and reach a new balance, to experience pain and learn to live with limitations and unsolvable problems.

Levinson et al. defined a "period" or a "stage" by its life structure and developmental tasks and not by concrete events such as marriage or retirement. Events of the latter type were labeled "marker events," conceived as critical parts of a period, but they do not *define* a period. Marker events change the person's life conditions, and adapting to new conditions is a significant developmental task. For example, the marriage in itself will have a meaning at age 22 that differs from its meaning at age 45.

Exercise 11.2

Write down the major characteristics of your own present life structure. Use the three perspectives mentioned above—sociocultural world, salient aspects of the self, participation in the world—as well as other concepts such as "developmental tasks." Please pay special attention to the relationships between this life structure and your other significant socio-identities.

Other theorists share this conception of characterizing each stage in adult life by a central cluster of concerns that must be dealt with. Erikson (1950, 1959) viewed each stage as characterized by a conflict between two poles that is accompanied by anxiety (industry versus inferiority, identity versus confusion, intimacy versus isolation, generativity versus stagnation, integrity versus despair). For Erickson, going successfully through a life stage means that one has experienced the positive and the negative sides of the conflict, reconciled them, and integrated them into an attained construct (competence, ideology, love, production, wisdom, and the like).

Levinson et al. distinguished between "stable periods" and "transitional periods" in adult life. Each stable period is followed by a transitional period. Stable periods are devoted to establishing and maintaining a life structure. Transitional periods are crisis periods, when an earlier life structure is terminated and one goes through the pain and distress of having to create another life structure.

Schlossberg (1981) developed a theoretical model for analyzing adaptation to transition. She defined transition as "an event or a non-event that results in a change in assumptions about oneself and the world, and thus requires a corresponding change in one's behavior and relationships" (1981, p.5). In her model she examines every transition in terms of the role changes it entails; its source and timing, onset, and duration; its degree of stress; the support systems (intimate relationships, family unit, network of friends) and institutional supports available to the individual in the crisis; and the various characteristics of the person him or herself (sex, age, race, ethnicity, socio-economic status, value orientation, psychosocial competence, and previous experience with similar transitions). All these factors contribute, according to Schlossberg, to the person's "adaptation"—the move from being totally preoccupied with the transition to integrating the transition into one's life.

Most writers (including Jung, Erickson, and Levinson) stress the significance of the distinction between early adulthood and late adulthood. One of the critical periods described by Levinson was the "mid-life transition," or, to use its more popular name, the "mid-life crisis."

In early adulthood, one creates one's "life enterprise" and acts to realize that enterprise. The enterprise is one's direction in life, in terms of broad aspirations and specific goals to be attained. The life enterprise takes the form of a "ladder" of goals and aspirations: When one step is attained, the objectives of the next step become more urgent. The "dream" is the more mythical and elusive component of the life enterprise. It is one's personal myth, the vision of imagined possibilities that generates excitement and vitality. The young person has a developmental task of giving the dream greater definition and finding ways to live it out. Levinson et al. argued that almost all persons have a dream, though it may be modest or heroic, vaguely defined or clear, passionate or quiet, a source of inspiration or a source of conflict.

In late adulthood, this forward motion is changed. One must reappraise the ladder of goals and aspirations, modify the life enterprise, and rework the dream. One must search for a new "meaning" of previous urges. This is a period not of examining simply success or failure in attaining goals, but of examining and modifying the basic meaning of success, failure, the ladder, and the dream. The major developmental tasks of that period are integration and individuation—learning acceptance of self with strengths and weaknesses, learning to live with existential realities, learning to live with pain and suffering, and creating a new balance of existence that is more deeply satisfying. Becoming "wiser" is more significant at that stage than being "more successful."

Beyond adulthood lies the period of old age. Getting old confronts the person with a variety of painful problems and changes: having to retire, becoming less competent and less healthy, facing a physical and mental decline, having to limit one's scope of activities, and eventually facing disability and death.

The growing number of older people in America ("the graying of America") poses serious problems in terms of social policies, social services, and the maintenance of communities. Given the dominant "youth culture" orientation in America, the treatment of the old-age stratum has become a psychological problem as well; old people are beginning to perceive themselves as a unique minority group that is the victim of prejudice and discrimination.

But there is also another view of old age. The cultural mythology has not totally relinquished the view of old age as associated with wisdom, knowledge, understanding, richness of spirit, depth of soul, and the ability to accept pain and suffering. The wise man and the prophet, the apostle and the angel are all mythologically held to be old, and this image is not apt to disappear even in this age of modernization and youth-oriented technology.

Exercise 11.3

Now that you are familiar with some major ideas in the sociology of age stratification and the psychology of age, we suggest that you conduct an interview with an old person, preferably one you know well, such as a grandparent. In this interview try to focus on life stages and changes in adult life, asking the person various questions about how he or she has changed over the years and how things are different today from the way they used to be.

Age Differences in Racial,
Ethnic, and Gender Groups

Academic psychologists have usually theorized about the middle-class stratum of Western society, and their generalizations about "human nature" have described their conceptions of this segment of the population. In the case of developmental life stages, the generalizations of many writers (Freud, Levinson) were also limited to men. These theories describe stages of development in assumed life cycles that are not interrupted by major crises and are characterized by relative affluence and comfort.

But in Western society many people are not affluent and verbal, and they do not have the leisure to deal with their personal development or to develop in uninterrupted patterns. Poverty, illness, a variety of personal and familial problems, as well as societal events such as wars, crime, and natural disasters, influence the lives of numerous people and interrupt the smoothness of their adult psychological development.

AGE DIFFERENCES IN MINORITY GROUPS

Age differences and age identities in racial, ethnic, and religious minorities are influenced by a variety of factors. The issues that may have an influence on minority age identity include:

- The culture of the group and its conception of various age groups (respect for old people, stereotypes of the old as wise or as a hindrance, and so forth).

- The differences in life experiences between members of the different age groups. This issue is relevant for majority groups as well, but sometimes the differences are much sharper for minorities (such as holocaust survivors or old black people born to liberated slaves).

- The differences in level of acculturation to the majority culture and the variance in resources among the minority age groups in coping and competing in the majority culture. In a heterogeneous society, the various age groups differ greatly in their degrees of alienation and familiarity with the culture of the majority.

- Conflicts between minority age groups concerning the "cause" of the group and the appropriate modes of action in their pluralistic struggle.

- Sharpening of differences and internal conflicts among the minority age groups due to the group's minority status.

- Levels of optimism of various minority age groups with regard to their future (and, indirectly, their past as well).

- The entry point into adulthood and the range of expectations with regard to the person's continued development as a minority group member in the majority culture.

Even without being culturally different and victims of prejudice and discrimination, minority groups most often occupy the lower socioeconomic status positions—and poverty, low education, and their resultant limited possibilities in themselves influence adult development and age identity. "Development" in adulthood may depend on the person's assumed possibilities: that one has the option of choosing a lifestyle, that one has a variety of challenges and satisfactions, that one can afford to "have a crisis" and to "change," and that one is not bothered by more basic needs so as to be free to search for "meaning." Most poor and uneducated people simply do not have these assumed possibilities. Their age identities have a narrower range of possibilities, the challenges posed by the most concrete aspects of just being able to survive and to satisfy their most basic needs are overwhelming, and their adult development is not characterized by the existential search for meaning and spiritual satisfaction as described by most theorists. We believe that a central aspect of age transitions and age-related conflicts under conditions of extreme poverty is hopelessness: learning to cope with the sadness and despair of the realization that things cannot and will not change and that one is powerless to improve the chances of one's children as well.

AGE AND SEX

Early writings on development in adult life were male-oriented. They were based on the relatively fixed life "schedule" characterizing middle-class males in Western society (studying, taking the first job, getting married, and the like). But most writers did not explicitly limit their theories to men, and the universality of their theories was subtly assumed. Levinson et al.'s (1978) theory of adult development was explicitly limited to men, and readers were cautioned against careless generalization of the theory to females. (Levinson and his colleagues are involved at present in studying lifelong development of women at home and in corporate settings.)

Women's life schedules in contemporary society are less fixed and more complex than men's. Men can concurrently develop a family and a career without facing the dilemma of maintaining one at the expense of the other. Women face a serious dilemma, having to carry the major burdens of child-bearing and childrearing at the same time that they would invest most of their energies in developing an occupation and a satisfying career. Women resolve this dilemma in various ways, each having its price and implications with regard to developmental life stages (for example, postponing marriage or postponing career development). The biological limits of the age of fertility narrow women's options in ways that men do not experience. Sheehy (1976) described five choices and roles that create greater variation in women's adult life development: caregiver, either-or, integrators, never-married women, and transients.

It is generally assumed that psychological development in infancy and childhood is quite similar in most domains for boys and girls. There is no consensus with regard to adult life, whether men and women develop differently and become psychologically distinguished groups. Robert May (1980) claimed there are deep psychological differences between men and women, who develop differently in adulthood. In a somewhat less conclusive way, Block (1971) described personality types that differ considerably for adult males and females. It is impossible to determine whether such differences are "cultural" and would disappear with the changing roles of women in society or whether there are innate and unchangeable differences. Regardless of what one wishes to believe about this issue, there is no doubt that in current Western society the adult life development of women is not identical to that of men.

Three decades ago, the major "mid-life crisis" discussed in the literature was women's menopause—the biological crisis marking the end of fertility and its accompanying manifestations of psychological stress. At that time, men were not viewed as experiencing such a crisis. Today, the term "mid-life crisis" is detached from the physical domain and discussed in the framework of male-oriented theories. Some writers may eventually raise the question whether women (who do not share men's fixed life schedule) have a mid-life crisis at all.

Interage Conflict

Age is a dimension of difference in society. It determines social roles and groups of membership. Age groups differ in "age-identity": in behavior, norms, concerns, and value orientation. Voluntary social interaction tends to be largely age-segregated; people prefer to spend time and socialize with their age group peers when they have the choice, because of the psychological similarities within the age group. Involuntary social interaction—in the family, in school, and at work—tends to cross age boundaries, forcing people of varied ages to interact with each other. These age-heterogeneous types of interactions are the major arenas of interage conflict in society.

Interage conflict has the same characteristics as other intergroup conflicts: tension, envy, competition for power and control, need to maintain self-image, exclusivity, polarization, stereotypy, and prejudice. But interage conflict is often more implicit than other intergroup conflicts. Unlike the explicit struggle between women and men, between black and white, between Catholic and Protestant, the struggling young and old are not always defined in age terms. In the 1960s, the "generation gap" *was* defined explicitly as an interage conflict, but in other historical periods the interage conflict has been disguised as a political or an ideological conflict (between conservatives and radicals, innovators and technocrats, a change orientation and a maintenance orientation). The disguise probably stems in part from the transiency of the age dimension. Being female, black, or Catholic is fixed characteristic, but being young or middle-aged is not a fixed membership, as people move from one age identity to another. It might therefore be more comfortable to identify the locus of conflict not in age itself but in an (age-related) issue or worthy cause.

THE "GENERATION GAP"

In the 1960s, the term "generation gap" gained salience in American culture (Coleman, 1961; Keniston, 1967, 1971; Kalish, 1969; Feuer, 1969; Mead, 1970). The gap between generations is as old as human civilization, but it is attributed to particular characteristics in each historical period. As McNeil and Rubin (1977) pointed out, the youngsters of the 1920s rebelled against puritanism, those of the 1930s rebelled against capitalism, in the 1950s they wanted to have more power in the political system, and in the 1960s they wanted to drop out of the system and/or destroy it. The intensity and explicitness of the interage conflict in the 1960s particularly attracted the attention of sociologists and other behavioral scientists, making the term "generation gap" become popular in that period. The protest movement against the war in Vietnam and against the middle-class establishment, the political and ideological alienation, the tendency to "drop out," and the use of drugs reached crisis proportions in the late 1960s and early 1970s.

The "generation gap" is a continual state of conflict between the young and the middle-aged. The young defy the entrenched position of the older generation, challenging their perspectives, ideology, and patterns of action. It is a conflict between the "youth culture" (Mead, 1970) and the "establishment." Like other intergroup conflicts, this conflict is characterized by an abundance of mutual stereotypes (restless and searching versus established and affluent) and prejudices (irresponsible, hedonistic, unrealistic, disrespectful, and naive versus corrupt, materialistic, over the hill, and reactionary). Each group believes that the other group "does not know what life is all about." Like other intergroup situations, the groups show lack of tolerance for each other's positions, and tension escalates quite readily. Essentially, this is a conflict between interest groups, a power struggle that keeps repeating itself with every cohort—some age groups growing up to demand more power, other age groups trying to keep and maintain the power they have already attained.

An interesting feature of the generation gap is that it is *expected* to take place. If the young generation does not rebel at all, educators and parents begin to wonder "What's wrong with this generation?" The older generation glorifies the memories of its own rebellion, but that does *not* make it more tolerant in dealing with the rebellion of the younger generation.

Adelson (1970) argued that there was no particular generation gap in the 1960s—that the literature about the generation gap was "pop sociology," an illusion shared by young and old about a particular and special conflict. We do not share Adelson's view: In the 1960s the anxiety about the possibility of being drafted to fight a political war of no ideological consequence and the power of one age group to force this unpleasant option on another age group probably contributed to the natural alienation between the generations.

In this struggle between the younger and the older generation, both sides experience a high level of *ambivalence*. The older generation views its own past nostalgically as "the good old days" and bemoans the fact that "nothing remains as it used to be." They also view nostalgically their own generation gap with their elders. Youth is admired, and the joys and innocence of the young are idealized. One wants to be young again—in body, in spirit, and in open horizons of potentials and possibilities. However, the middle-aged view the younger generation as naive, lacking in perspective, obstinate, and often downright stupid. Despite their own past, the older generation cannot understand why the young refuse to learn from their elders' experience and accumulated wisdom.

Members of the younger generation are also ambivalent. They wish to be "adults" in terms of power and control over societal resources; they wish to be taken seriously and treated like adults; yet they do not wish to take on the responsibilities and duties that "adulthood" entails. They enjoy their rebellious stance and are not yet confined by the limitations of the social realities their elders must face.

Exercise 11.4

Try to recall the circumstances and specific events of a "generation gap" conflict in which you were personally involved. If the conflict was resolved, analyze its entire course of development and its resolution. If the conflict has not yet been resolved, try to take the point of view of the other side, analyzing what would be necessary to resolve the conflict from the other's point of view.

It is understandable that the young cannot readily empathize with their elders. The older generation is in a life stage that the young have not yet experienced, and it is not easy to take an alien point of view. But why is it so difficult for the old to empathize with the young? Why are parents and teachers unable to understand the rebellion of the young, to show empathy and take their point of view, and to be more effective in dealing with the conflict? Haven't they gone through the same experience themselves? In fact, adults cannot readily empathize with the young, and we believe that this inability reflects the profound depth of developmental changes in personality. As people grow older they change in deep and significant ways, and memories are distorted and glorified. They no longer "know" their former, young selves; they are very different from what they used to be. But since the change is gradual rather than sudden, they sometimes think that they have not changed at all and are therefore intolerant of the young for being "different."

AGE-RELATED POWER CONFLICTS

Since society is age-stratified (Riley, Johnson & Foner, 1972), age groups struggle with each other for power and influence in all relevant arenas: the political system, the work market, the family, the educational system, and the community-at-large. The younger generation tries to penetrate into the "system" and attain power. Throughout their life span, the young have been controlled, shaped, and "dominated" by their parents' generation. Now, on the threshold of adulthood, they try to assert their independence and gain influence and power, particularly since they believe they can do a better job than their elders. But those in power are not willing to share it with another group, particularly not with those who lack wisdom and experience and who have not yet paid their "dues" to society.

On the other side of the age continuum, the group that approaches old age also experiences age-related power conflict, and their experience is quite painful. Unlike the young, who do not have power *yet* and who are struggling to attain it, the old group is losing power they once used to have, knowing they will not have it anymore. They are pushed out of their positions by the middle adult age group, they become technologically obsolete, and they must retire and relinquish their power. Their wisdom and experience often goes unappreciated, and decades of work and commitment are symbolically reduced to a gold watch delivered in an empty ritual. All of that occurs at the time that members of this generation must also deal with their physical decline and the issue of approaching death.

Some changes have been observed in the United States in the last few years with regard to age-related power conflict, namely, the emergence of old people in organized, struggling political interest groups. The "graying of America" has been accompanied by the appearance of the Gray Panthers. Old people have become politically active, forming lobbies to assert their particular interests as a "minority group," especially in the areas of urban living, health care, and social security. Organized in groups such as the American Association of Retired Persons and the National Association of Retired Teachers, they attempt to influence the political system to guarantee their rights and to satisfy their special needs.

In traditional, preindustrial society, old age was associated with the power of leadership and wisdom. But in the rapidly changing technological society the balance of power tilts toward the younger age groups, while the old become rapidly obsolete. As this trend continues, men and women in their fifties fight for power against those in their forties, and eventually those in their forties have to protect their positions against the pushing thirties. But the images of the wisdom and knowledge (and therefore power) of the old die hard: The most popular movies of the late 1970s were of the *Star Wars* type, which presented the cultural myth of the omnipotent power and moral superiority of the old, traditional, pretechnological Jedi knights. These movies transmitted the implicit message that young people approaching adulthood would "do better" by aligning themselves with the old against the dominant middle-age group.

AGE CONFLICTS IN THE FAMILY

The family is a basic social unit, a societal institution that is by definition age-heterogeneous. The major role of the family is to "produce" and social-ize the young, so that the foundation of the family lies upon its age-heterogeneous functions. Some writers see the family as the *source* of age conflict in society, while others view the family as functional in *reducing* age-related social cleavage (Foner, 1972). We believe that both views are probably correct.

The problems of pluralism in society are similar to the problems of pluralism in the family. The family is a *mirror of society,* and age is the central dimension creating its heterogeneity. It is through experiences in the family context that one attains one's initial and primary education in dealing with problems of similarity and difference, authority (Benne, 1943, 1970), political power, minority status, values, and ideology.

The family has an a priori political structure and a clear distribution of power, and it is the arena of continuous "political struggles" of various types. Some of these struggles take place within an age group (between the parents, for example), but most are interage conflicts (between children and parents). The parents' role is to raise the young and to take care of them until they can reach independence and self-sufficiency. But attainment of independence and self-sufficiency comes at the expense of the parents, since they are, by definition, the first victims of the assertiveness of the young, becoming the "enemy" and the "oppressors" in this intergroup conflict. Parents are torn between the wish to see their children grow and attain independence and assertiveness, and their wish not only to protect their children, but to form and mold them in their own image and prevent the children's rebellion and some of the inevitable age-related mistakes and pains. Parents are also angry and prone to fall into the polarization of conflict when their children rebel against them. The conflict is always related in part to the acceptance of the parents' value system and ideological perspective by the children, as part of a desired cultural, religious, ethnic, professional, or class "continuity."

At particular ages, a direct and dramatic age conflict becomes normative. A peer group of same-age adolescents then provides support to all its members, establishing the value system of that youth culture and developing effective strategies for dealing with parents. At other ages, there is a relative decrease in age conflict, up to the point when the parents' generation becomes dependent upon their children's generation.

Exercise 11.5

Examine your own family and your personal experiences with age heterogeneity and age conflict in the family. What were the major issues on which the conflict was focused? In tracing the historical development of this age conflict, can you identify the particular strategies that were useful? What were the main things you learned from these experiences? What will (did) you do differently when your children rebelled against you?

"Young" Radicals and "Old" Conservatives

It is widely held that adolescents and young adults are more radical, restless, leftist, and demanding of immediate change, while older people are more moderate and conservative, sometimes tending to be reactionary and even bigoted. In line with this prevalent image, we consistently described inter-age conflict as "the radical young against the conservative old" and *not* vice versa.

This view of young and old in society is stereotypic, but this stereotype seems to be quite valid, and evidence from a variety of sources supports this widely held notion that the young are more radical and the old more conservative (see Riley, Johnson, & Foner, 1972). Even valid stereotypes are overgeneralizations, and one must remember that not all old people are conservative, nor are all younger people radical, but this generalization describes true differences between the means of two age-based distributions. (Indeed, numerous historical instances have been recorded showing younger people supporting conservative causes and bigoted leaders and older people supporting more liberal causes. Some old persons, out of the occupational status "rat race," and feeling no need to be overcautious, become radicalized, at times siding with radical adolescents who have not yet "entered the system.")

The pattern of gradually shifting from radicalism to moderation to conservatism throughout the adult life cycle seems to be repeated in generation after generation. It is expressed in a great variety of ways: more reactionary patterns of voting among older citizens, greater resistance to new drugs on the part of older doctors, greater resistance to innovative instructional methods by older teachers, and so forth. In the 1950s and 1960s the *Commentary* was the voice of liberal, somewhat radicalized, anti-establishment intellectuals. As its editors and authors grew older in the 1970s, *Commentary* began shifting toward the right wing, from the "new left" to the "new right." Today, its editor, well in his upper middle age, describes himself as a "neoconservative."

A biologically based explanation would view attitudes as a reflection of physiological states. The young are bursting with energy and capable of excess activity. They enjoy being playful and find changing circumstances challenging and exciting. Adults are more settled down and economical, having learned to conserve their energies and use them efficiently. They are less excitable and curious, and they value moderation. Old organisms must face their physical decline and growing ridigity, when they are no longer able to do what they have been used to doing. They are invested in maintaining what already exists, fearing that new circumstances will tax their energies more than they can afford.

An economic explanation (see, for example, Parsons, 1959; Lipset, 1963;

Foner, 1972) would view old people's conservatism as a strategy for protecting their assets. Most people accumulate various assets in their lifetimes: money, property, reputation, prestige, and position. It would be reasonable for them to adopt attitudes that value, and guard, these advantages. Radical changes in society could rob older people of these assets and advantages; therefore they adopt a conservative, antichange stance to protect their assets. (One problem with this theory is that poor people who have not accumulated assets show a similar tendency toward conservatism.)

A modified sociological explanation (Foner, 1972) replaces "protection" with "societal commitment." Older people have made a lifelong investment in society and its existing institutions: They have learned to function in it, they have contributed to its maintenance, they have gained experience and have gotten used to its shortcomings, and they have learned to derive satisfactions in the existing society. Therefore, they become committed to keeping society the way it is and maintaining its stability. The younger generation, on the other hand, is "in a hurry." They are not committed to society and its institutions and had not received substantial satisfactions from it. They are more aware of society's shortcomings and less patient with them. They know that their youthful "blooming" is limited in duration, and they need to change society quickly so as to maximize their gratification while they are still young enough to enjoy it.

Psychological components might be added to the notions of asset protection and societal commitment. Through lifelong accumulation of experience, older adults have learned that "the more things change, the more they stay the same." They have witnessed the futility of sweeping changes, and they know that radical change does not make problems disappear. Therefore, they know that a radical view cannot be too beneficial, while it can become very destructive.

Psychological development in adult life leads older people to become more mature and wise. Maturity and wisdom include the loss of naivete and the avoidance of hastiness and rash action. People learn to respect internal stability and value small, slow, and gradual gratifications. Thus, according to

---

Exercise 11.6

This exercise should be conducted in a small group of learners, preferably of varying ages. Every one of you is instructed to draw a line on a sheet of paper or on the board. The line represents your life. Now put a dot on your line, representing where you feel you are right now in your life. Your assignment is to explore your own line and the lines and dots made by other people, trying to make meaning of these representations in light of what you read in this chapter.

this view, the growing conservatism is not defensive in nature, but rather an active, mature, and wise choice.

A simpler psychological notion would emphasize the *normative* nature of holding particular attitudes at particular ages. Regardless of the cause, young people are expected to be radical and older people are expected to be conservative. By holding age-appropriate attitudes, people simply fulfill the expectations they have learned, and they are rewarded for that by society. Mark Twain was quoted to be suspicious of people under twenty who are not radical and revolutionary, and of people after middle-age who are not conservative. "No life is perfect that has not been lived youth in feeling, manhood in battle, and old age in meditation" (Wilfrid Scawen Blunt, in *The Perfect Life*).

12

SOCIAL ROLES AND ROLE GROUPS

Roles and Social Behavior

Mother, student, critic, lover, joker, cook, driver, jock, expert, waiter, philosopher, sibling, inventor, policeman, senator, victim, doctor, boss, professional athlete, adolescent, arbitrator, grandparent. All of the foregoing are labels of social roles—positions that people occupy in the social system, accompanied by expectations as to how they should behave.

This chapter focuses on social roles that, like socio-identities, are determinants of similarity and difference in social interaction. Socio-identities are central (and relatively few) clusters in the social self that are mostly predetermined biosocially. Social roles are many and more varied, allowing more choice and flexibility of individual manifestations. Every person holds a large number of social roles, shifting constantly among roles in everyday conduct.

Most social behaviors are enacted as "role behaviors," that is, persons act, react, and interact in a framework of various and varying roles. Socio-identities, values, beliefs, and attitudes are expressed through specific roles and specific role behaviors. Perception of others and interaction with them always take place within a framework of social roles, the roles defining "who" the person is at a particular instance, how the person should be perceived, and how the person is expected to behave.

Roles are sets of expectations, rights, obligations, and patterns of predictable behaviors that persons employ when occupying particular positions. A "position" is a recognized shared attribute, behavior (such as playing basketball), or task (say, directing traffic). In other words, "role" refers to an identifiable group of people acting in predictable ways. Roles are also *labels* that people use to characterize themselves and others, and expectations about roles are generally shared. People readily identify the roles others play (the doctor about to examine you, the lover about to kiss you) and accommodate their behavior to create complementary interactions if they so wish.

Roles are functional like other social groupings: By partitioning people into clearly identifiable groups that perform as expected, they reduce informational overload, define situations clearly, minimize ambiguity and uncertainty, and maximize predictability. Roles define group boundaries and crystallize adaptable patterns of social behavior; in short, they function as organizers of the social environment. Also, like other social groupings, the cost of this functional consistency of social roles is rigidity and distortion—a loss of fluidity and flexibility in role definitions, role behavior, and social interaction.

Exercise 12.1
A Second Look at "Who Am I?"

This exercise takes you back to an exercise suggested in Chapter 1. You were asked then, and you are asked again now, to write as many short answers to the question, "Who am I?" as you can. Try to write one- or two-word labels or very short descriptive sentences.

Please do not read further until you have completed the task.

In Chapter 1, this exercise was used to focus your awareness on similarities and differences, group affiliations, and gaps between self-perception and perception by others. At this point, the intent of the exercise is to focus your attention on social roles and distinguish between roles and other group-related terms.

Please group your responses to the question "WHO AM I?" in the following categories:

(1) responses labeling your socio-identities;
(2) responses identifying your social roles (positions you occupy in your social setting, such as student or sibling);
(3) adjectives describing your values, attitudes, and beliefs;
(4) adjectives describing your personality traits and attributes; and
(5) other categories.

(Please note that the same response may be classified in more than one category).

Now, focus your attention on the category of social roles, and add to the list every role you consider yourself as occupying in your present life, even if less frequently than other roles.

Please keep your responses available for further analysis as you continue reading this chapter.

Reference Groups and
Membership Groups

As mentioned, social roles define groups and boundaries between groups. In the social-psychological literature, the concept "role" has been inseparable from "groups," and most writers on role theory base their discussion of roles on earlier conceptions of norms, reference groups, and membership groups (Hyman, 1942; Stouffer, 1949; Newcomb, 1950; Kelley, 1952; Merton & Kitt, 1950; Merton, 1957).

A membership group is a group to which one actually belongs. A reference group is a group to which one wishes to belong, to which one relates one's attitudes, or which one employs as a basis for comparison and self-appraisal. A membership group is an actual group, and membership can be experienced as emotionally positive, neutral, or negative. Reference groups are more abstract and idyllic, sometimes existing as clear groups only in imagination. A reference group is usually experienced as emotionally positive (only a few writers, such as McNeil and Rubin, 1977, have made use of the term in a negative way, describing a group with which one does not wish to identify and therefore adopts opposite attitudes as a "negative reference group").

Kelly (1952) distinguished between a reference group in which the individual seeks to gain or maintain *acceptance* and one that the person uses to define an abstract *standard of excellence*. The first type, a "normative reference group," involves conformity to the group's attitudes, assimilation of its values, and affiliation with its members. The second, a "comparative reference group," involves an internal standard of how one wishes to be rather than an actual membership in a real group. Seeking to be elected to office, being awarded a prize for service to the group, and being invited to serve on a board of directors of an important company or to the exclusive parties of the "jet set" are examples of the first type, while being an honest person, keeping impeccable table manners when one eats alone, or "thinking good of people" are examples of the second type. A given reference group can serve for the person both the normative and comparative functions or only one of the two.

There are four hypothetical combinations of reference and membership groups, presented in Figure 12.1. Merton (1957), who analyzed the considerations involved in people's choices of reference groups, gave special attention to reference groups that are nonmembership groups.

As can be seen in the figure, the most harmonious situation is when the same group serves as both a membership group and a reference group. "Involuntary membership" describes a case in which a person is a member of a particular group (ethnic, military, gender, or the like) that he or she does not accept as a reference group. On the other hand, when the person is not, or cannot be, a member of his or her reference group, the situation is one of

	Nonmembership Group	Membership Group
Reference group	WISH	HARMONY
Nonreference group	ALIENATION	INVOLUNTARY MEMBERSHIP

Figure 12.1:   Hypothetical Combination of Reference and Membership

"wish." The fourth cell, nonreference and nonmembership, describes maximal dissimilarity and "alienation." In that case, the person is not a member of a particular group nor does he or she wish to use that group as reference. Including this cell in the diagram, we had in mind not only the great variety of groups of nonmembership and nonreference about which a person has neutral feelings, but, more significant, those groups about which the person feels strongly negative, to which he or she objects as potential groups of membership and reference.

The phenomenon of "self-hate" would probably be associated with the "involuntary membership" cell in this model. Prejudice and discrimination would probably be employed by groups sensing themselves in the "harmony" cell, against those they consider to be in the "alienation" cell.

Central Concepts in Role Theory

"Role theory" is an aggregate of terms and concepts that have become household words among educated and socially conscious people. The concepts we present were derived from various authors, including Goffman (1959), Secord and Beckman (1964), Biddle and Thomas (1966), and Sarbin and Allen (1969). For application of these concepts to your own self-inquiry, it is suggested that you pick three or four of your central roles, and for each of the concepts to be discussed, jot down some notes to illustrate how this concept relates and applies to your own experiences.

"ACTOR" AND "TARGET" IN ROLE BEHAVIOR

The term "role" is taken from the world of theater, where actors assume particular roles and perform them in front of an audience. In his analysis of the presentation of self in everyday life, Goffman (1959) used theater-related terms such as "parts", "acts", and "routines". Other writers tried to limit the analogy between theater and "life", suspecting that people might react negatively to the characterization of real-life role behavior as "putting on an act".

Role behavior involves two parties—the person who enacts the role, and the "receptor" of this behavior (also called "the target", "the audience", or simply "the other".) Role behavior can be examined from the viewpoint of the actor or from the viewpoint of the other, yielding quite disparate observations. In your application exercise, try to identify instances where you are required to be mostly an actor and instances where you are required to serve as the recipient. How do these experiences differ from each other?

ROLE EXPECTATIONS

Both the actor and the audience have role expectations, which determine to a large extent actual role behaviors and the ways people interpret and react to them. In fact, role expectations are so strong and prevalent that people can readily identify roles enacted by others, much as they can enact various roles without preparation. Young children can easily take a variety of roles, "knowing" implicitly their role expectations.

Exercise 12.2

In this exercise you can apply the model in Figure 12.1 to your own groups of reference and membership. Please prepare an enlarged diagram and fill in the names of your own groups that fit in each of the four cells.

You can now analyze (alone or with a group of readers who have filled in their own diagrams) the personal antecedents of your division of groups and examine how you view and relate to people belonging to groups in each of your four cells.

Role expectations have anticipatory and normative elements: the anticipatory element is the ability to predict what will happen; the normative element is the prescription of what "should" happen. Role expectations vary in their levels of clarity: Sometimes they are extremely clear and explicit; at other times they are vague and ambiguous. The clarity of role expectations is higher for roles that are more formal and demanding, for roles that are enacted more frequently, and for roles that might carry more severe repercussions for violation of role expectations. As you do Exercise 12.2, please describe specific role expectations, comparing them to those provided by other participants for similar roles.

ROLE DEMANDS, NORMS, AND SANCTIONS

Some, but not all, role expectations are "role demands." A role expectation becomes a role demand when it is highly normative and has clear consequences and sanctions. When a role expectation is not normative (that is, when violation of that expectation carries no serious consequence) its function is predictive rather than prohibitive. Role demands may at times be very strict (as in the changing of the guard in London), but more often they are less explicit. Nevertheless, strict sanction and punishment can be invoked even if role demands are ambiguous. This is particularly true for role interactions involving a power differential: superior-subordinate relations, teacher-student relations, and the like. The role of student, for instance, has many unclear demand elements, yet compliant students are amply rewarded, while violators of the implicit demands of the student role may be severely punished. In doing Exercise 12.2, identify role demands as distinguished from role expectations, and examine various consequences of role-appropriate and role-inappropriate behavior that you have experienced.

ROLE SKILLS

A wide array of cognitive, emotional, and motoric skills are involved in role interaction. The ability "to act" is not necessarily the most important skill; perceiving nuances of the actor's role behavior and being able to take the actor's point of view are as crucial for effective interaction as the acting ability. Thus, both transmission and reception, encoding and decoding role skills are important. In Exercise 12.2, try to trace and describe general and specific role skills, and examine their effects on particular events that you have experienced.

ROLE PERFORMANCE

This concept shifts attention from the prerequisites (expectations, demands, skills) and the products (norm and sanction) of role situations to the actual performance of the role itself. In spite of the relative stability in role expectations and role evaluation, there is great variability among people in role performance. That variability stems from several sources: (1) Individuals differ in levels of involvement and preemptiveness of particular roles. Role performance may vary from noninvolvement to ecstasy or bewitchment (Sarbin & Allen, 1969). (2) People vary in their perceptions of role expectations and role prescriptions. There are many different ways a role such as "good parent" or "good teacher" can be enacted. (3) People differ from each other in behavioral style and personality, so that the same role expectations lead to a varied range of performances. In your Exercise 12.2, compare your own role performance with the performances of others who are enacting similar roles.

ROLE EVALUATION

Role evaluation is the retrospective examination of role performance, which is strongly influenced by the person's values. In role evaluation, the examination includes role expectations and role demands, norms and sanctions, the social setting, the actual role performance, and the outcomes of the role interaction.

ROLE CONFLICT

Probably the best-known term from role theory, "role conflict," refers to several kinds of conflict. One type is *intrarole conflict,* when elements within the same role contradict or exclude each other (as when "good parents" are strict with their child, thereby hurting the child's feelings). Another type is *interrole conflict,* when the demands of different roles clash with each other, so that effective performance of one role comes at the expense of another role—in terms of commitment (such as the conflict of a student-athlete), conflicting interests (the professor's roles as teacher and scientist), or conflicting values (loyalty to a friend who has acted immorally).

Due to the multiplicity of roles in every person's life and the internal complexity of most roles, the experience of role conflict is very common. Most people become quite adept in dealing with their role conflicts, developing strategies for resolving, or at least relieving, the tension of their role conflicts. In Exercise 12.2, first describe some of the role conflicts you have experienced and then examine your particular ways of dealing with role conflicts

ROLE LEARNING

The learning of social roles is the essence of socialization and enculturation, a long, complex, and most implicit process. Almost none of the person's roles is taught explicitly. Some roles are learned in a trial-and-error fashion, the consequences of one's behavior serving as informational feedback for future conduct. Other roles are adopted from role models, picked up vicariously by observing others, made up piece by piece by utilizing various sources, or even invented by the individual. Society provides many types of stimuli that facilitate the development of roles (media, folklore, literature, and so on), but these influences are unfocused, and role learning can rarely be attributed to one identifiable source. In your application exercise, try to trace the various sources involved in your learning of a particular role.

Inquiry Into Roles and Role Systems

Family and work constitute the two major "occupations" for adults, and people spend the highest proportions of time and mental energy in enacting their family and vocational roles. Freud capsulated his view of mental health as "the ability to love and work."

Family and vocational roles are enacted in *role systems*—social organizations of various role holders, some complementary and others conflicting with each other. To understand a given role fully, inquiry must encompass the entire system within which that role is enacted.

In this section we provide guidelines for inquiry into a major role and the social system in which it is enacted. A "major role" is one (such as "family role") that can be broken into several more specific roles (father, husband, sibling, uncle, son) and a series of highly specific "miniature roles" (strict father, tender husband, sexist husband, generous uncle, miserly uncle).

We recommend that you focus the suggested inquiry on your vocational role. If you do not yet have a clear professional role, we recommend that you focus your inquiry on your professional *aspirations*. Try to imagine and project your professional role and its role system, taking information from various sources to create that picture. Another possibility (if applicable) is to investigate the role of "student" and the role system (college) in which it is enacted. Finally, you can also focus your inquiry on your family role.

The suggested inquiry into roles and role systems can be most effective in a group discussion by a relatively homogeneous small group (2-5 participants). Using the following guidelines, the discussants formulate their personal data, sharing it with other members and analyzing the emerging issues through contrast and comparison.

ROLE DEFINITION AND EXPECTATIONS

Labeling the Roles. We mentioned previously that a major role is divided into several roles and numerous miniature roles. Therefore, the first task is to list the various labels and sublabels of the role you investigate. Roles can be perceived as concentric circles, their views changing as a function of the perceiver's psychological distance from the role holder. For instance, the role "doctor" is viewed differently by supermarket buyers and by patients, administrators, nurses, and other doctors within the hospital. For the doctor's colleagues, the label "doctor" is meaningless, and they need to know exactly "what kind of doctor" he or she is.

Defining Role Expectations. To define role expectations, one must first decide *who* defines these expectations (the role holder or others) and whether the existing definitions (*if* they exist) are clear and explicit. Roles prescribe norms, but these are often implicit and latent. Sometimes clear norms are provided in some areas while in other areas norms remain latent. Sometimes explicit norms might be contradictory to implicit norms (as when a teacher states: "I want you to be original and write in this exam any interesting ideas that come to your mind," or a boss invites a subordinate "to give me honest and direct feedback").

Identifying the Appropriate Cognitive Style. A role is a psychological point of view, an orientation that determines how information will be processed and how it will lead to actual behavior. People adopt for each role an appropriate cognitive style: critical, analytical, intuitive, emotional, abstract, solution-oriented, and so forth. A teacher cannot deal with her own children as she does with students in class; books are read differently for exams and for pleasure; and the policeman's view of the street is different from the cabdriver's view. Many problems in communication are caused by misidentification of cognitive style. We believe that subroles within a major role would indicate different cognitive stances, much as the same specific role might include several different orientations.

ROLE PERFORMANCE

In trying to define and describe the nuances of role performance, please pay attention to the following issues. First, it is important to delineate the *range* of relevant role performances: What *must* happen and what *can* happen in performing the role? How much flexible "free play" do you have in performing the role (compared to others performing that role and compared to self-role performance on different occasions)? How unique can you be in role performance?

PATTERNS OF SOCIAL CONTACT

Formal and Informal Contact. Every role involves contact and interaction with other people, some sharing the same role and others carrying different and/or complementary roles in the role system. Therefore, to investigate roles, the patterns of social contact in the role system must be delineated: How much contact does the role entail? With whom is the contact made? What proportions of contact are voluntary and involuntary? formal and informal? central to the role or marginal? To what extent is the scenario of role contact predetermined and to what extent is it open and free-floating? To what extent is the interaction made with persons sharing the role or whose roles are complementary or adversary?

Power relations. Role interaction usually involves competition and power relations. Competition may be explicit or implicit, and often the parties collude (knowingly or unknowingly) to present a facade of equality and cooperation. Competition may be between holders of the same role as well as between holders of different roles. The power struggle is most evident when the role system stratifies various role holders in authority relationships. In investigating your role, we believe that the explication of power relations is of particular significance.

SOURCES OF CONFLICT IN ROLE BEHAVIOR

In the previous discussion of role conflict, we emphasized that role conflict can take place *within* a role as well as *between* roles. In this inquiry it is important that you examine not only the interpersonal conflicts the role entails, but also the internal role conflicts you experience, such as the conflict between two incompatible subroles that are part of the major role.

Another source of conflict concerns role evaluation and sanction: Who evaluates role performance and what is their power to sanction? To what extent can you become a victim of role evaluation? To what extent are the criteria for role evaluation clear and agreed upon? What would be the consequences for you of "good behavior" and "bad behavior"?

The Power of Social Roles

In this section we illustrate the power of roles in three areas: the power of roles in creating a mental perspective, their power "in the eyes of the beholder," and their power in making people cruel and inhuman. Some of the following examples are quite dramatic; they are by no means exceptional or unique.

THE POWER OF ROLES IN CREATING A MENTAL PERSPECTIVE

Folk wisdom has it that "the role makes the person." In a sense, the world is a stage, and people are actors on that stage. People believe, and wish to believe, that their actions are products of their thoughts, attitudes, and rational, free decisions. This is not incorrect, but the reverse is also true, and many thoughts and values are products of the roles people have enacted. Roles are powerful in that they create an entire mental perspective that role holders accept and adopt, often without questioning. This mental perspective has cognitive aspects (what and how to think), emotional aspects (how to feel towards whom), and behavioral aspects (norms and prescriptions). It has repeatedly been found in attitude change research (McGuire, 1969; Oskamp, 1977) that forcing persons to assume a position contrary to their views and making them advocate those views publicly can produce a noticeable and persistent attitude change.

Entering the new role involves shifting from one mental perspective to another. The concurrent appearance of two disparate perspectives provides material for slapstick comedy (for example, the psychiatrist who brought his little daughter to a psychiatric convention in the Mel Brooks movie, *High Anxiety*) or evokes tension or conflict that people are motivated to reduce (as when the college instructor discovers his mother attending his class for credit). When people must enter new, unfamiliar roles, they are tense until they learn the role and acquire the appropriate mental perspective. Most entering college or graduate school students remain tense until they figure out how to be a "student" in that particular place.

Over the years, we have taught and trained hundreds of school principals, superintendents, teachers, and other educators. We found that a substantial proportion of these responsible educators undergo a magic mental and behavioral metamorphosis when they enter the role of student: They do not listen; they pass notes and interrupt the instructor; they celebrate any opportunity to break or to cancel a session; and they become passive and dependent, wishing to be "spoon fed" and to avoid mental effort. Their mental perspective changes when they enter the new role and they "become" students.

In school, teachers often make use of the power of roles in creating a mental perspective: A common way of dealing with a disruptive child is to delegate a particularly prestigious and responsible role to that child. Teachers have a high rate of success in using such changes in role perspective to solve behavioral problems.

In politics, power relations between political parties dictate rather rigid and inflexible mental perspectives. In Britain, for example, when the Conservatives run the government, the Labour Party becomes "Her Majesty's Opposition," whose role it is to criticize the government and expose its mistakes. When the balance of power is tilted, yesterday's critics take a constructive perspective, while the ousted "doers" shift to the criticizing role. Similar shifts take place in any democracy, where political roles define and prescribe the mental perspective of the politicians. It takes a particularly grave crisis and a great threat from outside to make politicians abandon these ritualized roles and unite to act together.

When the Chrysler Corporation appointed a leader of the United Auto Workers union as a member of its board of directors several years ago, many eyebrows were raised—either to wonder how this person could function in his dual role or to admire the stroke of genius involved in this "neutralization" of a labor leader by the creation of an internal role conflict. In Israel, a university professor, expert in labor relations, was appointed several years ago to be the State Controller, responsible for labor negotiations with all branches of public service. In that capacity he received a delegation of professors who submitted a report on the attrition in professors' salaries in Israeli universities, demanding changes in their pay structure. The State Controller rejected the professors' demands altogether, although ironically he happened to be one of the authors of the professors' report (written in the previous year).

THE POWER OF ROLES IN THE
EYES OF THE BEHOLDER

Roles influence not only the mental perspective and behavior of their holders, but also the ways in which role holders are perceived and judged by others in their social environment. The power of roles is thus mediated through stereotypes of role holders and expectations about their attributes, behaviors, and performances. The accumulated research on expectancy bias and self-fulfilling prophecies (Rosenthal, 1971, 1976; Rosenthal & Rubin, 1978) shows that the expectations of the beholder can influence the behavior and performance of role holders. Babad (1979; Babad & Inbar, 1981; Babad, Inbar, & Rosenthal, 1982a, 1982b) showed that this is particularly true for "beholders" who are susceptible to stereotypically biasing information and who have power to influence role holders' behavior (as in a teacher-student relationship). Thus, perceptions not only can act as cognitive organizers, but also can become actual determinants of behavior.

A particularly dramatic illustration of the power of roles in the eyes of the beholder was provided by David Rosenhan (1973) in his article, "On Being Sane in Insane Places." Rosenhan and several co-workers gained admission to psychiatric wards of several hospitals by claiming to hear voices saying such things as "empty" or "hollow." Most of these pseudo-patients had been labeled schizophrenic. On entering, each had been told that he or she would be discharged when the staff became convinced of his or her sanity. As soon as they were admitted, all pseudo-patients began to behave normally and stopped simulating *any* symptoms. They stayed in the wards an average of 19 days, and one person stayed as long as 52 days. *Not one* of these pseudo-patients was ever deemed sane by the staff and discharged from the psychiatric ward. They were never detected in spite of their normal, appropriate, and sane behavior. On the contrary, Rosenhan showed that the staff at times seemed to receive confirmation of their diagnoses from observing the behavior of these pseudo-patients.

THE POWER OF ROLES IN
MAKING PEOPLE INHUMAN

Since roles involve norms and expectations, they are inevitably tied to issues of conformity and compliance. Not only are people ready to enter a role in a way that involves cognitive distortion, but when a role calls for cruel and inhuman behavior, many people are willing to enter that role and behave inhumanly. They seem to give up their own sense of moral judgment and follow the role's prescriptions, passing the responsibility for their acts on to "the authority."

In Asch's (1952, 1955) famous studies on conformity, substantial proportions of subjects showed conformity to a group opinion, responding to a task in a way they knew to be incorrect. Over the years, numerous studies have repeatedly shown the prevalence of conformity and compliance under group pressure. Milgram (1963, 1974) conducted famous (and quite controversial) studies on obedience. A substantial proportion of people—in the role of

subjects in a scientific investigation—showed readiness to administer elec-
tric shocks to others in obedience with the instructions of a "scientist." Many
subjects experienced considerable stress when they "shocked" their victims
yet continued to administer shocks as instructed. Milgram (1974) concluded
that many people will do what they are told in an obedient role as long as they
perceive the order as coming from "a legitimate authority." They are obedient even when ordered to perform acts that they know, in their consciences, to
be morally wrong.

Working directly in a role system, Zimbardo and his associates (Zimbardo, Haney, Banks, & Jaffe, 1973) created a role-play simulation of a jail,
where some subjects were to play prisoners, and others, the role of guards.
The simulation was planned to last two weeks, but Zimbardo was forced to
disband it after six days because of the emergence of extremely destructive
manifestations and psychogenic symptoms of high intensity. "Prisoners"
showed withdrawal and depression symptoms, while "jailers" became extremely tough and cruel. Although Zimbardo's work is controversial, it is at
least suggestive of the power of social roles in making people inhuman. Over
the years, we have often witnessed artificial role-playing situations turning
into extremely destructive, nasty, and cruel confrontations, which role play-
ers justified as demanded by the roles.

In a previous chapter we mentioned a report by Jones (1976), a history
teacher in a California high school, who tried to demonstrate to his students
that most people can turn into Nazis when such a role is enforced. Jones
created the Third Wave Movement in his school, a movement allegedly
stressing strength, discipline, and authority and directly encouraging intolerance, authoritarianism, and an anti-intellectualism. Within several days
the "movement" mushroomed in that high school, more and more enthusiastic students joining every day. The students adopted a group salute, self-
appointed body guards "protected" the leader, and an aggressive "gestapo"
began to operate in the school.

Jones's report might be overdramatic and somewhat sensationalistic, but
Nazi Germany of the 1930s and 1940s will remain forever a painful historical
testimony to the power of roles in making people inhuman. The nation that
had been considered most cultured and civilized had become a murderous
monster, violating any possible human right and executing mass genocide.
Its citizens not only complied obediently, but they participated in playing
their inhuman roles with German precision and effectiveness. In the war
trials after the war, Nazi defendants repeated the same excuse: "I only did
what I had been told to do."

We are aware of various methodological and conceptual reservations that
have been raised about the works of Milgram, Rosenthal, Zimbardo, Rosenhan, and Jones. However, we believe that some social scientists find it hard
to accept that roles can be so powerful in making people inhuman. When

racial, ethnic, religious, ideological, and gender struggles are concerned, the moral and ideological cause and the intensity of the socio-identity make it somewhat more palatable to accept extremity and destructiveness. But it is harder to accept that roles that are not anchored in socio-identities, minority status, or violations of human rights would be as powerful in making people cruel and inhuman.

Roles and Intergroup Processes

Roles partition people into groups, groups of role holders interact with each other and often have conflicting interests, and therefore the various intergroup processes take place for role groups much as they take place for other types of groups. Following the description of some typical role-related intergroup processes, we describe a unique type of role-related process: ritualized interrole conflict.

ROLES AND SOCIO-IDENTITIES

Roles are experienced differently from socio-identities. A person has a variety of different roles and shifts constantly from role to role, but only a few socio-identities, and these are more fixed and constant. People invest large amounts of mental energy in role management and role performance, but these investments are experienced largely in a situation-specific way and are not particularly "meaningful" in terms of one's identity. Socio-identities are in the "core" of one's social existence, highly meaningful and central group identifications.

For many people, socio-identities act as agents of "segregation," limiting their interactions with out-groups and gratifying their needs within their own group. This is not true of role behavior, where people continuously interact with holders of different roles and must continuously negotiate interrole issues with other people.

There are some situations in which a role can acquire the attributes of a socio-identity, or, in effect, "become" a socio-identity. This happens often in the work domain, where people identify so strongly with their professional role and invest so much mental energy in it that it becomes a salient socio-identity. Once a role becomes a socio-identity, the various intergroup processes (stereotypy, prejudice, ethnocentrism, and particularly intense and polarized interrole conflict) are manifested.

The shift of the professional role into a socio-identity is experienced quite positively by those who make it. This socio-identity is one of free choice, and the person exercises control over the formation and shaping of this identity. It is formed on the basis of identification with one's professional role and satisfies various needs. A professional socio-identity (a scientist, a teacher, a manager, and so on) can be more neutral and apolitical than other socio-identities and can therefore often bridge some cleavages caused by other differences (racial, national, religious, and the like). Thus, as an identity of choice, the professional socio-identity not only provides various satisfactions but also can relieve some of the frustrations persons experience in their other socio-identities.

"Minority status" means, among other things, that a group is limited in its access to particular roles and positions in society or that the range of free play in performing specific roles is limited for members of that minority group compared to members of non-minority groups. Therefore, the struggle of a minority group is aimed at gaining access to a larger range of positions, and eliminating the limitations on the roles available to its members. Groups fight against the stereotypes that identify them as holding only certain roles and against the prejudices and discriminatory practices that maintain that limited access. This has been particularly salient in recent years in gender-related conflict, where feminists have been fighting against oppressive sex roles and tendentious sex-role socialization.

ROLE-RELATED STEREOTYPES AND PREJUDICE: ROLES AND POWER RELATIONS

As mentioned, the various intergroup phenomena (stereotypes, prejudice, discrimination) are as observable for roles as they are for other dimensions of difference, since roles partition people into definable groups. A very large number of role-related stereotypes are held and used by most people. These stereotypes characterize either "pure" role groups (teachers, politicians, adolescents, soldiers, and the like) or groups that combine roles with race, ethnicity, gender, or another dimension of societal heterogeneity (such as Jewish mothers, southern belles, Catholic nuns, Jewish American Princesses, and Latin lovers). Role-related prejudices (against policemen, "jocks," poets, disc jockeys, or secretaries) are probably as prevalent in society as racial, ethnic, religious, and ideological prejudices.

Exercise 12.3

Please generate a list of role-related stereotypes and prejudices that are familiar to you either from your own life experiences or the experiences of your family members, friends, or acquaintances. In analyzing these instances, pay special attention to interrole conflict and power relations between role holders. Can you identify instances when the same role evokes different stereotypes in distinguishable groups of "others," according to the others' role vis-à-vis the subject of the stereotype?

The existence of role-related stereotypy, prejudice, and discrimination is not surprising, since these phenomena accompany any partition of individuals into distinguishable groups in human society, and most roles clearly identify individuals as members of role groups. Not every role has an inherent power orientation, yet interrole relations almost inadvertently involve power relations and a power struggle. Therefore it is possible to view role groups as minority or majority groups and to analyze role-related oppression and discrimination in the full, intense sense of these terms. However, it is probably correct to state that conflicts between role groups often do not carry the same "flavor" and ideological fervor as a racial, ethnic, religious, or gender-based pluralistic struggle.

By their very definition, many social roles are in conflict with other roles, so that the conflict is a built-in characteristic of the role. This is not to say that the conflict is the *central* feature of the role, but only that the conflict is "programmed" into the role and a power struggle is expected a priori to take place. Many examples of preprogrammed power relations are available: student and teacher, worker and boss, policeman and delinquent, principal and superintendent, and so forth. Through folklore, literature, jokes, and movies, as well as through administrative policies and social customs, society creates images of particular roles (such as mother-in-law), reinforcing their power relations with other roles and often even "ritualizing" interrole power struggle (see next section).

To conclude, we believe that the *political view* of role relations is important, as it illuminates aspects that are sometimes hidden and implicit, and yet have a strong influence on role behavior and on the ways people interact with each other. The political view is more salient when role groups explicitly struggle with each other, but it may have an implicit influence even on seemingly innocent role interactions between two individuals (father and son, lovers, salesperson and buyer, and the like).

RITUALIZED INTERROLE CONFLICT

A unique set of phenomena that illuminates issues of intergroup conflict is the "ritualized intergroup conflict." Ritualized conflicts are adversary role situations that are preprogrammed and "choreographed" in society. Through the preplanning and the predictability of their scenarios, these conflicts can be kept under control. They are functional in allowing conflict to take place, at the same time keeping it from exploding beyond its expected boundaries.

Some of society's major institutions are organized in adversary systems that create ritualized interrole conflicts. We illustrate this process through examples from the political system, the legal system, and labor relations. Now that you are familiar with our way of analyzing the functionality of social phenomena, you are encouraged to provide and explicate your own examples, analyzing their functionality for society and for the persons who play roles in them.

The political systems of the United States, Britain, and other countries are organized so that two parties or political blocs are in ritualized conflict with each other. One is the "minority party" and the other, the "majority party." The conflicts between the parties (with regard to legislation, international diplomacy, and so on) are preprogrammed, and a politician knows the "appropriate" point of view, which depends on membership in the minority or the ruling party. Most critical votes follow the planned, predicted scenario of party line. One group takes a criticizing stance and is generally dissatisfied with the administration, and the other takes a constructive role, supporting the administration. (At the same time, the system allows for some flexibility of free play and individual opinion, so that the representatives are not be perceived as puppets. Moreover, the politicians themselves do not wish to appear to be conforming to a party line and try to assert the independence of their opinions. Nevertheless, most important decisions in democratic governments are highly predictable on the basis of party membership.)

When the balance of power shifts from one party to another in the election, there is an awkward period when the previous majority must enter the role of minority, while the minority must assume the majority's responsibilities. By law, the new roles cannot be enacted for some weeks. This awkward period is called in American politics the "lame duck" period.

In countries that do not operate on a two-party system, the process of ritualized conflict becomes more complicated. In Russia, for example, only one party legally exists, making it impossible to ritualize a clear role conflict. In Israel, there are numerous parties and the government is a coalition government. The Israeli system has maintained the ritualized roles of "coalition" and "opposition," but marginal parties can gain power by being unpredictable when both sides need their votes.

Another example of ritualized conflict in the American political system is the famous system of "checks and balances" among the executive, legislative, and judiciary branches of government. Checks and balances illustrate most explicitly the needs and functions of ritualized interrole conflicts in a political system.

In the legal system, the "court battle" is the prominent ritualized interrole conflict. Two professionals, representing adversary positions, figuratively wrestle with each other. A judge who is an objective interpreter of the law, or a jury that represents objectivity of the public-at-large, will hand down the verdict. Each lawyer is supposed to be loyal and committed to his or her side's point of view, and "justice" emerges out of their clash. To control the boundaries of this ritualized and symbolic conflict, the language, dress, and behavior of both lawyers are highly ritualized, and the authority of the court is never to be questioned in a democratic society. Only a higher court, prelegislated as well, can overturn a lower court's decision, and *nobody* can challenge the authority of the Supreme Court. This scenario is in some ways reminiscent of the biblical myth of David and Goliath, in which representatives of nations at war (Israelites and Philistines) fought each other to determine which nation would be victorious.

The same type of ritualization (maybe somewhat less formalized) is found in labor relations. "Management" and "labor" take adversary, ritualized positions, negotiating according to established rules and procedures. Each side takes an extreme position, and there are particular behaviors that are permitted (such as going on strike or verbally abusing the other side) and others that are prohibited (such as physical attacks or actually damaging goods). As long as both sides adhere to the ritualized scenario, a compromise resolution will eventually by negotiated. Violation of the choreographed roles makes the process "go wild" and is perceived to be highly destructive.

A major goal of the socialist movement has been to provide workers with access to the power of this ritualized conflict. In the United States, workers attained the right to unionize following a long and bitter pluralistic struggle. In some areas (mostly in the South) unions are still almost nonexistent. At the same time, the professional roles of "labor representative" and "negotiator" are recognized professions today, and the federal government employs people in these capacities. In communist countries (the "workers' heaven"), workers are not permitted to enter this kind of ritualized conflict, as recent events in Poland have shown.

13

VALUE ORIENTATION AND IDEOLOGY: UNIFIERS AND DIVIDERS

Values, Ideology, and Identity

The shift from foregoing areas of discussion to the domain of value orientation and ideology opens a new window on inquiry into the social self. The individual is born into a racial or gender group and must "make meaning" of this membership by creating an appropriate perspective and socio-identity. Values and ideology do not follow existing and innate group memberships in the same way. A person can choose a value orientation and an ideology, thereby defining his or her membership in a desired group ("responsible people," liberals, and so on). A person cannot exercise any degree of choice concerning what biosocial group (race, ethnicity, nationality, gender) he or she is born into and has no control over the social consequences of such group memberships. Value orientation and ideology (as well as professional and social roles) are *voluntary* memberships of the social self. One can choose values and ideologies and exercise control by changing and modifying them in light of their consequences. A person is *defined by* biosocial attributes, but *defines* him- or herself in terms of value orientation and ideology.

As in the treatment of other dimensions of the social self, we distinguish in this chapter between ideological socio-identity and ideological intergroup conflict. The first focus emphasizes the importance of values in the social self and examines the processes involved in the creation and maintenance of value orientation and ideological socio-identity. The second focus emphasizes the political struggle between ideological groups in society and the effects of ideological fanaticism.

We also distinguish in this chapter between "value orientation" and "ideological socio-identity." Every person has various values, and the integration of these values into one perspective is the person's value orientation. Value orientation is an important component of the social self, regardless of whether it is explicitly defined or remains implicit. We use the term "ideological socio-identity" to refer to an explicit and salient membership in a defined ideological group (such as feminists or communists). Membership in a certain ideological group must be important to the person, and he or she must be intensely committed to the group for the term "ideological socio-identity" to apply. Thus, while almost every person has a value orientation (although people differ in how articulated, integrated, salient, and consistent their value orientations are), relatively few people have clear and salient ideological socio-identities. Readers should note that we use the term "ideology" in this chapter in a *social* or *group* sense, as distinct from other—more personal, ideational, or "theoretical"—connotations of this term.

In dealing with ideological socio-identities, we further distinguish between their "pathological" and "nonpathological" manifestations. Pathological manifestations include fanaticism, dogmatism, and instances in which beliefs and values are used as weapons in punitive and destructive ways. Pathology of ideology is evident when groups (such as Catholics and Protestants) whose stated values are almost identical can mercilessly kill and destroy each other. Nonpathological manifestations of ideology are reflected in great religious, political, and social contributions of ideologies and ideologues to the progress of human civilization.

Value Orientation and the Social Self

CONCEPTIONS OF BELIEFS, ATTITUDES, AND VALUES IN SOCIAL PSYCHOLOGY

"Johnny is sad today." "I love hamburgers." "Polish people are hardworking." "Familiarity breeds contempt." These are random examples of the hundreds of thousands of thoughts that can pass through a person's mind. A large number of terms can be used to describe and define people's verbal statements (observation, opinion, belief, idea, conclusion, thought, image, attitude, notion, assumption, value, and so on), and distinguishing among these types of terms can be an exasperating task. Social psychologists have focused research and theory on some of these concepts (mostly beliefs and attitudes) and neglected others.

The classical view in social psychology (Allport, 1935; McGuire, 1969) held that an "attitude" is made up of three components that are consistent with each other:

- *Cognitive component.* Beliefs and ideas about the attitude object ("Germans are methodical and not humorous").
- *Affective component.* Positive or negative feelings and a value judgment about the attitude object ("I don't like Germans").
- *Behavioral component.* Tendency to act or respond in a particular way toward the attitude object ("I stay away from Germans").

Over the years, most writers on attitudes held in consensus that (1) attitudes include value judgments, (2) most attitudes are focused on identifiable objects, and (3) attitudes do not "stand alone" but are organized in consistent and meaningful clusters.

Most of the research on attitude formation, organization of attitudes, and attitude change over the years has been based on this conception of the three components of attitudes (see Oskamp, 1977). "Belief" was considered to be the cognitive component of attitudes, and "value" was vaguely identified as the affective/judgmental component of attitudes. Thus, "attitude" was the superconcept that included beliefs and values as subcategories. Rokeach (1968) pointed out that to some writers (such as Jones & Gerard, 1967) "value" seemed synonymous with "attitude" because the attitude object has valence.

In a noted reformulation of this concept, Fishbein and Ajzen (1975) separated the three components and conceptualized their sequential order. They used the term "attitude" to refer only to the affective component, the term "belief" to refer to the cognitive component, and the term "intention" to refer to the behavioral component. According to Fishbein and Ajzen, the attitude toward an object is based on the belief about it. In turn, the attitude determines the behavioral intentions. Thus, the sequential order of components according to Fishbein and Ajzen is as follows:

$$\text{Belief} \longrightarrow \text{Attitude} \longrightarrow \text{Intention} \longrightarrow \text{Behavior}$$

In these conceptions and the research based on them, values were largely neglected. Many current textbooks in social psychology (such as Shaver, 1981) do not define or index values at all (much as they ignore ideology). Among the reasons that could account for the neglect of values are the facts that experimental social psychologists currently prefer to focus on social cognition and information processing, rather than affective factors (see Carrol & Payne, 1976), and that attitudes—being more specific, less idiosyncratic, and focused on definable subjects—are more amenable to experimental laboratory research than are values.

Writers who emphasized the significance of values doubted the exclusive scientific validity of controlled experimental manipulations conducted in the social-psychological laboratory. They were more concerned about the real-life influences of people's orientations toward their social environments on their actual daily conduct. Kurt Lewin (1948; or Lewin & Grabbe, 1945) strongly emphasized the significance of values and value orientation in processes of reeducative change and in understanding "social conduct." Katz and Stotland (1959) theorized about "value systems," which they conceived as larger structures that organize and integrate sets of more specific attitudes. Allport, Vernon, and Lindzey (1960) developed a well-known instrument measuring six major classes of values (theoretical, social, political, religious, aesthetic, and economic). More recently, Rokeach (1968, 1973) was the most vocal advocate of the significance of values, attacking the futility of the current treatment of attitudes in social psychology.

Rokeach (1968) argued that conventional theorizing in social psychology did not distinguish clearly among beliefs, attitudes, and values and did not analyze them in distinctively different ways. An adult person has tens or hundreds of thousands of beliefs and thousands of attitudes, but only dozens of values. Unlike other writers who viewed beliefs as representing the cognitive component of attitudes, Rokeach argued that beliefs have all three components: cognitive, affective, and behavioral. A belief can be any of a large variety of propositions held by a person: It can be descriptive ("the sun rises in the east"), evaluative ("ice cream is good"), prescriptive ("children should obey adults"), or existential ("death is inevitable"). Beliefs can be expectations, interpretations, hypotheses, inferences about underlying states, opinions, observations, and stereotypes. Rokeach (1968, p. 112) defined "attitude" as a "relatively enduring and persistent organization of beliefs around a common social object or situation, predisposing the person to respond in some preferential manner." Thus, people can have the same attitude but base it on different, even disparate, beliefs.

In Rokeach's conceptualization, "value" is a type of central belief about how one should or should not behave or about some end state of existence that is or is not worth attaining. Values are centrally located within the person's total belief system. They are *abstract ideals* or "generalized beliefs," not tied directly to a specific attitude, object, or situation. Examples of values include truth, beauty, freedom, thrift, responsibility, duty, and order.

Rokeach (1968, p. 160) argued that values, not attitudes, are the most significant constructs in accounting for human conduct: "Once a value is internalized, it becomes a standard or criterion for guiding action, for developing and maintaining attitudes toward relevant objects and situations . . . for morally judging self and others, comparing self with others . . . a standard employed to influence the values, attitudes, and actions of others (e.g., children)."

Exercise 13.1 Inquiry Into Value Orientation

Please write down the values that you consider most significant and central. After you write down up to fifteen values, arrange them hierarchically according to your own order of priority. Then write next to each entry the major behaviors you enact in order to realize that particular value.

We recommend that you share your data with other learners, comparing and contrasting the emerging value orientations.

Rokeach saw values as organized hierarchically in the individual's value system according to their relative importance to the individual. In our terms in this chapter, "value orientation" is this integrated value system of the person.

THE GENESIS OF VALUES IN SOCIETY

"Civilization" is "a relatively high level of cultural and technological development," and "to civilize" is "to bring about a technically advanced and rationally ordered stage of cultural development" (*Webster's New Collegiate Dictionary,* 1970). Using their superior brain power, human beings have developed over many centuries a civilization that enables them to control their environment and to live in relative comfort and security. Civilization is a system of norms and rules that regulate the behavior of the members of human society so as to guarantee its smooth maintenance and progress. Societal norms are in essence compromises that balance society, preventing a situation in which a few can freely satisfy all their needs at the expense of all others. In Freudian terms, norms of civilization reflect the victory of "the reality principle" over "the pleasure principle."

Values are transformations of societal norms, redefined in moral terms and internalized by the individual members of society. To murder or to steal might not have been "bad" originally. But if such acts are permitted without sanction, they may hamper the effective functioning of human civilization. When the prohibition against murdering or stealing becomes sanctified and internalized by individuals, it constitutes a value (the value of human life or of human property).

Human culture has developed through the progressive construction and application of a system of functional norms. The law in modern society is one reflection of these norms, while the internalization of these norms is reflected in the value system. The more successful society becomes in the socialization of value orientation, the less it needs to police its citizens in maintaining these norms, since people become self-directed by being "value-oriented."

VALUE ORIENTATION AND THE SOCIAL SELF

The process of socialization involves both learning and more global education. "Learning" refers to the acquisition of specific knowledge and intellectual attainments, while "education" refers to the acquisition of values and a value orientation. In early socialization, specific behaviors must be taught, since the child lacks the ability to abstract hypothetical values. But as persons grow, they are expected to internalize the standards and form a system of values. A value acts as an abstract principle to guide behavior in a variety of concrete situations that have not been experienced before. For example,

young children are specifically taught to behave honestly in concrete situations. Later they are expected to abstract "honesty" as a value that directs
their future behavior. Attaining a value orientation makes the person "self-
directed," acting in a functionally effective and "civilized" way.

Values are central and influential in all areas of human life, and most
everyday behaviors reflect underlying values, usually even without the conscious awareness of their holders. Values are expressed choices about how to
behave in particular situations, in orders of priorities, and in the ways people
think about their behavior. If you stopped for a minute to scrutinize one day in
your life, you would probably be surprised to discover the great array of
underlying values that would emerge as relevant to that day's behaviors.

Values operate in two major ways to influence behavior. First, values influence people's thinking, shaping their social perceptions, interpretations, and
judgments. With internalized values, one "thinks" patriotically, religiously,
ethically, charitably, responsibly, honestly, and so forth, and the values become ingrained as ways of thinking. Second, values become "internal rein-
forcers," serving to reward persons internally for appropriate behavior. One
"feels good" about losing weight or telling the truth and is encouraged to
internalize more values and to act in a value-appropriate way.

But acting in value-appropriate ways involves losses as well as gains.
Some needs canot be constantly gratified; people must give up some hedonistic wishes and urges, be considerate of others, and often make sacrifices
for their values. Thus, value orientation and hedonism are in constant struggle. Indeed, we all "sin" at times, acting in some way against a value we hold,
trying to gratify an immediate need. But such violations do *not* imply (as
parents, teachers, and the internal superego sometimes insist) that we are bad,
valueless, spineless persons. At other times we experience a clash between
different values we hold (say, between the need to complete a commitment on
time as promised, and the need to give time and support to a troubled friend),
and in the moral dilemma we violate some values so that we can realize
others.

FROM VALUE ORIENTATION TO IDEOLOGY

Webster's New Collegiate Dictionary offers the following definitions of
"ideology": "visionary theorizing"; "a systematic body of concepts, especially about human life or culture"; "the integrated assertions, theories, and
aims that constitute a socio-political program"; and "a system of beliefs to
which people can have a strong commitment." Adding up elements from
these definitions illuminates the complex facets of ideology: a way of thinking . . . comprehensive nature . . . a group of people sharing a common view
or a common ideal . . . belongingness and commitment . . . socio-political.

We stated earlier that we view value orientation and ideology as disparate

(but related) concepts. Most people have an explicit or implicit value orientation, but only some people have a full ideology that constitutes a socio-
identity. Value orientation is central in every individual's social self, reflected
in various socio-identities and touching all areas of life. An ideological
socio-identity involves actual and committed membership in an ideological
group. An ideological socio-identity is always central and salient for its
holder, often to the exclusion of other identities and memberships. "Being
ideological" means, in our working definition, more than having values; it
means having a *cause* and a set of ideals (political, religious, social, or "cos-
mic") for which one would actively struggle or even die. To believe in God is
part of value orientation; deciding to dedicate one's life to God is ideological.
To believe in the value of socialized medicine is a socialist view; being a
communist is an ideological membership. To believe in equality is a value;
being a feminist is ideological.

We are aware that our working definition of ideological socio-identity is
strict and somewhat exclusive, implying that most people do not have clear
ideological socio-identities. We understand that many readers would find a
more flexible definition of "being ideological"—one that incorporates an
integrated set of values and beliefs with a compatible style of social conduct—sufficient, without including the necessary component of an intense
group membership. While such an orientation is certainly appropriate for
analysis of any person's ideology, we find our view of ideological socio-
identities as intense, powerful, and central group memberships more functional in understanding intergroup phenomena and critical events in human
history that are directly tied to ideology.

The Functions of Ideology

Ideology serves many social functions and satisfies various needs for its
holders. Ideological groups continue to grow and flourish, new groups are
continuously emerging, and many people are "seeking" ideological and spiritual groups. In this context, we use "ideology" as "ideology of choice": One
can be born into an ideological group (a Kibbutz, Catholicism, and so forth),
but this innate membership does not automatically become an ideological
socio-identity. A person can choose to make a commitment that will turn an
innate membership into an ideological socio-identity (making a conscious
choice, for example, to be an adult "member" of the kibbutz in which one has
grown up). The choice element in itself is a major function of ideology:
Having made one's choice and accepted the responsibilities and commitment
it entails is highly satisfying and rewarding.

Ideology functions like other group memberships and other socio-identities of the social self. In the following discussion, we analyze the psychologi-

cal functions that are unique to ideology, over and above the functions of most types of groups.

FUNCTIONS OF BELIEVING

Ideology is fundamentally based on faith—in a cause, in an idea, in a supervalue, or in an image of some type. Therefore, "believing" is a major function of ideology, and believers receive a variety of gratifications. ("Believing" is used here in a global way, bearing no resemblance to the use of "belief" by Rokeach or other social psychologists earlier in this chapter.) Human society respects intense believers and rewards them for their faith. As the slogan "you've got to believe" implies, one is considered a better person and a better citizen if one believes in some ideological cause, be it religious, political, social, environmental, or the like. As long as their ideologies are not aimed directly at destroying the foundation of society itself, society is very tolerant of believers, including their shortcomings and intolerance.

How does believing gratify the individual believer? We think that the major function of believing is *integration*. Believing is an integration of cognition and emotion, of affective elements and ideational elements. Believing is simultaneously an emotional experience and a cognitive experience. Furthermore, believing integrates values, thoughts, and opinions with behavior. Most ideologies prescribe specific codes of behavior, and believers' faith is expressed through these normative rituals and behaviors. Thus, for the believer, thought, feeling, and behavior are integrated and synchronized. Finally, believing also integrates the individual person with the "universe." By believing in a cause or in a basic organizing principle, one reaches an integrated perspective that directs one's functioning and makes one a meaningful part of the universe. The significance of what one believes makes the believer him- or herself meaningful and significant as well. (Believing in Christ gives the believer Christlike qualities; if you have "faith," you are "faithful").

A second function of believing is the *idealization* of the subject of faith. Idealization takes two major forms: an ideal end state of existence (communist society, democratic society, "heaven") and a personification of the ideal (Lenin, Mao, Buddha, Jesus, and, most important, God). The belief in an ideal state of existence makes the dreariness of daily existence more bearable, lifting the believer above the pettiness of reality. Sometimes it even sanctifies the routine, daily existence. Belief in the personification of an ideal satisfies deep-seated needs of dependency and esteem. God or godlike objects of belief are perceived as ideal images, with endless wisdom, goodness, and power. By believing in them, one both "shares" and is helped.

FUNCTIONS OF BELONGING

A few people have an intense, personal, idiosyncratic ideology that is *not* a clear group membership. But almost invariably the membership in an ideological group is a most salient and psychologically rewarding aspect of being ideological. The various characteristics of group membership described in Chapter 7 (group cohesion and solidarity, mutual support and protection, pressure against deviation, separatism, exclusivity, and so on) become more emphasized and intense when a group is identified on an ideological basis. This special significance of belonging to ideological groups is contributed by several factors:

(1) Membership in the ideological group is neither innate nor forced; it is, rather, an expression of the member's free choice.
(2) The dimension of similarity among members is ideational rather than biosocial: Members are bound together by shared ideals and a common belief in worthy causes.
(3) Members are unique and special in their willingness to make sacrifices for the group. They share an acceptance of "duty" as defined by the group's norms. Ideological groups often show "shared righteousness," where being together with other members and doing the group's "thing" constitute a spiritual experience.

People with a strong ideological identification use ideology as the major criterion of similarity for selection of friends. They do interact with relatives and work colleagues, but most often their "real" friends are chosen on the basis of ideological similarity. Similarity of attitudes is known to be a strong determinant of attraction between people (Byrne, 1971), but in the case of ideology the exclusion of out-groups (that is, those who do not share the particular ideology) is more extreme. This exclusivity serves to strengthen commitment to the group and to increase in-group cohesion.

An ideological group typically needs to have an identifiable out-group that is distinguishable from the in-group. To maintain its purity and uniqueness, the boundaries of the ideological group must be rigid, and some people must be excluded. The Soviet Union provides a fascinating example of this process: Only one major political ideology is legal in Russia, and citizens are not permitted to form or join anticommunist groups. Nevertheless, the Communist Party is a highly selective and exclusive group, and only a few people are allowed the privilege of actual membership in the Party. Similar manifestations of exclusivity are found in most revolutionary and extreme ideological groups. This process is symbolized by the biblical hero Gideon, who, under grave threat, reduced the size of his volunteer army to those few who (figuratively) licked water without kneeling down.

COGNITIVE FUNCTIONS OF IDEOLOGY

Ideology is adopted as a complete perspective that touches all or most important aspects of life. As such, ideology functions for its holders as a cognitive organizer and clarifier: It defines basic assumptions and ways of dealing with important issues; it sets the order of priority of various life issues; it shapes social perception and ways of interpreting social information; it removes doubt and cognitive dissonance; and it provides a total point of view that serves as a cognitive "anchor."

Ideology (particularly religious ideology) legitimizes nonrational thinking (please note that "nonrational" is not identical with "irrational"), doing away with the premise that the only way of examining any idea is through scientific, logical, empirical reasoning. It allows (indeed, sometimes demands) people to hold nonrational beliefs that cannot be proved empirically (such as beliefs concerning the existence of God, the creation of the universe, the basic nature of man, and the goals of society). Ideology makes it clear which basic premises must be accepted without question, and which domains and ideas are open to debate, scholarly work, and intellectual challenge.

Finally, most ideological systems are explicit in determination of "right" and "wrong." Not only are these judgments prescribed, but it is also made clear who has the (religious, political, spiritual) authority to determine right and wrong when doubt arises.

These factors help to make ideology functional from the cognitive point of view, simplifying issues and clarifying ways of thinking for its believers. But these same factors can also make ideology a cognitive distorter, intensifying dogmatism, increasing rigidity and intolerance of ambiguity, and restricting cognitive "freedom." In fact, the modern term "dogmatism" is derived from the ancient concept "dogma." According to the *Encyclopaedia Britannica* (Vol. 7, 1971, p. 553), "Dogma in Christian theology is a doctrine set down in the deposit of divine revelation and authoritatively defined by the entire church as a truth to be believed and accepted by all orthodox Christians. From this definition it is evident that the meaning and the status of dogma dependent upon the prior conviction of Christians that the mystery of God had been definitely revealed in Jesus Christ, and that the church, in response to and responsibility for this revelation, has both the right and the duty to define dogma in the formal and ecclesiastical sense of the word." In our opinion, this quote exemplifies both the positive and the negative functions of ideology in the cognitive domain.

EXISTENTIAL FUNCTIONS OF IDEOLOGY

Life in a human society brings up a series of existential issues and paradoxes that every thinking person must face. The riddle of life and the "program" of the universe, the underlying "order of things," issues of the meaning of life, the basic nature and purpose of individuals and society, the meaning of happiness and self-worth, issues of ethics and morality, of good and bad, and the meaning of death—these are but a few of the numerous existential issues with which a person must come to grips. The inability to resolve such existential issues leads many intelligent thinkers to cynicism and despair.

A significant function of ideology is that it provides answers to many existential questions, reducing perplexity and doubt and offering a global perspective that provides not only answers but meaning and purpose as well. The existential answers often lie in the basic premises of an ideology—those premises that are to be accepted on faith and not be questioned by believers. Thus, ideology can have a relieving power that is reserved only for true, committed believers. Indeed, highly "orthodox" ideological believers (in religion, communism, and other ideologies) are complacent, satisfied with having clear answers and few existential doubts. The opponents of ideology view this complacency as "an escape from freedom"—the avoidance of taking personal responsibility for continuously coping with life's existential issues.

Exercise 13.2

Focus your thinking on one individual whom you know quite well personally, whom you perceive as having a clear ideological socio-identity. First, identify this socio-identity, and then analyze the various functions this ideology seems to serve for that person. Consider the functions discussed above, but try to generate more specific and personalized functions that are relevant to this individual's situation and life history.

Pros and Cons of Ideology

Political and social ideologies bloomed in the nineteenth century. As a result of reactions to drastic changes in society and in the polity (the decline of monarchies, the industrial revolution, and so forth), new ideologies emerged, capturing the imagination of many people. Marxism and other political-social ideologies had millions of followers, and educated people in general were enchanted with "being ideological." In the twentieth century, strong shifts both toward *and* away from ideology were observable in both Europe and the United States. The implementation of Marxist ideology in communist countries, economic crises, World War II, the cold war, the end of colonialism and the emergence of the Third World, and the war in Vietnam were events that influenced these shifts toward and away from ideology. In general, it seems that new ideologies can emerge under a variety of societal conditions, including stress and crisis as well as excess affluence and security, political uncertainty as well as strong-hand regulation.

In the last few decades there has been a decline in the power and popularity of sociopolitical and religious ideologies. In the United States, the more prevalent ideologies in recent years have been associated with minority status and struggle (such as feminism and Black Power) or with other forms of an antiestablishment orientation. Some thinkers who have been highly ideological earlier in their lives have become disenchanted with ideology, turning to a "postideological" intellectual stance that criticizes the "cons" of ideology. Daniel Bell's (1960) *The End of Ideology* is an example of this process.

The arguments against ideology fall into three major categories: (1) the extremity and unreasonableness of ideology; (2) the politicization of ideology; and (3) the existential futility of ideology.

The first category emphasizes the dangers of extremity and fanaticism in the practice of ideology. Ideology acts as a distorter, simplifying ideas, ignoring disconfirming information, and increasing, often even encouraging, dogmatism. Implicitly or by design, it intensifies prejudice against out-groups, which is used to justify oppression and discrimination. Ideology claims monopoly on truth, intolerantly rejecting dissonant views or facts. It demands total commitment of intellect and emotion, and what makes ideology powerful is its fanatic force of passion. Bell wrote: "For the ideologue, truth arises in action. . . . He comes alive not in contemplation, but in the deed. One might say, in fact, that the most important latent function of ideology is to tap emotion" (1960, p. 371). "The ideologist—communist, existentialist, religionist—wants to live at some extreme, and criticizes the ordinary man for failing to live at the level of grandeur" (p. 289).

The second argument is that ideology is often only a facade of universal values that masks political self-interest. Bell argued that ideology involves the conversion of ideas into social levers, and the use of ideas as weapons. The politicization of ideology inevitably corrupts its ideals and values. Examples of this phenomenon are the oppressive nature of communist regimes that presumably implement communist ideology, or the known cycle of South American freedom fighters, who defeat an oppressive regime, and become quickly corrupted—the oppressive targets for the next generation of ideological freedom fighters.

The third argument against ideology involves a rather cynical view of change in human systems. According to this view, the potential for constructive change in persons and in society is very limited; ideology tends to deepen social cleavage and intensify conflict in society, decreasing rather than increasing the chances of resolving social problems. In other words, given that most serious problems of human society cannot be effectively resolved, ideology only contributes to destructive conflicts and cannot facilitate real social progress.

In response to these arguments against ideology, the supporters of ideology maintain that distortion, extremity, politicization, and corruption are basic characteristics of any struggle and any society, notwithstanding whether or not ideology is involved. Ideology in itself does not *create* these destructive phenomena, and if it sometimes intensifies them, that damage is balanced by ideology's great constructive contributions. Society, they argue, would be worse off without ideology: Its ideals and moral principles keep individuals from being alienated, helping them to maintain their level of commitment and value orientation and enhancing their moral standards and moral behavior.

The "pros" of ideology include the functions discussed above: believing, belonging, cognitive functions, and existential functions. Ideology is a significant human motivator and direction giver; it enables people to be spiritual and value-oriented, providing their lives with meaning and purpose and giving them moral ideals they will aspire to achieve and an overall "ethic" that can make them happier and more fulfilled members of society.

The supporters of ideology are well aware of the dangers of fanaticism and extremity, but they oppose "throwing out the baby with the bathwater." Even extremity and fanaticism can sometimes serve significant psychological functions, and the pros of ideology can be utilized in effective ways without falling blindly into distortion, extremity, and prejudice. The supporters of ideology believe that it is a major educational task to teach people how to develop and maintain meaningful ideological socio-identities without throwing society into bitter and unsolvable ideological conflicts.

The Role of Ideology
in Human History

Ideology is political as much as it is spiritual, moral, and social. It is an image of a desired end state of individual and society, coupled with a strong urge to *change* society and to realize this end state. Acts of social change are basically political acts. (We use the term "political" not necessarily in relation to government.)

From a societal perspective, ideology is a way of formulating the moral codes of society and causing change processes that will bring about particular states. The struggle among ideological groups to determine these ideals and the methods for their realization is certainly a political struggle. Politicization of ideology in itself is *not* corruption of ideology. Ideology becomes corrupted when values serve as a facade for self-interest or when terrible crimes are committed in the name of ideology.

The picture of the contributions of ideology to society in human history is ambivalent: Over the centuries, ideologies have made great contributions to social progress, yet ideologies have also become extremely destructive and "pathological."

CONTRIBUTIONS OF IDEOLOGY TO SOCIAL PROGRESS

The great contributions of ideology to human civilization have usually taken place through dramatic and revolutionary events. An idea or a moral perspective turns into a political cause, a group of believers is recruited to fight for their cause, and their victory marks an ideologically based change in society.

We illustrate historical changes rooted in ideology in four major domains: *religious* (centered on ideas of faith and ethics), *political* (centered on the idea of freedom), *social* (centered on the idea of human rights), and *moral/existential* (centered on ideas of personal freedom, existential concerns, and the like). These domains are distinguishable from each other, yet they are not mutually exclusive.

Major examples of the contributions of ideology in the religious domain include the emergence of monotheism and the elimination of paganism in the ancient world, the growth of Christianity as the central ethical and religious ideology of Western civilization, and the growth of Islam into an empire encompassing the entire Arab world. The struggle of Martin Luther and the Protestant revolt against the Catholic Church in the sixteenth century are other illustrations of ideologically based conflicts that reflect the powerful wish to have freedom of faith and flexibility in determining moral codes. Still another type of significant religiously rooted historical event is the return of the Jews to Israel after a long history of persecution in exile, to build their own society in their own country. The Puritans who left Europe aboard the *Mayflower* to sail to America and the Amish in Pennsylvania present examples of the same general type.

Historical changes in society due to political ideologies are very salient, due to the politicization of most ideological struggles. While religious ideology is focused on issues of faith and ethics, political ideology deals with issues of freedom, control, and the "correct way" of managing society. The very idea of "democracy" and the gradual emergence of democracies to replace monarchies, empires, and other nondemocratic forms of government are due to the persistence of various political ideologies. Some of the most notable examples include the American Revolution and the way it established a constitution and a bill of rights, laying the foundation for a highly ideological democratic republic; the communist revolution, which was based on Marxist ideology and led to the creation of communist governments in two of the largest countries on earth (China and the USSR); and the French Revolution, which put an end to the French monarchy and led to the creation of the Republic.

"Social ideologies" have added to religious faith and ethics and to political freedom and democracy a focus on the ideal of human rights. Social ideologies have gone beyond the abstract idea of freedom to focus on the equity among groups, their equal opportunities, and the division of power and resources in society. In a sense, Marxist ideology dealt with similar ideas. The creation of the modern "welfare state" and the legislation of civil rights in recent decades are reflections of the political impact of social ideologies.

The Israeli kibbutz is another example of the realization of a social ideology. Communal living that prohibits private property, use of money, wages, and materialism and requires democratic self-governance is the social reality for the thousands of kibbutz members.

A special group of social ideologies that has been particularly influential in recent years consists of ideologies held by minority groups in their pluralistic struggle for equal rights and more access to power positions in society. The struggle of racial, ethnic, religious, national, and gender groups in the last decades certainly has had a great impact in the United States and other Western countries, leading to a great variety of planned and unplanned changes in society.

The last category of the contributions of ideology to society—the moral / existential— is less clearly defined than the previous ones. We include in this category historical events that have become symbols of the value of specific ideas. Galileo become the historical symbol of the freedom of thought and the value of science; Jean d'Arc became the symbol of martyrdom—the readiness to die for one's ideology; England's King Edward VIII became the symbol of the power of love, having given up his throne in order to marry the woman he loved; Albert Schweitzer came to symbolize the value of sacrifice in the service of humanitarian ideals; and the Watergate incident in the United States became a symbol of how truth and justice and citizens' moral outrage can defeat the political "system."

THE PATHOLOGY OF IDEOLOGY

Ideology is a powerful source of intergroup conflict in society. Throughout human history an incredibly large number of crimes against humanity have been committed in the name of ideology. The Crusades, the Spanish Inquisition, the American Civil War, Communist totalitarianism, and the war in Ireland are but a few examples of the lethal and destructive potential of ideology. Ironically, the very same factors (extremely strong beliefs, total commitment to the group, willingness to sacrifice for the group's cause) that make ideology so valuable and constructive for society are also the roots of its pathology.

The pathology of ideology stems in part from its complex relationship with power politics. We explained earlier how ideology becomes politicized and how it can become corrupted in this process. Next, we describe several scenarios of historical events reflecting the relationship between ideology and politics, demonstrating the pathology of ideology.

One scenario is what Bell (1960) defined as an ideological facade covering self-interest. In this situation, a purely political struggle is "dressed" in an ideological facade. Politicians are always searching for a moral or ideological facade to cover their bare ambitions. In order to be elected, candidates feel they must identify and develop a "cause" in which they presumably believe for which they are fighting (be it law and order, civil rights, reducing the power of government, or the like). They then imply that it is only because of these serious causes that they are so eager to be elected. We do not argue that real ideological causes are always missing, but we view the political game as encouraging and rewarding the creation of ideological facades. This scenario may appear quite cynical, but one of its most atrocious illustrations took place in this century, when the German Nazis dressed their expansionism and totalitarianism in a facade of a racial and cultural "ideology."

In the second scenario, a political or social conflict in which ideology initially plays a minor role escalates into an "ideological conflict." The conflict can be an economic competition between groups or a struggle for power and control. But if the fighting groups differ along an ideological dimension, the salience of ideology as the cause and the central issue of the conflict can intensify to the point that the conflict is erroneously perceived as an ideological struggle. One example of this process is the past conflict in Ireland, where a clash between social class groups and a struggle for political independence have come to be perceived by many as an ideologically based conflict between Protestants and Catholics. Similarly, the current conflict in Lebanon was *not* a struggle between Christianity and Islam, but a political and economic war between the long-established resident Arabs (who happen to be mostly Christian) and the aspiring and power-hungry newcomers—the Palestinians (who are Moslem). Most American historians think that the war between the northern and southern states in the nineteenth century was caused, to a large extent, by the competition between two disparate and incompatible economic systems, which disrupted the potential for maintaining a viable federal government. Yet the Civil War is conveniently thought of as an ideological war that was meant to abolish slavery.

In another scenario, ideology plays a major role in the uprising of the oppressed, only to "disappear" when the ideological group attains its goals and reaches a power position. Ideology disappears from practice, but *not* from rhetoric. The best illustration of this scenario is the rise of communism. From being highly ideological at the onset, before the Revolution, communism has turned into totalitarian and oppressive regimes, violating citizens' civil rights and personal freedom. Poland provided an ironic illustration of this phenomenon in 1981: Workers had to fight a communist government for their rights, and the tanks of another communist government were used to threaten them. Eventually, martial law was declared to restrain the popular workers' movement. Nevertheless, in every May Day parade the slogan "Workers of all nations unite" is prominently flashed.

In the last scenario, ideology remains genuinely important in actual practice, but it is righteously used as an instrument for oppression and persecution. This scenario is reflected in the ways Eastern European communist countries run their economies and social systems; how cruel, fundamentalist religion is practiced in countries such as Saudi Arabia, Libya, and Iran; and how Chinese society is managed. In the name of zealous ideology, citizens are deprived of basic liberties, discriminated against, and often even persecuted.

In the intergroup domain, the pathology of ideology lies in its extremity and fanaticism. An ideological position is often an uncompromising position, marked by righteousness and lack of self-criticism. An "ideological position" is most often a morally superior position that encourages prejudice against the out-group and intensifies dogmatic trends (cognitive *and* affective) among the believers. Most important, an "ideological position" often discourages a person from making an effort to resolve a conflict.

On the individual level, "becoming ideological" often means becoming dogmatic and close-minded. It signals a shift to a level of righteous principle that is intended to be uncompromising and unyielding. An interaction between individuals can become ideological, thereby turning explosive and unresolvable. For instance, an argument between a husband and a wife about the children's carpool arrangements can become a fight between a "feminist" and a "sexist"; a dinnertable conversation can become a clash between political ideologues; a parent's reaction to a child's behavior can turn into a confrontation between child-rearing ideologies.

The intergroup processes described in earlier chapters emerge with particular bitterness and extremity when the conflict is ideological. Prejudices are stronger and scapegoating is more cruel, righteous, and remorseless (for example, killing Jews on the basis of the false allegation that they use Christian blood for their rituals, or believing that every conservative is by definition bigoted and prejudiced). The concept of martyrdom has a most "noble" and functional origin. Martyrdom is total self-sacrifice that exposes the cruelty and moral inferiority of the out-group, at the same time confirming the moral superiority and sanctity of the in-group perspective, fueling conflict and intensifying the ideological fervor of the believers.

In pluralistic struggle, both minority and majority groups gain from taking an ideological stance. For the minority group, adopting an ideological position is quite easy, since minority status in itself reflects some sort of social injustice. The position that a particular biosocial attribute (such as color or gender) should in no way lead to differential treatment, and the demand for equality among groups are basically ideological positions. Furthermore, in Western societies a special value is attached to "supporting the underdog" no matter who the underdog is. Indeed, minority groups frequently make use of powerful ideological positions in their pluralistic struggles.

It seems that the majority group needs the ideological cloak even more than the minority group. It is almost the only way (and certainly the most respectable one) to justify holding on to their power rather than relinquishing it or sharing it with others. If the majority group represents a particular ideology and its cause is compelling enough (as in the cases of fundamental religion, communism, and law and order), and if the majority group is convinced that other groups would not be as committed to "keeping the faith," there is justification for holding on to the power and discriminating against minority groups.

Concluding Comments

Our foregoing discussion of the constructive contributions and the pathology of ideology demonstrates most sharply the ambivalence we have expressed throughout this book with regard to dimensions of heterogeneity and difference in society and their ensuing phenomena of intergroup processes.

Societal heterogeneity and division of people into distinct groups are inevitable, and groups cannot be expected ever to stop struggling with each other. Socio-identities that develop around significant group memberships carry the seeds for many positive and satisfying "fruits": a sense of identity and belongingness, uniqueness, channeling of thought and affect, contact with similar others, a solid social framework, participation in a meaningful group culture, and so on. But this very "groupness" also carries the seeds of destruction: intergroup competition leads to a variety of dangerous and explosive phenomena, from cognitive distortions in information processing, through prejudicial attitudes and feelings, to acts of discrimination, oppression, and even crimes against humanity.

These processes are universal and inevitable, deeply ingrained in human nature. In a way, they help to make human nature so fascinating and paradoxical—simple and complex, predictable and unpredictable at the same time.

But human beings can exercise a certain degree of control over their internal processes through the use of knowledge and inquiry that lead to better understanding of the psychological processes governing their conduct. In this book we have attempted to provide the knowledge we think is relevant to issues of societal heterogeneity, central dimensions of the social self, and intergroup processes. We have also provided guidelines and suggestions for self-inquiry, in the hope of deepening your awareness and integrating your knowledge so that you will be able to cope more effectively with issues of self and identity, similarity and difference, and conflict between groups.

We do not believe that stereotypy, prejudice, discrimination, and group warfare will ever disappear from human society. We do, however, believe that conflicts can be managed more rationally and extreme fanaticism can be curbed when people educate and reeducate themselves, inquiring into their social selves and applying the lessons of their inquiry to their social conduct.

BIBLIOGRAPHY

Adelson, J. What generation gap? *New York Times Magazine*, January 18, 1970.

Adorno, T. W., Frenkel-Brunswick, E., Levinson, D. J., & Sanford, R. N. *The authoritarian personality.* New York: Harper & Row, 1950.

Allport, G. W. Attitudes. In C. Murchison (Ed.), *Handbook of social psychology.* Worcester, MA: Clark University Press, 1935.

Allport, G. W. *The nature of prejudice.* Reading, MA: Addison-Wesley, 1954.

Allport, G. W., Vernon, P. E., & Lindzey, G. *A study of values.* Boston: Houghton Mifflin, 1960.

Amir, Y. Contact hypothesis in ethnic relations. *Psychological Bulletin*, 1969, *71*, 319-342.

Amir, Y. The role of intergroup contact in change of prejudice and ethnic relations. In P. A. Katz (Ed.), *Towards the elimination of racism.* New York: Pergamon, 1975.

Amir, Y. The ethnic contact and its implications to attitudes and inter-group relations: Summaries and re-evaluations. *Megamot*, 1977, *23*, 41-76. (in Hebrew)

Anderson, D. F., & Rosenthal, R. Some effects of interpersonal expectancy and social interaction on institutionalized retarded children. *Proceedings of the 76th Annual Convention of the American Psychological Association*, 1968, 479-480.

Aronson, E. *The social animal.* San Francisco: Freeman, 1972. (2nd ed., 1976)

Asch, S. Forming impressions of personality. *Journal of Abnormal and Social Psychology*, 1946, *41*, 258-290.

Asch, S. *Social psychology.* Englewood Cliffs, NJ: Prentice-Hall, 1952.

Asch, S. Opinions and social pressures. *Scientific American*, 1955, *193*, 31-35.

Ashmore, R. D. Prejudice: Causes and cures. In B. Collins (Ed.), *Social Psychology.* Reading, MA: Addison-Wesley, 1970.

Ashmore, R. D., & Del Boca, F. K. Psychological approaches to understanding intergroup conflict. In P. A. Katz (Ed.), *Toward the elimination of racism.* New York: Pergamon, 1976.

Ashmore, R. D., & Del Boca, F. K. Sex stereotypes and implicit personality theory: Toward a cognitive-social psychological conceptualization. *Sex Roles*, 1979, *5*, 219-248.

Ashmore, R. D., & Del Boca, F. K. Conceptual approaches to stereotypes and stereotyping. In D. L. Hamilton (Ed.), *Cognitive processes in stereotyping and intergroup behavior.* Hillsdale, NJ: Erlbaum, 1981.

Austin, W. G., & Worchel, S. (Eds.). *The social psychology of intergroup relations.* Monterey, CA: Brooks/Cole, 1979.

Babad, E. Y. A multi-method approach to the assessment of humor: A critical look at humor tests. *Journal of Personality*, 1974, *42*, 618-631.

Babad, E. Y. Pygmalion in reverse. *Journal of Special Education*, 1977, *11*, 81-90.

Babad, E. Y. President Sadat's visit to Jerusalem: Some observations of an Israeli social psychologist. *APA Monitor*, February 1978.

Babad, E. Y. Personality correlates of susceptibility to biasing information. *Journal of Personality and Social Psychology*, 1979, *37*, 195-202.

Babad, E. Y., Birnbaun, M., & Benne, K. D. The C-Group approach to laboratory learning. *Group and Organization Studies*, 1978, *3*, 168-184.

Babad, E. Y., & Inbar, J. Performance and personality correlates of teachers' susceptibility to biasing information. *Journal of Personality and Social Psychology,* 1981, *40,* 553-561.

Babad, E. Y., Inbar, J., & Rosenthal, R. Pygmalion, Galatea, and the Golem: Investigations of biased and unbiased teachers. *Journal of Educational Psychology,* 1982, *74,* 459-474. (a)

Babad, E. Y., Inbar, J., & Rosenthal, R. Teachers' judgments of students' potential as a function of teachers' susceptibility to biasing information. *Journal of Personality and Social Psychology,* 1982, *42,* 541-547. (b)

Babad, E. Y., Mann, M., & Mar-Hayim, M. Bias in scoring the WISC subtests. *Journal of Consulting and Clinical Psychology,* 1975, *43,* 268.

Bardwick, J. *The psychology of women.* New York: Harper & Row, 1971.

Barry, H., III, Bacon, M. K., & Child, I. L. A cross-cultural survey of some sex differences in socialization. In J. M. Bardwick (Ed.), *Readings on the psychology of women.* New York: Harper & Row, 1972.

Bell, D. *The end of ideology.* New York: Free Press, 1960.

Bell, D. (Ed.). *The radical right.* Garden City, NY: Doubleday, 1964.

Bell, D. Socialism. *International Encyclopedia of the Social Sciences,* 1968, *14,* 506-534.

Bell, D. Ethnicity and social change. In N. Glazer & D. P. Moynihan (Eds.), *Ethnicity: Theory and experience.* Cambridge, MA: Harvard University Press, 1975.

Bem, D. J. Self perception: An alternative interpretation of cognitive dissonance. *Psychological Review,* 1967, *74,* 183-200.

Bem, D. J. The epistemological status of interpersonal stimulations: A reply to Jones, Linder, Kiesler and Brehm. *Journal of Experimental Social Psychology,* 1968, *4,* 270-274.

Bem, D. J. *Beliefs, attitudes, and human affairs.* Monterey, CA: Brooks/Cole, 1970.

Bem, D. J. Self-perception theory. In L. Berkowitz (Ed.), *Advances in experimental social psychology* (Vol. 6). New York: Academic Press, 1972.

Bem, S. L. The measurement of psychological androgyny. *Journal of Consulting and Clinical Psychology,* 1974, *42,* 155-162.

Bem, S. L. Androgyny vs. the tight little lives of fluffy women and chesty men. *Psychology Today,* September 1975.

Bem, S. L. On the utility of alternative procedures for assessing psychological androgyny. *Journal of Consulting and Clinical Psychology,* 1977, *45,* 196-205.

Bem, S. L., & Lenney, E. Sex typing and the avoidance of cross sex behavior. *Journal of Personality and Social Psychology,* 1976, *33,* 48-54.

Benjamin, A. J., & Levi, A. M. Process minefields in intergroup conflict resolution: The Sdot Yam workshop. *Journal of Applied Behavioral Science,* 1979, *15,* 507-519.

Benne, K. D. *A conception of authority.* New York: Teachers College, Columbia University, 1943.

Benne, K. D. History of the T Group in the laboratory setting. In L. P. Bradford, J. R. Gibb, & K. D. Benne (Eds.), *T-Group theory and laboratory method.* New York: Wiley, 1964.

Benne, K. D. Something there is that doesn't love a wall (a rejoinder to the preceding article). *Journal of Applied Behavioral Science,* 1965, *1,* 327-336.

Benne, K. D. Authority in education. *Harvard Educational Review,* 1970, *40,* 385-410.

Benne, K. D. The processes of re-education: An assessment of Kurt Lewin's views. *Group and Organization Studies,* 1976, *1,* 26-42.

Benne, K. D. Societal changing and organizational development. *Southern Review of Public Administration,* 1978, *1,* 416-432.

Benne, K. D., Bradford, L. P., Gibb, J., & Lippitt, R. (Eds.). *The laboratory method of changing and learning.* Palo Alto, CA: Science & Behavior Books, 1975.

Bennis, W. G., Benne, K. D., Chin, R., & Corey, K. E. *The planning of change* (3rd ed.). New York: Holt, Rinehart & Winston, 1976.

Berube, M. R., & Gittell, M. (Eds.). *Confrontation at Ocean Hill Brownsville.* New York: Praeger, 1969.

Berzins, J. I. *New perspectives on sex roles and personality dimensions.* Paper presented at the meeting of the American Psychological Association, Chicago, September 1975.

Bettelheim, B., & Janowitz, M. *Social class and prejudice, including dynamics of prejudice.* New York: Free Press, 1964.

Biddle, B. J., & Thomas, E. J. (Eds.). *Role theory: Concepts and research.* New York: Wiley, 1966.

Birnbaum, M. Whose values should be taught? *Saturday Review,* June 20, 1964.

Birnbaum, M. The Clarification Group. In K. D. Benne, L. P. Bradford, J. Gibb, & R. Lippitt (Eds.), *The laboratory method of changing and learning.* Palo Alto, CA: Science & Behavior Books, 1975.

Blake, R. R., & Mouton, J. S. Reactions to intergroup competition under win-lose conditions. *Management Science,* 1961, *7,* 420-435.

Blake, R. R., Mouton, J. S., & Sloma, R. I. The union-management laboratory: Strategy for resolving intergroup conflict. *Journal of Applied Behavioral Science,* 1965, *1,* 25-57.

Blalock, H. M., Jr. *Toward a theory of minority-group relations.* New York: Wiley, 1967.

Block, J. *Lives through time.* Berkeley, CA: Bancroft Books, 1971.

Block, J. Issues, problems, and pitfalls in assessing sex differences: A critical review of *The Psychology of sex differences. Merrill-Palmer Quarterly,* 1976, *22,* 283-308.

Block, J., & Block, J. An investigation of the relationship between intolerance of ambiguity and ethnocentrism. *Journal of Personality,* 1951, *19,* 303-311.

Brehm, J. W. *A theory of psychological reactance.* New York: Academic Press, 1966.

Brewer, M. B. In-group bias in the minimal intergroup situation: A cognitive-motivational analysis. *Psychological Bulletin,* 1979, *86,* 307-324. (a)

Brewer, M. B. The role of ethnocentrism in intergroup conflict. In W. G. Austin & S. Worchel (Eds.), *The social psychology of intergroup relations.* Monterey, CA: Brooks/Cole, 1979. (b)

Brigham, J. C. Ethnic stereotypes. *Psychological Bulletin,* 1971, *76,* 15-38.

Brophy, J. E., & Good, T. L. Teachers' communication of differential expectation for children's classroom performance: Some behavioral data. *Journal of Educational Psychology,* 1970, *61,* 365-374.

Broverman, J. K., Vogel, S. R., Broverman, D. M., Clarkson, F. E., & Rosenkrantz, P. S. Sex-role stereotyping: A current appraisal. *Journal of Social Issues,* 1972, *28,* 59-78.

Brown, L. D. Can "haves" and "have-nots" cooperate? Two efforts to bridge a social gap. *Journal of Applied Behavioral Science,* 1977, *13,* 211-224.

Brown, P. (Ed.). *Radical psychology.* New York: Harper & Row, 1973.

Brown, R. *Social psychology.* New York: Free Press, 1965.

Byrne, D. *The attraction paradigm.* New York: Academic Press, 1971.

Cameron, C. Sex-role attitudes. In S. Oskamp (Ed.), *Attitudes and opinions.* Englewood Cliffs, NJ: Prentice-Hall, 1977.

Campbell, D. T. Common fate, similarity and other indices of the status of aggregates of persons as social entities. *Behavioral Science,* 1958, *3,* 14-25.

Campbell, D. T. Stereotypes and the perception of group differences. *American Psychologist,* 1967, *22,* 817-829.

Campbell, E. Q. (Ed.). *Racial tensions and national identity.* Nashville: Vanderbilt University Press, 1972.

Carithers, M. W. School desegregation and racial cleavage, 1954-1970: A review of the literature. *Journal of Social Issues,* 1970, *26,* 25-47.

Carroll, B. A. (Ed.). *Liberating women's history.* Urbana: University of Illinois Press, 1976.

Carroll, J. S., & Payne, J. W. (Eds.). *Cognition and social behavior.* Hillsdale, NJ: Erlbaum, 1976.

Cauthen, N. R., Robinson, I. E., & Krauss, H. H. Stereotypes: A review of the literature 1926 1968. *Journal of Social Psychology,* 1971, *84,* 102-125.

Chafetz, J. S. *Masculine/feminine or human? An overview of the sociology of sex roles.* Itasca, IL: Peacock, 1974.

Chandler, R. *Public opinion: Changing attitudes on contemporary political and social issues.* New York: Bowker, 1972.

Chapman, L., & Chapman, J. Illusory correlations as an obstacle to the use of valid psycho-diagnostic signs. *Journal of Abnormal Psychology,* 1969, *74,* 271-280.

Chen, M., Levi, A., & Adler, C. *Towards an evaluation of the junior high school's contribution to the educational system.* Jerusalem: National Council of Jewish Women Research Institute, School of Education, Hebrew University of Jerusalem, 1978.

Chin, R., & Benne, K. D. Generalized strategies for effecting change in human systems. In W. G. Bennis, K. D. Benne, & R. Chin (Eds.), *The planning of change* (3rd ed.). New York: Holt, Rinehart & Winston, 1976.

Christie, R., & Jahoda, M. (Eds.). *Studies in the scope and method of "The Authoritarian Personality."* New York: Free Press, 1954.

Clark, K. B., & Clark, M. P. Racial identification and preference in Negro children. In E. E. Maccoby, T. M. Newcomb, & E. L. Hartley (Eds.), *Readings in social psychology.* New York: Holt, Rinehart & Winston, 1958.

Clausen, J. A. The life course of individuals. In M. W. Riley, M. Johnson, & A. Foner (Eds.), *Aging and society, Volume III: A sociology of age stratification.* New York: Russell Sage Foundation, 1972.

Cohen, S. P., Kelman, H. C., Miller, F. D., & Smith, B. L. Evolving intergroup techniques for conflict resolution: An Israeli-Palestinian pilot workshop. *Journal of Social Issues,* 1977, *33,* 165-189.

Coleman, J. S. *Community conflict.* New York: Free Press, 1957.

Coleman, J. S. *The adolescent society.* New York: Free Press, 1961.

Coleman, J. S., Campbell, E. Q., Hobson, C. J., McPartland, J., Mood, A. M., Weinfeld, F. D., & York, R. L. *Equality in educational opportunity.* Washington, DC: U.S. Government Printing Office, 1966.

Constantinople, A. Masculinity-femininity: An exception to the famous dictum? *Psychological Bulletin,* 1973, *80,* 389-405.

Cottle, T. J. Strategy for change. *Saturday Review,* September 20, 1969, pp. 70-73.

Dahrendorf, R. On the origin of inequality among men. In A. Béteille (Ed.), *Social inequality.* Baltimore: Penguin, 1969.

D'Andrade, R. G. Sex differences and cultural institutions. In E. E. Maccoby (Ed.), *The development of sex differences.* Stanford, CA: Stanford University Press, 1966.

de Beauvoir, S. *The second sex.* New York: Knopf, 1949.

Deckard, B. S. *The women's movement* (2nd ed.). New York: Harper & Row, 1979. (1st ed., 1975)

Deutsch, M. *The resolution of conflict.* New Haven, CT: Yale University Press, 1973.

Deutsch, M., & Hornstein, H. A. (Eds.). *Applying social psychology.* New York: Wiley, 1975.

Dion, K. Physical attractiveness and evaluations of children's transgressions. *Journal of Personality and Social Psychology,* 1972, *24,* 207-213.

Dollard, J. *Caste and class in a southern town.* New Haven, CT: Yale University Press, 1937.

Downing, L. L., & Monaco, N. R. *Ingroup-outgroup bias formation as a function of differential ingroup-outgroup contact and authoritarian personality: A field experiment.* Schenectady, NY: Union College, 1979. (Mimeo)

Ehrlich, H. J. *The social psychology of prejudice.* New York: Wiley, 1973.

Encyclopaedia Britannica. Chicago: Author, 1971.

Erikson, E. H. *Childhood and society.* New York: Norton, 1950.

Erikson, E. H. Identity and the life cycle. In G. S. Klein (Ed.), *Psychological issues.* New York: International Universities Press, 1959.

Erikson, E. H. The concept of identity in race relations: Notes and queries. In T. Parsons and K. B. Clark (Eds.), *The Negro American.* Boston: Beacon, 1965.

Erikson, E. H. *Identity, youth and crisis.* New York: Norton, 1968.

Erikson, E. H. *Dimensions of a new identity.* New York: Norton, 1974.

Eysenck, H. J. *The psychology of politics.* London: Routledge & Kegan Paul, 1954.

Festinger, L. *A theory of cognitive dissonance.* Evanston, IL: Row, Peterson, 1957.

Feuer, L. *The conflict of generations: The character and significance of student movements.* New York: Basic Books, 1969.

Firestone, S. *The dialectic of sex.* New York: Bantam, 1970.

Fishbein, M., & Ajzen, I. Attitudes towards objects as predictors of single and multiple behavioral criteria. *Psychological Review,* 1974, *81,* 59-74.

Fishbein, M., & Ajzen, I. *Belief, attitude, intention, and behavior: An introduction to theory and research.* Reading, MA: Addison-Wesley, 1975.

Foner, A. The polity. In M. W. Riley, M. Johnson, & A. Foner (Eds.), *Aging and society* (Vol. 3). New York: Russell Sage Foundation, 1972.

Frazier, N., & Sadker, M. *Sexism in school and society.* New York: Harper & Row, 1973.

Freeman, J. *The politics of women's liberation.* New York: David McKay, 1975.

Frenkel-Brunswick, E. Intolerance of ambiguity as an emotional and perceptual personality variable. *Journal of Personality,* 1949, *18,* 108-143.

Freud, A. *The ego and the mechanisms of defense.* New York: International Universities Press, 1946.

Friedan, B. *The feminine mystique.* New York: Dell, 1964.

Gerbner, G., & Signorielli, N. *Women and minorities in television drama 1969-1978.* Philadelphia: University of Pennsylvania, Annenberg School of Communications, 1979.

Gergen, K. J., & Gergen, M. M. *Social psychology.* New York: Harcourt Brace Jovanovich, 1981.

Gilbert, G. M. Stereotype persistence and change among college students. *Journal of Abnormal and Social Psychology,* 1951, *46,* 245-254.

Glazer, N., & Moynihan, D. P. *Beyond the melting pot.* Cambridge, MA: MIT Press, 1963.

Glazer, N., & Moynihan, D. P. (Eds.). *Ethnicity: Theory and experience.* Cambridge, MA: Harvard University Press, 1975.

Goethals, G. R., & Reckman, R. F. The perception of consistency in attitudes. *Journal of Experimental Social Psychology,* 1973, *9,* 491-501.

Goethals, G. R., & Worchel, S. *Adjustment and human relations.* New York: Knopf, 1981.

Goffman, E. *The presentation of self in everyday life.* Garden City, NY: Doubleday, 1959.

Goldberg, P. Are women prejudiced against women? In A. Theodore (Ed.), *The professional woman.* New York: Schenkman, 1971.

Hamilton, D. L. Cognitive biases in the perception of social groups. In J. S. Carroll & J. W. Payne (Eds.), *Cognition and social behavior.* Hillsdale, NJ: Erlbaum, 1976.

Hamilton, D. L. A cognitive-attributional analysis of stereotyping. In L. Berkowitz (Ed.), *Advances in experimental social psychology* (Vol. 12). New York: Academic Press, 1979.

Hamilton, D. L. (Ed.). *Cognitive processes in stereotyping and intergroup behavior.* Hillsdale, NJ: Erlbaum, 1981.

Hamilton, D. L., & Gifford, R. K. Illusory correlation in interpersonal perception: A cognitive basis of stereotypic judgments. *Journal of Experimental Social Psychology,* 1976, *12,* 392-407.

Harvey, J. H., Ickes, W. J., & Kidd, R. F. (Eds.). *New directions in attribution research* (Vol. 1). Hillsdale, NJ: Erlbaum, 1976.

Henley, N. M. The politics of touch. In P. Brown (Ed.), *Radical psychology.* New York: Harper & Row, 1973.

Herman, S. N. *Jewish identity: A social psychological perspective.* Beverly Hills, CA: Sage, 1977.

Hole, J., & Levine, E. *Rebirth of feminism.* New York: Quadrangle, 1971.

Horowitz, D. L. Ethnic identity. In N. Glazer & D. Moynihan (Eds.), *Ethnicity: Theory and experience.* Cambridge, MA: Harvard University Press, 1975.

Horwitz, M., & Berkowitz, N. *Attributional analysis of intergroup conflict.* Paper presented at the meeting of the American Psychological Association, Chicago, 1975.

Horwitz, M., & Rabbie, J. M. Individuality and membership in the intergroup system. In H. Tajfel (Ed.), *Social identity and intergroup relations.* New York: Columbia University Press, 1982.

Hovland, C. I. Reconciling conflicting results derived from experimental and survey studies of attitude change. *American Psychologist,* 1959, *14,* 8-17.

Hovland, C. I., & Sears, R. Minor studies of aggression: Correlation of lynchings with economic indices. *Journal of Psychology,* 1940, *9,* 301-310.

Hyman, H. H. The psychology of status. *Archives of Psychology,* 1942, *38,* Whole no. 269.

Hyman, H. H., & Sheatsley, P. B. Attitudes toward desegregation. *Scientific American,* 1964, *211,* 16-23.

Isaacs, H. R. *Idols and the tribe, group identity and political change.* New York: Harper & Row, 1975. (a)

Isaacs, H. R. Basic group identity: The idols of the tribe. In N. Glazer & D. P. Moynihan (Eds.), *Ethnicity: Theory and experience.* Cambridge, MA: Harvard University Press, 1975, 29-52. (b)

Jones, E. E., & Davis, K. E. From acts to dispositions: The attribution process in person perception. In L. Berkowitz (Ed.), *Advances in experimental social psychology* (Vol. 2). New York: Academic Press, 1965.

Jones, E. E., & Gerard, H. B. *Foundations of social psychology.* New York: Wiley, 1967.

Jones, E. E., Kanouse, D. E., Kelley, H. H., Nisbett, R. E., Valins, S., & Weiner, B. *Attribution: Perceiving the causes of behavior.* Morristown, NJ: General Learning Press, 1971.

Jones, R. Take as directed. *The Co-Evolution Quarterly,* 1976, 132-139. (Box 428, Sausalito, CA 94965)

Jones, R. A. *Self fulfilling prophecies.* Hillsdale, NJ: Erlbaum, 1977.

Jones, R. A., Hendrick, C., & Epstein, Y. M. *Introduction to social psychology.* Sunderland, MA: Sinauer Associates, 1979.

Kalish, R. A. The old and new as generation gap allies. *Gerontologist,* 1969, *9,* 83-89.

Kanowitz, L. *Women and the law.* Albuquerque: University of New Mexico Press, 1969.

Kariel, H. S. Pluralism. In D. L. Sills (Ed.), *International encyclopedia of the social sciences* (Vol. 12). New York: Macmillan, 1968.

Karlines, M., Coffman, T. L., & Walters, G. On the fading of social stereotypes: Studies in three generations of college students. *Journal of Personality and Social Psychology,* 1969, *13,* 1-16.

Katz, D. The functional approach to the study of attitudes. *Public Opinion Quarterly,* 1960 *24,* 163-204.

Katz, D. Consistency for what? The functional approach. In R. P. Abelson, E. Aronson, W. J. McGuire, T. M. Newcomb, M. J. Rosenberg, & P. H. Tannenbaum (Eds.), *Theories of cognitive consistency: A sourcebook.* Chicago: Rand McNally, 1968.

Katz, D., & Braly, K. Racial stereotypes of one hundred college students. *Journal of Abnormal and Social Psychology,* 1933, *28,* 280-290.

Katz, D., & Stotland, E. A preliminary statement to a theory of attitude structure and change. In S. Koch (Ed.), *Psychology: A study of a science* (Vol. 3). New York: McGraw-Hill, 1959.

Kelley, H. H. Two functions of reference groups. In G. E. Swanson, T. M. Newcomb, & E. L. Hartley (Eds.), *Readings in social psychology* (Rev. ed.). New York: Holt, Rinehart & Winston, 1952.

Kelly, J. A., & Worell, J. New formulations of sex roles and androgyny: A critical review. *Journal of Consulting and Clinical Psychology,* 1977, *45,* 1101-1115.

Keniston, K. The sources of student dissent. *Journal of Social Issues,* 1967, *23,* 108-132.

Keniston, K. *Youth and dissent.* New York: Harcourt Brace Jovanovich, 1971.

Kirschner, B. F. Introducing students to women's place in society. In J. Huber (Ed.), *Changing women in a changing society.* Chicago: University of Chicago Press, 1973.

Klineberg, O. *The human dimension in international relations.* New York: Holt, Rinehart & Winston, 1964.

Kraditor, A. *The ideas of the woman suffrage movement, 1890-1920.* New York: Columbia University Press, 1965.

Kreps, J. M. *Sex in the market place: American woman at work.* Baltimore: Johns Hopkins University Press, 1971.

Kreps, J. M., & Clark, R. *Sex, age, and work: The changing composition of the labor force.* Baltimore: Johns Hopkins University Press, 1975.

Kurland, P. B. Ruminations on the quality of equality. *Brigham Young University Law Review,* 1979, *1,* 1-23.

Laumann, E. O. *Bonds of pluralism: The form and substance of urban social networks.* New York: Wiley, 1973.

Levin, J. *The functions of prejudice.* New York: Harper & Row, 1975.

LeVine, R. A., & Campbell, D. T. *Ethnocentrism: theories of conflict, ethnic attitudes, and group behavior.* New York: Wiley, 1972.

Levinson, D. J., with Darrow, C. N., Klein, E. B., Levinson, M. H., & McKee, B. *The seasons of a man's life.* New York: Knopf, 1978.

Lewicki, R. J., & Alderfer, C. P. The tension between research and intervention in intergroup conflict. *Journal of Applied Behavioral Science,* 1973, *9,* 424-468.

Lewin, K. *Resolving social conflicts.* New York: Harper, 1948.

Lewin, K. *Field theory in social science* (D. Cartwright, Ed.). New York: Harper, 1951. (Also London: Tavistock, 1952)

Lewin, K., & Grabbe, P. Conduct, knowledge, and acceptance of values. *Journal of Social Issues,* 1945. (Also in K. Lewin, *Resolving social conflicts.* New York: Harper, 1948)

Lippmann, W. *Public opinion.* New York: Harcourt Brace Jovanovich, 1922.

Lipset, S. M. *Political man.* Garden City, NY: Doubleday, 1963.

Maccoby, E., & Jacklin, C. *The psychology of sex differences.* Stanford, CA: Stanford University Press, 1974.

Mannheim, K. *Ideology and utopia.* New York: Harcourt Brace Jovanovich, 1955.

Marrow, A. J. *The practical theorist: The life and work of Kurt Lewin.* New York: Basic Books, 1969.

May, R. *Sex and fantasy.* New York: Norton, 1980.

McGuire, W. J. The nature of attitudes and attitude change. In G. Lindzey & E. Aronson (Eds.), *The handbook of social psychology* (Vol. 3) [2nd ed.]. Reading, MA: Addison-Wesley, 1969.

McNeil, E. B., & Rubin, Z. *The psychology of being human.* San Francisco: Canfield, 1977.

Mead, M. *Sex and temperament in three primitive societies.* New York: Morrow, 1935. (Also New York: Dell, 1968)

Mead, M. *Male and female.* New York: Dell, 1949.

Mead, M. *Culture and commitment: A study of the generation gap.* New York: Doubleday, 1970.

Merton, R. K. *Social theory and social structure.* New York: Free Press, 1957.

Merton, R. K., & Kitt, A. S. Contributions to the theory of reference group behavior. In R. K. Merton & P. F. Lazarsfeld (Eds.), *Studies in the scope and method of "The American Soldier".* New York: Free Press, 1950.

Milgram, S. Behavioral study of obedience. *Journal of Abnormal and Social Psychology,* 1963, *67,* 371-378.

Milgram, S. *Obedience to authority.* New York: Harper & Row, 1974.

Millett, K. *Sexual politics.* Garden City, NY: Doubleday, 1969.

Minkowich, A., Davis, D., & Bashi, J. An evaluation study of Israeli elementary schools. Jerusalem: School of Education, Hebrew University of Jerusalem, 1977.

Money, J., & Ehrhardt, A. *Man and woman, boy and girl.* Baltimore: Johns Hopkins University Press, 1972.

Neugarten, B. (Ed.) *Personality in middle and late life.* New York: Atherton, 1964.

Neugarten, B. L. Continuities and discontinuities in psychological issues into adult life. In B. Sutton-Smith (Ed.), *Readings in child psychology.* New York: Appleton-Century-Crofts, 1973.

Newcomb, T. M. *Social psychology.* New York: Holt, Rinehart & Winston, 1950.

Nisbett, R. E., Caputo, C. G., Legant, P., & Maracek, J. Behavior as seen by the actor and as seen by the observer. *Journal of Personality and Social Psychology,* 1973, 27, 154-164.

Nisbett, R. E., & Wilson, T. D. Telling more than we can know: Verbal reports on mental processes. *Psychological Review,* 1977, 84, 231-259.

Novack, M. *The rise of the unmeltable ethnics.* New York: Macmillan, 1973.

Ortega Y Gasset, J. *Man and crisis.* New York: Norton, 1958.

Oskamp, S. *Attitudes and opinions.* Englewood Cliffs, NJ: Prentice-Hall, 1977.

Parsons, T. "Voting" and the equilibrium of the American political system. In E. Burdick & A. Brodbeck (Eds.), *American voting behavior.* New York: Free Press, 1959.

Parsons, T. Some theoretical considerations on the nature and trends of change in ethnicity. In N. Glazer & D. P. Moynihan (Eds.), *Ethnicity: Theory and experience.* Cambridge, MA: Harvard University Press, 1975.

Parsons, T., & Platt, G. M. Higher education and changing socialization. In M. W. Riley, M. Johnson, & A. Foner (Eds.), *Aging and society. Volume III: A sociology of age stratification.* New York: Russell Sage Foundation, 1972.

Pettigrew, T. F. Social psychology and desegregation research. *American Psychologist,* 1961, 16, 105-112.

Pettigrew, T. F. *A profile of the Negro American.* New York: Van Nostrand, 1964.

Pettigrew, T. F. Racially separate or together? *Journal of Social Issues,* 1969, 25, 43-69.

Pope, K. S., Levenson, H., & Schover, L. R. Sexual intimacy in psychology training: Results and implications of a national survey. *American Psychologist,* 1979, 34, 682-689.

Pressey, S. L., & Kuhlen, R. C. *Psychological development through the life span.* New York: Harper & Row, 1957.

Rabbie, J. M., & Horwitz, M. The arousal of ingroup-outgroup bias by a chance win or loss. *Journal of Personality and Social Psychology,* 1969, 13, 269-277.

Riley, M. W., & Foner, A. *Aging and society* (Vol. 1). New York: Russell Sage Foundation, 1968.

Riley, M. W., Johnson, M., & Foner, A. (Eds.). *Aging and society, Volume III: A sociology of age stratification.* New York: Russell Sage Foundation, 1972.

Rogers, C. *Client centered therapy.* Boston: Houghton Mifflin, 1951.

Rokeach, M. Generalized mental rigidity as a factor in ethnocentrism. *Journal of Abnormal and Social Psychology,* 1948, 43, 259-278.

Rokeach, M. *The open and closed mind.* New York: Basic Books, 1960.

Rokeach, M. *Beliefs, attitudes and values: a theory of organization and change.* San Francisco: Jossey-Bass, 1968.

Rokeach, M. *The nature of human values.* New York: Free Press, 1973.

Roper, E. The politics of three decades. *Public Opinion Quarterly,* 1965, 29, 368-376.

Rosen, R. Sexism in history or writing women's history is a tricky business. *Journal of Marriage and the Family,* 1971, 33, 541-544.

Rosenhan, D. L. On being sane in insane places. *Science,* 1973, 179, 250-258.

Rosenkrantz, P., Vogel, S. R., Bee, H., Broverman, J. K., & Broverman, D. M. Sex-role stereotypes and self concepts in college students. *Journal of Consulting and Clinical Psychology,* 1968, 32, 287-295.

Rosenthal, R. *Experimenter effects in behavioral research.* New York: Appleton-Century-Crofts, 1966. (Rev. ed., 1976)

Rosenthal, R. Teacher expectations and their effects upon children. In G. S. Lesser (Ed.), *Psychology and educational practice.* Glenview, IL: Scott, Foresman, 1971.

Rosenthal, R., & Jacobson, L. *Pygmalion in the classroom.* New York: Holt, Rinehart & Winston, 1968.

Rosenthal, R., & Rubin, D. B. Interpersonal expectancy effects: The first 345 studies. *Behavioral and Brain Sciences,* 1978, 3, 377-415.

Ross, L. The intuitive psychologist and his shortcomings: Distortions in the attribution process.

In L. Berkowitz (Ed.), *Advances in experimental social psychology* (Vol. 10). New York: Academic Press, 1977.

Roszak, B., & Roszak, T. (Eds.). *Masculine/feminine.* New York: Harper & Row, 1969.

Rubovitz, P. C., & Maehr, M. L. Pygmalion black and white. *Journal of Personality and Social Psychology,* 1973, *25,* 210-218.

Sadker, M. P., & Sadker, D. M. Sexism in teacher-education texts. *Harvard Educational Review,* 1980, *50,* 36-46.

Sarbin, T. R., & Allen, V. L. Role theory. In G. Lindzey & E. Aronson (Eds.), *The handbook of social psychology* (Vol. 1) [2nd ed.]. Reading, MA: Addison-Wesley, 1969.

Schlossberg, N. K. A model for analyzing human adaptation to transition. *The Counseling Psychologist,* 1981, *9,* 2-18.

Secord, P. F., & Beckman, C. *Social psychology* (2nd ed.). New York: McGraw-Hill, 1964.

Shaver, K. G. Principles of social psychology. Cambridge, MA: Winthrop, 1981.

Shaw, M. E., & Constanzo, P. R. *Theories of social psychology.* New York: McGraw-Hill, 1970.

Sheehy, G. *Passages.* New York: Dutton, 1976.

Sherif, M., Harvey, O. J., White, B. J., Hood, W. E., & Sherif, C. W. *Intergroup conflict and cooperation: The Robber's Cave experiment.* Norman: University of Oklahoma Book Exchange, 1961.

Sherif, M., & Sherif, C. *Groups in harmony and tension.* New York: Harper & Row, 1953. (2nd ed., 1964)

Small, J., & Birnbaum, M. The structured group interview. *Training and Development Journal,* 1971 (September), 26-32.

Stouffer, S. A. An analysis of conflicting social norms. *American Sociological Review,* 1949, *14,* 707-717.

Stryker, S. Developments in "two social psychologies": Toward an appreciation of mutual relevance. *Sociometry,* 1977, *40,* 145-160.

Sumner, W. G. *Folkways.* Boston: Ginn, 1906.

Tajfel, H. (Ed.). *Differentiation between groups: Studies in the social psychology of intergroup relations.* London: Academic Press, 1979.

Tajfel, H., Billig, M. G., Bundy, R. P., & Flament, C. Social categorization of intergroup behavior. *European Journal of Social Psychology,* 1971, *1,* 149-178.

Tajfel, H., & Turner, J. An integrative theory of intergroup conflict. In W. G. Austin & S. Worchel (Eds.), *The social psychology of intergroup relations.* Monterey, CA: Brooks/Cole, 1979.

Tavris, C. Who likes women's liberation and why: The case of the unliberated liberals. *Journal of Social Issues,* 1973, *29,* 175-198.

Thibaut, J. W., & Kelley, H. H. *The social psychology of groups.* New York: Wiley, 1959.

Thompson, R. C., & Michel, J. B. Measuring authoritarianism: A comparison of the F and D scales. *Journal of Personality,* 1972, *40,* 180-190.

Turner, J. Social categorization and social discrimination in the minimal group paradigm. In H. Tajfel (Ed.), *Differentiation between social groups: Studies in the social psychology of intergroup relations.* London: Academic Press, 1979.

Wasserman, E., Lewin, A. Y., & Bleiweiss, L. H. (Eds.). *Women in academia: Evolving policies toward equal opportunities.* New York: Praeger, 1975.

Websters New Collegiate Dictionary (7th ed.). Springfield, MA: G. & C. Merriam, 1970.

Weisstein, N. Psychology constructs the female. In P. Brown (Ed.), *Radical psychology.* New York: Harper & Row, 1973.

Williams, R. M., Jr. The reduction of intergroup tensions: A survey of research on problems of ethnic, racial, and religious group relations. *Social Science Research Council Bulletin,* 1947, *57,* 1-153.

Women on words and images. *Channeling children: Sex stereotyping on prime time TV.* Princeton, NJ: Author, 1975. (a)

Women on words and images. *Dick and Jane as victims: Sex stereotyping in children's readers.* Princeton, NJ: Author, 1975. (b)

Worchel, S., Lind, E., & Kaufman, K. Evaluation of group products as a function of expectations of group longevity, outcome of competition, and publicity of evaluations. *Journal of Personality and Social Psychology,* 1975, *31,* 1089-1097.

Wrightsman, L. S. *Social psychology in the 70s.* Monterey, CA: Brooks/Cole, 1972.

Wrightsman, L. S., & Deaux, K. *Social psychology in the 80's* (3rd ed.). Monterey, CA: Brooks/Cole, 1981.

Yalom, I. D. *Theory and practice of group psychotherapy.* New York: Basic Books, 1975.

Zimbardo, P. G., Haney, C., Banks, W., & Jaffe, D. A Pirandeloian prison: The mind is a formidable jailer. *New York Times Magazine,* April 8, 1973, pp. 38-60.

Zimbardo, P. G., & Meadow, W. *Sexism springs eternal in* The Reader's Digest. Paper presented at the meeting of the Western Psychological Association, San Francisco, April 1974.

REFERENCE INDEX

Adelson, J. (1970): 204, 249

Adorno, T. W., E. Frenkel-Brunswick, D. J. Levinson, and R. N. Sanford (1950): 94-96, 249

Allport, G. W. (1935): 230, 249

Allport, G. W. (1954): 77-80, 90, 102, 127, 249

Allport, G. W., P. E. Vernon, and G. A. Lindzey (1960): 231-232, 249

Amir, Y. (1969): 115, 249

Amir, Y. (1975): 115, 249

Amir, Y. (1977): 115, 116, 117, 118, 249

Anderson, D. F. and R. Rosenthal (1968): 27, 249

Aronson, E. (1976): 50, 89, 104, 129, 249

Asch, S. (1946): 249

Asch, S. (1952): 222, 249

Asch, S. (1955): 222, 249

Ashmore, R. D. (1970): 249

Ashmore, R. D. and F. K. Del Boca (1976): 249

Ashmore, R. D. and F. K. Del Boca (1979): 76, 249

Ashmore, R. D. and F. K. Del Boca (1981): 176-177, 178, 249

Austin, W. G. and S. Worchel (1979): 249

Babad, E. Y. (1974): 191, 249

Babad, E. Y. (1977): 27, 249

Babad, E. Y. (1978): 52, 249

Babad, E. Y. (1979): 92, 98, 99, 191, 222, 249

Babad, E. Y., M. Birnbaum, and K. D. Benne (1978): 12, 39, 42, 61, 139, 249

Babad, E. Y. and J. Inbar (1981): 99, 191, 222, 250

Babad, E. Y., J. Inbar, and R. Rosenthal (1982a): 28, 100, 222, 250

Babad, E. Y., J. Inbar, and R. Rosenthal (1982b): 27, 99-100, 222, 250

Babad, E. Y., M. Mann, and M. Mar-Hayim (1975): 250

Bardwick, J. (1971): 165, 250

Barry, H. III, M. K. Bacon, and I. L. Child (1972): 163, 166, 250

Bell, D. (1960): 240, 244, 250

Bell, D. (1964): 250

Bell, D. (1968): 250

Bell, D. (1975): 152, 250

Bem, D. J. (1967): 129, 250

Bem, D. J. (1968): 250

Bem, D. J. (1970): 250

Bem, D. J. (1972): 250

Bem, S. L. (1974): 191, 250

Bem, S. L. (1975): 191, 250

Bem, S. L. (1977): 191, 250

Bem, S. L. and E. Lenney (1976): 190, 250

Benjamin, A. J. and A. M. Levi (1979): 115, 250

Benne, K. D. (1943): 207, 250

Benne, K. D. (1964): 39, 139, 250

Benne, K. D. (1965): 250

Benne, K. D. (1970): 207, 250

Benne, K. D. (1976): 39, 137, 139, 196, 250

Benne, K. D. (1978): 129, 131, 132, 250

Benne, K. D., L. P. Bradford, J. Gibb, and R. Lippitt (1975): 250

Bennis, W. G., K. D. Benne, R. Chin, and K. E. Corey (1976): 127, 250

Berube, M. R. and M. Gittell (1969): 113, 250

Berzins, J. I. (1975): 191, 251

Bettelheim, B. and M. Janowitz (1964): 251

Biddle, B. J. and E. J. Thomas (1966): 214, 251

Birnbaum, M. (1964): 251

Birnbaum, M. (1975): 12, 37, 39, 61, 139, 251
Blake, R. R. and J. S. Mouton (1961): 110, 115, 251
Blake, R. R., J. S. Mouton, and R. I. Sloma (1965): 251
Blalock, H. M. (1967): 251
Block, J. (1971): 202, 251
Block, J. (1976): 178, 251
Block, J. and J. Block (1951): 251
Brehm, J. W. (1966): 51, 54, 130, 251
Brewer, M. B. (1979a): 108, 109, 251
Brewer, M. B. (1979b): 119, 251
Brigham, J. C. (1971): 251
Brophy, J. E. and T. L. Good (1970): 27, 99, 251
Broverman, J. K., S. R. Vogel, D. M. Broverman, F. E. Clarkson, and P. S. Rosenkrantz (1972): 251
Brown, L. D. (1977): 115, 251
Brown, P. (1973): 251
Brown, R. (1965): 251
Byrne, D. (1971): 237, 251

Cameron, C. (1977): 134, 166, 177, 179, 180, 187, 188, 251
Campbell, D. T. (1958): 108, 251
Campbell, D. T. (1967): 120, 251
Campbell, E. Q. (1972): 152, 251
Carithers, M. W. (1970): 118, 251
Carroll, B. A. (1976): 180, 251
Carroll, J. S. and J. W. Payne (1976): 86, 231, 251
Cauthen, N. R., I. E. Robinson, and H. H. Krauss (1971): 251
Chafetz, J. S. (1974): 165, 177-178, 179, 182, 183, 251
Chandler, R. (1972): 187, 252
Chapman, L. and J. Chapman (1969): 252
Chen, M., A. Levi, and C. Adler (1978): 118, 252
Chin, R. and K. D. Benne (1976): 128, 129, 130-131, 136, 252
Christie, R. and M. Jahoda (1954): 252
Clark, K. B. and M. P. Clark (1958): 252
Clausen, J. A. (1972): 197, 252
Cohen, S. P., H. C. Kelman, F. D. Miller, and B. L. Smith (1977): 115, 252
Coleman, J. S. (1957): 252
Coleman, J. S. (1961): 203, 252

Coleman, J. S., E. Q. Campbell, C. J. Hobson, J. McPartland, A. M. Mood, F. D. Weinfeld, and R. L. York (1966): 118, 252
Constantinople, A. (1973): 191, 252
Cottle, T. J. (1969): 252

Dahrendorf, R. (1969): 101, 147, 252
D'Andrade, R. G. (1966): 166, 167, 252
de Beauvoir, S. (1949): 252
Deckard, B. S. (1975-1979): 168, 180, 183, 189, 252
Deutsch, M. (1973): 42, 115, 158, 252
Deutsch, M. and H. A. Hornstein (1975): 252
Dion, K. (1972): 252
Dollard, J. (1937): 102, 252
Downing, L. L. and N. R. Monaco (1979): 107, 108, 252

Ehrlich, H. J. (1973): 252
Erikson, E. H. (1950): 197, 198, 252
Erikson, E. H. (1959): 197, 198, 252
Erikson, E. H. (1965): 197, 252
Erikson, E. H. (1968): 197, 252
Erikson, E. H. (1974): 253
Eysenck, H. J. (1954): 97-98, 253

Festinger, L. A. (1957): 253
Feuer, L. (1969): 203, 253
Firestone, S. (1970): 189, 253
Fishbein, M. and I. Ajzen (1974): 253
Fishbein, M. and I. Ajzen (1975): 137, 231, 253
Foner, A. (1972): 207, 209, 253
Frazier, N. and M. Sadker (1973): 181, 182-183, 253
Freeman, J. (1975): 253
Frenkel-Brunswick, E. (1949): 96, 97, 253
Freud, A. (1946): 50, 253
Friedman, B. (1964): 253

Gerbner, G. and N. Signorielli (1979): 179, 253
Gergen, K. J. and M. M. Gergen (1981): 90, 253
Gilbert, G. M. (1951): 84, 253
Glazer, N. and D. P. Moynihan (1963): 123, 90,
Glazer, N. and D. P. Moynihan (1975): 101, 147, 253

Neugarten, B. L. (1973): 197, 255
Newcomb, T. M. (1950): 213, 255
Nisbett, R. E., C. G. Caputo, P. Legant, and J.
    Maracek (1973): 57, 256
Nisbett, R. E. and T. D. Wilson (1977): 47-48,
    54, 57, 109, 256
Novack, M. (1973): 28, 256

Ortega Y Gasset (1958): 197, 256
Oskamp, S. (1977): 137, 220, 256

Parsons, T. (1959): 208, 256
Parsons, T. (1975): 152, 256
Parsons, T. and G. M. Platt (1972): 197, 256
Pettigrew, T. F. (1961): 104, 256
Pettigrew, T. F. (1964): 123, 152, 256
Pettigrew, T. F. (1969): 256
Pope, K. S., H. Levinson, and L. R. Schover
    (1979): 183, 256
Pressey, S. L. and R. C. Kuhlen (1957):
    197, 256

Rabbie, J. M. and M. Horwitz (1969):
    108, 256
Riley, M. W. and A. Foner (1968): 256
Riley, M. W., M. Johnson, and A. Foner
    (1972): 195, 205, 208, 256
Rogers, C. (1951): 49, 256
Rokeach, M. (1948): 256
Rokeach, M. (1960): 97, 256
Rokeach, M. (1968): 137, 231, 232-233, 256
Rokeach, M. (1973): 137, 232, 256
Roper, E. (1965): 187, 256
Rosen, R. (1971): 180, 256
Rosenhan, D. L. (1973): 222, 256
Rosenkrantz, P., S. R. Vogel, H. Bee, J. K.
    Broverman, and D. M. Broverman
    (1968): 176, 256
Rosenthal, R. (1966)-(1976): 222, 256
Rosenthal, R. (1971): 27, 99, 222, 256
Rosenthal, R. and L. Jacobson (1968): 27,
    99, 256
Rosenthal, R. and D. B. Rubin (1978): 27,
    222, 256
Ross, L. (1977): 25, 53, 57, 256-257
Roszak, B. and T. Roszak (1969):
    188-189, 257
Rubovitz, P. C. and M. L. Maehr (1973): 27,
    99, 257

Sadker, M. P. and D. M. Sadker (1980):
    181, 257
Sarbin, T. R. and V. L. Allen (1969): 214,
    216, 257
Schlossberg, N. K. (1981): 199, 257
Secord, P. F. and C. Beckman (1964):
    214, 257
Shaver, K. G. (1981): 231, 257
Shaw, M. E. and P. R. Constanzo (1970): 257
Sheehy, G. (1976): 197, 202, 257
Sherif, M., O. J. Harvey, B. J. White, W. E.
    Hood, and C. W. Sherif (1961): 42,
    109-110, 114-115, 116, 257
Sherif, M. and C. Sherif (1953): 42, 257
Small, J. and M. Birnbaum (1971): 40,
    61, 257
Stouffer, S. A. (1949): 213, 257
Stryker, S. (1977): 37, 257
Sumner, W. G. (1906): 118-119, 257

Tajfel, H. (1979): 108, 257
Tajfel, H., M. G. Billig, R. P. Bundy, and
    C. Flament (1971): 107, 108, 257
Tajfel, H. and J. Turner (1979): 108, 257
Tavris, C. (1973): 187, 188, 257
Thibaut, J. W. and H. H. Kelley (1959): 257
Thompson, R. C. and J. B. Michel (1972):
    98, 257
Turner, J. (1979): 108, 257

Wasserman, E., A. Y. Lewin, and L. H.
    Bleiweiss (1975): 183, 257
Weisstein, N. (1973): 180, 189, 257
Williams, R. M. (1947): 42, 257
Women on words and images (1975a):
    179, 257
Women on words and images (1975b):
    179, 258
Worchel, S., E. Lind, and K. Kaufman (1975):
    109, 258
Wrightsman, L. S. (1972): 89, 258
Wrightsman, L. S. and K. Deaux (1981):
    90, 258

Yalom, I. D. (1975): 55, 258

Zimbardo, P. G., C. Haney, W. Banks, and
    D. A. Jaffe (1973): 223, 258
Zimbardo, P. G. and W. Meadow (1974):
    179, 258

SUBJECT INDEX

ABOUT THE AUTHORS

ELISHA Y. BABAD teaches social and educational psychology at the School of Education and the Department of Psychology of the Hebrew University, Jerusalem, Israel. He received his Ph.D. degree in psychology from Duke University. He has been involved in training group trainers at the Hebrew University and in application of the C-group method in various settings in Israel (the military, development towns, Arab-Jewish relations).

MAX BIRNBAUM is professor emeritus of sociology and human relations, Boston University. He was formerly director of Boston University's Human Relations Laboratory and of its Center for Applied Social Science. He is a member of the American Sociological Association and a founding member of the International Association of Applied Social Scientists. He has participated as director or staff member of more than a hundred training institutes and laboratories.

KENNETH D. BENNE is professor emeritus of philosophy and human relations, Boston University. He has taught at every level of the educational system and in a variety of continuing education programs. Charter member of the Philosophy of Education Society, co-inventor of Laboratory Training, one of the founders of National Training Laboratories, of Boston University's Human Relations Center, and of the International Association of Applied Social Scientists, he has worked as consultant and trainer in religious, industrial, educational, health, and community settings.